Fifty Years Of The
FINAL FOUR

Fifty Years Of The
Final Four

GOLDEN MOMENTS OF THE NCAA BASKETBALL TOURNAMENT

By Billy Packer
With Roland Lazenby

A FULL COURT PRESS BOOK

TAYLOR PUBLISHING
DALLAS, TEXAS

Library of Congress Cataloging in Publication Data

Packer, Billy.
    Fifty years of the final four : golden moments of the NCAA basketball tournament /
by Billy Packer with Roland Lazenby.
        p.   cm.
    "A Full Court Press book."
    ISBN 0-878333-592-7 : $19.95
    1. National Collegiate Athletic Association--History.
2. Basketball--Tournaments--United States--History. I. Lazenby.
GV885.49.N37P33 1987
796.32'372--dc19   87-18134

Dedicated to John Wooden

Contents

Foreword By Senator Bill Bradley

U.S. Senator Bill Bradley, Democrat-New Jersey, was named the Most Valuable Player of the 1965 Final Four in Portland, Oregon, where he scored a record 58 points in the consolation game against Wichita State.

Much is said and written about the magic and drama of the Final Four, the hype, the hoopla, the glitz. Yet the drama and the magic relate to the nature of the event itself, to the fact that these are college students. They are still young. They are well trained and well coached in most cases. But in every Final Four the human factor looms large: who rises to the occasion; who makes a mistake; what were the reasons for the mistake. While there is a great deal at stake for the players and the coaches, the Final Four is still part of a larger continuum, which is the college experience. The sanctity of the Final Four is that it is an amateur event, albeit one that today generates millions of dollars in income. I think the appeal of it is that there is still enough veneer covering the commercialism, still enough amateurism, still enough unusual, unpredictable things that happen, to give the drama a particular human dimension.

For the player, the event is appealing because of its challenge, because you are still unformed as a talent, even as a senior. This grand basketball drama, this pageant requires you to be at your peak as a player. In my day, we played before a crowd of 12,000 or so, and it seemed like the entire basketball world was looking on. Today, the audience *is* the basketball world, with millions watching on television.

Even so, there is a special flavor to the college competition. Certainly there are abuses of the system, as any system is open to abuse. But college athletes still have to be students, still have to go to school, still have to earn passing grades. What they do beyond that as athletes is merely another large part of their college experience, as valuable as any other part of college.

The Final Four itself is an educational experience for those who are fortunate enough to participate. I always think of the coaches in the arena as teachers approaching a special class, waiting to see who will really excel, who

Opposite —Bill Bradley with Princeton's third-place trophy in 1965.

will not. And the spectators approach the event much like an audience approaches a college drama or a special presentation of university musical talent.

That's why it's important to see the Final Four and other special college athletic competitions as part of the larger continuum, the college experience. They present the opportunity for a generation to display its talents.

For those reasons, the 1965 Final Four holds very special memories for me. It was a culmination of all of my work and the team's work during my years at Princeton. Our reaching the semifinals demonstrated that a team of students could compete against the best. It was tremendously reassuring that we got to the Final Four. Even today, everyone from our team regrets that we didn't go to the finals and win it. Yet even our loss was educational. Sometimes dreams aren't fulfilled.

Although we didn't win the championship, that weekend in March 1965 brought its rewards, particularly when Hank Iba came to the locker room after the consolation game to congratulate me on my college career. He was the Olympic coach in 1964, a great coach, and he meant a lot to me.

People sometimes ask me if I still find time to play the game. I tell them that occasionally I shoot around. When I turned 40, a member of my staff gave me a video of the seventh game of the 1970 NBA championship. I took it home and watched it, and that kind of gave me a little excitement. I hadn't really touched a ball for maybe six years. So the next day I went down to a playground two or three doors away and started to go through my practice routine. I was down there about 45 minutes and the shot was dropping. I came back to the house, and the next day I could hardly get up. I realized that my heart might be willing but my knees said no. For this reason, old players have their memories. They replay their Final Fours from the pages of a book. I hope you enjoy this one, and while you read it, keep in mind that the NCAA tournament is more than simply basketball. It's a half century of the college experience.

The Spectacle

Over the past 50 years, the NCAA basketball tournament has cut and polished its glittering jewel of a championship, an event that has come to be known as the Final Four. In its half century of life, the tournament has mirrored the face of modern American society: the upheaval of World War II, the boom of the early 50s, the pain of the Civil Rights era and the 60s, the uncertainty of Vietnam and the 70s. Arriving in the 80s, the NCAA tournament has become one of the grand spectacles of sport, a month-long extravaganza of television, an event exceeded in range only by the Olympics.

This book is an unabashed attempt to marvel at the tournament's successes, at its growth from the age of radio and passenger trains and dank college gyms to the dawn of video and jets and superdomes. Perhaps, as much as anyone, I am fascinated by the developments. Since 1962, when I had the good fortune to play in the Final Four as a guard for Wake Forest, the tournament has been a force carrying my professional life on its back. It has lifted me from a career of sales and regional broadcasting to the challenges of network television.

But, no matter how much I feel a part of it, this story is not mine. It's an account of championships and defeats, players and coaches. In reviewing 50 years of their trials and tribulations, of the tournament's growth, the immediate overwhelming question is, Why? Why did it boom?

Certainly, anyone asked that question would leap to the answer: television. But it's not so simple. In fact, I'm not sure there is a definitive answer, only good guesses.

I think you must begin with the people. The legends immediately come to mind. Behind every one of them are a dozen role players and an entire network of people working to bring their schools victory—assistant coaches, trainers, managers, secretaries, publicists. Before moving to the glitter, let's tip our hats to the grit.

But in all truthfulness, the legends are the essence of the tournament, the sensational force that pulls the crowds through the turnstiles. Many great coaches have left their mark on the finals: Branch McCracken, Hank Iba, Adolph Rupp, Phog Allen, Phil Woolpert, Pete Newell, Fred Taylor, George Smith, Ed Jucker, Vic Bubas, the incomparable John Wooden, Bob Knight, Al McGuire, John Thompson, Denny Crum, Guy Lewis, and Dean Smith, each of them weaving some personal thread through the fabric of the sport.

The vital warp to their weft is the players: Bob Kurland, Tom Gola, Bill Russell, Wilt Chamberlain, John Havlicek, Jerry Lucas, Walt Hazzard, Gail Goodrich, Lew Alcindor, Bill Walton, David Thompson, Magic Johnson, Larry Bird, Darrell Griffith, Isiah Thomas, Michael Jordan, James Worthy, Elgin Baylor, Bill Bradley and others, many of them beginning the strands of professional greatness during their NCAA tournament appearances.

Esteemed even more than each great individual are the great teams, such as Cincinnati, 1961-62, or the Cinderella clubs of NC State in '83 and Villanova in '85, with victories that stirred the underdog soul of America.

None of these, however, is a bigger factor than the development of the game itself, beginning as indoor pastime in the cold cities of the East, gathering its momentum in the Midwest and West with the running one-hander in the 40s. Basketball then became a battle of control offense vs. the fast break. To that collision of styles came the innovations of defense, a myriad of presses and zones and gimmicks.

Another vital strand was the evolution of the tall, modern athlete. The long-delayed arrival of civil rights opened college basketball to blacks, to players dedicated to long hours polishing their craft. Coincidentally, the wonderments of modern science brought advances in diet and weight training.

Just as the decades had built the substance of basketball, the age of television preened its image and fattened its profitability. A team in the finals in the early 40s was lucky to net $100 after travel expenses. Phil Woolpert's University of San Francisco champions in 1956 took home about $12,000. Today, the payoff for each Final Four team is more than a million. Where has the money come from? Television rights fees. The fast pace of basketball in its rather limited playing area is a near perfect fit for video production. That makes for great television entertainment.

North Carolina Coach Dean Smith has seen the tournament through four of its five decades, as a player and assistant coach in the 50s and as a head coach in the 60s, 70s, and 80s. "There was more to the tournament in the 60s than in the 50s," he told me, "but there still wasn't that tremendous energy. The Final Four in '62 was big in Louisville, but in '72 it still wasn't real big when we played Florida State in the semis. But then we hit Atlanta in 1977 and found a media blitz, and it was on. I mean, what a change."

Big East Conference Commissioner Dave Gavitt was a member of the NCAA tournament's television committee just as the Final Four's popularity soared. There were two things that served as a catalyst for the growth, Gavitt said in an interview for this book. "One was to open the tournament up to multiple teams from the same conference. If you go back to the days when the ACC could send only one team to the NCAA, think how many great Duke teams never got there because they lost in the ACC tournament. When the NCAA tournament was opened up, every team that had a legitimate chance to win the national championship was assured of being there.

"The second important development was the balancing of the regional tournament pairings. The idea was to make sure that every team that reached the finals had to travel equally hazardous roads. We didn't realize it at the time, but that set up incredible intersectional matchups. In the second round, you would have a Georgetown playing a Memphis State or a Notre Dame against TCU.

"I think the impact of the Final Four became apparent in New Orleans in 1982 when 63,000 people showed up in the Superdome. The final, Georgetown against North Carolina, was such an unbelievable game. It really took the lid off the place. I thought Seattle in 1984 really took the tournament to the next level by wrapping an entire community effort around it.

"Those two things made the tournament a more saleable product. If the Masters golf tournament didn't have all the best players in the world, it wouldn't command the attention or broadcasting rights fees that it does. The NCAA tournament didn't have all the best until it opened up. Once it had all the great teams, it became a totally different property. NBC was paying about $18 million for three years (1979-80-81) until all three networks began bidding in 1980-81. CBS got it for 1982-83-84 by bumping the rights fees to about $48 million. The next time around (for 1985-86-87) CBS almost doubled the rights to about $93 million to make sure they could keep it. Then last year, when CBS again acquired the rights, they paid more than $161 million for 1988-89-90."

The sums of money are mind boggling. In fact, they're fascinating, but they aren't why I'm in love with the NCAA tournament. I remember being a kid in Bethlehem, Pennsylvania (where my father was a basketball coach). I listened on the radio as my hero, Tom Gola, and his LaSalle teammates, won the 1954 NCAA championship. I was heartbroken the next year when Gola and LaSalle were beaten in the NCAA finals by San Francisco and a player I'd never heard of, Bill Russell.

As a young fan, my infatuation with the tournament burned after that. Then, in 1962, I was a senior guard on Bones McKinney's Wake Forest team that made it to the Final Four in Louisville. Ohio State with John Havlicek and Jerry Lucas had a stronger team and beat us in the semifinals. Our prize came in the consolation game, where we played John Wooden's first UCLA team to reach the Final Four. At the time, Wooden was just another good college coach, yet to soar into the realm of legend. We beat his team for third place, the last NCAA tournament loss a Wooden team would suffer until the national semifinals in 1974.

For all the talk of money, entertainment and the modern tournament, I think television's crowning achievement is the capturing of the emotion of the NCAAs. Their charm is the feeling the amateur players bring to the competition, a feeling that quite often seems lost in the professional game.

"I think you almost get too wrapped up in it," Virginia's Lee Raker said before the 1981 Final Four in Philadelphia. "You have such incredible highs, such expectations. Then you don't win. All the emotion that could go one way, could go the other way real quickly."

Different people have responded to that pressure in different ways. At the press conference after his 1975 semifinal win over Louisville, John Wooden told reporters, "I've enjoyed coaching this last team as much as the first." It was a subtle announcement of his retirement, as subtle as the way he coached.

In 1977, Marquette Coach Al McGuire was a city tough crackerjack, talking his crazy lingo and joking loosely in his interview before the championship game with North Carolina. But when his team won, he sat on the bench mindless of the national audience and cried like a baby.

Nothing in my tournament experience was heavier, more somber, than Kentucky in 1978. Coach Joe B. Hall had a great team and was under tremendous pressure to win the national championship. That Monday of the finals I was walking through the hotel and happened upon the Kentucky team at its pre-game meal. It was almost as if the players were at a funeral. There was no joking, no laughing, very little conversation. The players were sullen under their burden. I could sense that anything less than a national championship would bring them no respect in their basketball-crazy Bluegrass.

The 1979 final pitted Larry Bird and Indiana State against Magic Johnson and Michigan State. It's still amazing to me that that game has the highest TV ratings of any Final Four game. If anything, it shows the massive audience has a sixth sense for history.

Earlier in the season, I had said Larry Bird and his team were not worthy of their number-one national ranking. Later, of course, I came to admire Bird's putting his teammates on his back and carrying them to the top of college basketball. During the final shootaround before the championship tipoff, I went onto the floor to talk to Indiana State guard Carl Nicks, who was wearing a T-shirt lampooning me. While I had my back turned, Bird lined his teammates up each with a basketball. And when I turned around, they all tossed a pass at my head. Fortunately, they weren't trying to take my head off. With the way Bird passes, he could have done that easily. Instead, it was a rare flash of his sense of humor during a

Oregon Fans Celebrate the return of the Ducks after their 1939 NCAA championship.

season in which his burden had made him sullen.

For Georgetown Coach John Thompson and Hoya guard Fred Brown, the emotion was born of a very human error, Brown's mistaken pass in the closing moments of 1982's dramatic final against North Carolina. The Tar Heels' James Worthy was out of position on defense as Georgetown, down 63-62, worked the ball for one final shot. Brown mistook Worthy for a teammate and passed him the ball. Astonished, then gleeful, Worthy raced downcourt to preserve Carolina's championship. Brown was disconsolate afterward, until Thompson stepped up and hugged him coming off the floor. It was one of the grand gestures in all of sport.

For many others, the emotion has come in cascades of joy. Foremost among those images is NC State's Jim Valvano immediately after the 1983 upset of Houston in Albuquerque. I remember watching Houston's Phi Slamma Jamma and Louisville put on a dunking exhibition in the semifinal—perhaps the finest display of athleticism in tournament history—and thinking there was no way State could beat the Cougars in the championship.

I wish I could say the game had been a learning experience, but I distinctly remember thinking the same thing two years later before the Villanova/Georgetown final.

The following pages of the Final Four offer a strange mix, of the historical and the personal. If you squint, you can look past the glitter and the klieg lights, past the video cameras and microphones, beyond the technicolor scoreboards, over the bank of word processors on press row, and if you strain your eyes hard enough, you can gaze beyond the Superdomes and Kingdomes, and you just might get a glimpse of the NCAA tournament in its infancy, in simpler days when even the university gyms were little more than dungeons with lumpy, old wrestling mats hung on the walls behind the baskets.

At first, it's an elusive vision. But if you try you can see an America of running boards and passenger trains, and you can see basketball as a game of two-handed set shots and center jumps after each basket. Don't worry if you have trouble connecting the game that was to the game that is. The tournament has come a long way.

An Interview With Curt Gowdy

Over the years, Curt Gowdy has played a major role in the development of the NCAA basketball tournament. His appreciation of college basketball began during his days as a player for the University of Wyoming. Through the 1960s, he repeatedly urged television network officials to broadcast the spectacle and excitement of the games. Finally, network television accepted Gowdy's idea, and the growth of the NCAA tournament hasn't stopped since. As a broadcaster, Gowdy covered the Final Four from 1965 to 1978, an experience that has provided him with a unique perspective of the event.

Packer—Do you recall first hearing of the Final Four?

Gowdy—It wasn't called the Final Four then. It was called the NCAA Basketball Championship, and I heard about it with Oregon winning it in 1939. I had just entered the University of Wyoming. In 1941, we won the Skyline Conference, I believe it was called, or the Rocky Mountain Conference, and went to Kansas City to play in the NCAA tournament. In those days there were four teams from the West—Wyoming, Creighton, Arkansas and Washington State—and four teams from the East—Dartmouth, Pittsburgh, North Carolina, and Wisconsin. We went to Kansas City and we were beaten by Arkansas, a team I still think was one of the greatest college teams I ever saw. They had Pop Freiberger and Shorty Carpenter, and the smallest man was Red Hickey, who later was a great pro football player. He was about 6-foot-2 or -3 and weighed over 200 pounds. I had to cover him. They were upset in the finals in the West by Washington State. Wisconsin won the East, then held off Washington State for the national title.

That was really my first involvement with the NCAA basketball tournament. When I think of the many times I've been in places like New Orleans at the Final Four and watched what was going on, I realize how small it was in those early days. Yet it was still big in the players' minds. The arena was sold out in Kansas City. There was no television of course, and it wasn't the national attraction.

Our 1942 Wyoming team was better than the '43 team, which won the national championship with Kenny Sailors against Georgetown. In '42 we had a better team then the '43 team, but '43 with Kenny Sailors won the championship against Georgetown. Then Wyoming played a charity game with St. John's, the winner of the NIT. And even in Wyoming the NIT, in most peoples' minds, was still the biggest tournament. Wyoming beat St. John's, so the Cowboys enjoyed kind of a double slam in being the NIT and NCAA champs.

The NIT was definitely the better known tournament in those days. I knew all about Ned Irish (the college basketball promoter) and all the college doubleheaders in Madison Square Garden through the 30's. He got great publicity. Irish really did a great job of promoting. I'm surprised they don't mention his name as much today as they used to, because he really made college basketball in New York.

But gradually, as time went on, the NIT waned and the NCAA grew bigger, the field grew bigger. When I became a sports announcer and joined NBC (in 1965) no network would pick up NCAA basketball. It was carried by independent producers. Never was on a national network. I talked with Roone Arledge, who was a young guy then and head of ABC Sports. I said, "I think the biggest bargain today in sports in America is the semifinals of the National Collegiate Basketball Tournament. Name me any other sport where the four best in one sport get together one afternoon in one arena and play. The four best baseball teams don't play in one day. This is a great affair to me when the final four teams play and then the winners play for the national championship."

So I talked him into doing the NCAA tournament in 1962 in Louisville. ABC crammed it down to an hour-and-a-half and put it on Wide World of Sports.

Packer—You were the announcer?

Gowdy—I was the announcer on it.

Packer—Did you have a color man as such in those days?

Gowdy—I don't remember who worked with me. ABC eliminated the halftime. They had to condense it down to an hour-and-a-half to put it on the Wide World of Sports. I'll never forget it. We went down there I think on a Thursday for a Saturday game; and UCLA had a sophomore guard named Walt Hazzard, and Gary Cunningham and Fred Slaughter. They had a small team with Cunningham being the tallest at about 6-foot-5. UCLA played Cincinnati and Wake Forest played Ohio State. Havlicek, Lucas, Knight—these guys, they were all seniors. This was their last shot. Remarkable era for Ohio State in three years. They won the National Championship their sophomore year, then got beat the next two years by Cincinnati. How about two teams from the same state meeting twice in the finals?

Anyway, I'll never forget '62, sitting there and getting ready, scouting the players and everything. UCLA got behind Cincinnati in the semifinals 25 to 4 or something like that, a tremendous deficit, but they came back and

The Final Four has become a premier event of sports television.

tied the game. Then Tom Thacker hit a line drive shot at the buzzer—his only field goal of the afternoon—and won the game for Cincinnati. If he hadn't won that game I'm sure UCLA would have won the title because Jerry Lucas of Ohio State hurt his knee in the other semifinal against the Wake Forest team you played on, Billy.

So then we had Ohio State and Cincinnati going at it, which turned out to be a one-sided affair, a 12-point game. Cincinnati beat them easily and later Ohio State Coach Fred Taylor told me that even with Jerry Lucas healthy he didn't think his team could have beaten them. He was very disappointed about it. ABC took that game and condensed it Saturday afternoon on Wide World of Sports.

Packer—Was it the same Saturday or was it replayed the next week?

Gowdy—No, they showed it the same day. The game was played at two o'clock but the Wide World didn't come on until 6:30. There was no showing of the semifinal games. I kept talking to Arledge. He and I were very close but nobody at ABC really expressed any interest in it. Then NBC got into it. NBC, as you know, really deserves a lot of credit for developing the NCAA tournament television package.

Packer—How many games did you really broadcast on network television?

Gowdy—I did the 1962 game. Then I did them right in a row, '65 through '78.

Packer—What was the first game to be broadcast live?

Gowdy—That started, I think, in 1966. I left ABC at the end of 1965 when they gave up the American Football League package. NBC got the rights to do the AFL and also picked up the baseball game of the week. So the NBC people came to me and said, "Look, the AFL is now ours, and we want you and Christman. We had developed quite a reputation. Paul and I moved over to do the football, and the network people said, "Look, as long as we've got you to do the football, we want you to do the baseball, too."

Then in 1966 NBC came up with the NCAA basketball championship. What a lucky guy I was. Suddenly I was doing the World Series, the Rose Bowl game, the All-Star game, the NCAA basketball championship, the Super Bowl game. How could one guy be that lucky to be with one network that had the rights to all these events?

Now the NCAA semifinals then were played Thursday night, and the final game was played on Saturday. At first, we just did the championship game, and gradually things slid to where they put the semifinal on Saturday afternoon and put the championship game on at night. I

15

Curt Gowdy, veteran broadcaster. Opposite—David Thompson celebrates NC State's 1974 championship.

did that first prime-time game at night and continued to do so as long as I was there. I think the first one at night was in 1970, the year St. Bonaventure made the Final Four, only to have center Bob Lanier get hurt.

Packer—How about the Wooden years, the truly golden period of college basketball? Would you agree that the string of UCLA victories was a big factor in making the tournament a major television event?

Gowdy—Well, it was like the 1987 Kentucky Derby. There was no big horse. When UCLA started its string there was no dominant team. Different teams won it all the time. In a way, the Bruins were a great attraction because everybody loves a winner and soon appreciates the dynasty, which was what they had. And then the burning question became, Could anybody conquer them next year? They were so good and so overpowering; there were only two close championship games that I remember. Florida State gave them a great game out in Los Angeles but lost, 81-76. Hugh Durham was the coach, and the thing that surprised me about Florida State was the defense they played. Durham played UCLA belly-to-belly, met them right at midcourt, and played a tough defensive game.

Another club that gave them a great game was Drake University, who lost, 85-82, in the 1969 semis against Alcindor. Drake gave them a great spurt at the end of the game. Outside of that, most of the championship games were blowouts during Wooden's dynasty. Remember Rick Mount of Purdue? They were beaten badly. It got to be so you really, like most of the Super Bowl games, you started looking forward to something and it just wasn't there. UCLA was so good.

Packer—That string wasn't broken until they lost in the semis to NC State.

Gowdy—I did that game. And the thing I remember about that was the reaction of the UCLA kids. They were very disappointed. Walton and Greg Lee, the guard, said they were going home and weren't going to play in a consolation game. That was another controversy, with the guys who didn't want to play in that third-place game on Monday night. I guess they had a meeting and decided they weren't going to play in the consolation game. And Walton's father—I talked to Walton's father—he came to Walton and said, "Look, these guys gave you a scholarship for four years. With Coach Wooden, you got your college education. If you don't play in that game, don't come home."

So they changed their minds. That 1974 semifinal against NC State is one of the games UCLA, that right now as you and I are talking, John Wooden is sitting at home reliving again. I think UCLA was five to seven points ahead in the second overtime. Tommy Curtis lost a dribble. Lee threw the ball away. They should have won that game. Of all the games I'd seen them play, they blew it in the second overtime to North Carolina State, 80-77, which then won the title. That was the one time I saw them lose in the NCAA. The other time was in Philly, when they lost in the semifinals with Gene Bartow. Here's a guy, Bartow, who takes them to the Final Four, and the big supporters want to fire him out there.

Packer—So you worked the first game, when John Wooden took UCLA to the finals against Cincinnati in 1962, and then the last time, with Gene Bartow.

Gowdy—The last time Wooden ever coached, Billy, you and I worked that one together in San Diego, when they beat Kentucky, 92-85. And one of the finest games I ever saw—you and I saw it together—was the 1975 semifinals, when they beat Louisville in overtime. Richard Washington hit that bucket to tie the game at the buzzer, then they won in overtime. The story about that is that Wooden could have been beaten in the West Regionals. Jud Heathcote's Montana team had them beaten. Heathcote had a guy named Eric Hays, who got 32 points. Hays was a left-handed kid and a brilliant student. The referee accidentally struck Hays in the face late in the game, knocked him to his knees. I tell you, UCLA was very lucky to win that game, but they won the West Regionals. Marques Johnson, a sophomore, got 30 points, and they handily beat Arizona State. But John could have

ended up disappointed by ending a great career by being beaten in the West Regionals. Then he went down to San Diego and walked out a winner and said good-bye to everybody.

I did the first time he played in the Final Four and the last time he played in the Final Four. The teams were different. That first team I saw was a little team. Then he had another little team, Goodrich and those guys, and won with them. Then he had Alcindor and Walton. Wooden won with all kinds of teams. He had two of the greatest centers that ever played who made it a jinx to dominate. One fellow I remember at UCLA—and I kidded Gary Cunningham about it when he was athletic director at Wyoming—was the guy who played his best basketball, John Vallely in the 1969 and '70 NCAA tournaments. You look up his record—he scored 29 points in the '69 semis and 23 points in the '70 semis. He was superb. Vallely is hardly mentioned by UCLA among all their great players and great teams.

Cunningham was a blue chip player and always played the best in the tough games. The Wooden teams were all different but all alike in the regimen. They ran those high-post offenses. I noticed little things about them, how they'd hold their arms up in the free throw lane ready for the rebound, how they'd always banked their side shots. When they'd practice they had a drill where they'd come down, bounce to the baseline and shoot a little bank shot outside the baseline. I asked Wooden about that. He just thought it was an easier way to shoot than aiming straight for the hoop. His teams had beautiful skills fundamentally.

Wooden was a deceiving man in that he mildly rolled up his program during the games. In practice he was tough. When he was a player he was tough. He would drive and crash into the bleachers on layups and played the game hard. His teams played that way.

Packer—Which player had the greatest game you ever saw in the Final Four?

Gowdy—Bill Walton missed one shot, made 21 out of 22 against Memphis State. He got hurt, I remember, toward the end of the game. He crashed to the floor. But that was about the best single performance I've ever seen. Walton was the best passing center I ever saw. He could have played outside. It's a shame he got hurt. His career could have been something. The one thing I'll always remember about Walton was when I went out to do the Rose Bowl game and I wrote a story for a magazine and it came out in December predicting the All-America team. UCLA was playing their opening game of the season that night, and I went out to watch them play. Some guy from the team comes to me and asks, "You know Bill Walton?"

I said, "Yes, he's a new center."

"He wants to see you."

Al McGuire shouts instructions during the 1977 final.

Well, Walton tore into me for not picking him for the All-Star team. He was a sophomore and he was going to play his first college game that night. He pointed out that his freshman team had beaten the varsity by 20 points.

I said, "No, I didn't pick you. I didn't know much about you."

He said, "Well, you should have done better research."

He really jumped all over me. I watched him play that night, and I could tell he was going to be great. He was a very emotional type. Every time he'd come down the court he'd look over at Wooden to see if he'd done all right, and Wooden would shake his head at him.

Packer—Who had the best team you ever saw? What team would you want to take out on the court and win with?

Gowdy—I suppose either the Walton team that won

the title or Alcindor's team. Knight had a great team in '76. The thing we forget about Knight is he lost one game in two years. The 1975 Indiana team was a great one. Scott May, their best player, had a broken arm when they lost to Kentycky by one point. Listen, Bobby always claimed that 1975 team was better than the one that won it all the next year.

Packer—The first game that you covered, how many cameras were used?

Gowdy—Three or four. And we had no slow motion then. The Japanese invented slow motion...But NBC every year kept adding more cameras, and they became more prepared and they really built that package up. One thing that was very important was Tom Gallery, a legendary guy in our business, a former sports director at NBC, used to pound his fist: "Where's the sound? I want to hear the ball bouncing, I want to hear those bodies running, I want the sound." NBC planted those mikes all over everywhere. Sound is so important to video. NBC worked hard to bring that sound off the court; they were good at that.

Packer—What about broadcasting in the early days of the Final Four. Was radio big? What were the early rights fees for television?

Gowdy—There was little broadcasting in the early days. When we broadcast our Wyoming game back home, the radio networks wouldn't even touch it back then. Why I don't know. The first NCAA tournament game ever played, Oregon lost money. They went home and had to pay some of their expenses out of their own pockets. The first TV rights fees were probably one or two million dollars to start. From there, it's done nothing but escalate. When the tournament got to 32 teams, I thought that was big enough. But I will have to say that the 64-team format has become to me a giant Indiana or Illinois state basketball tournament.

Packer—Do you like it that way?

Gowdy—I like it. I think it added a tremendous excitement. Every part of America is represented. There are a lot of teams in there, Cleveland State beating Indiana, Arkansas beating Notre Dame. Suddenly you hear about teams that had no name scoring upsets, and it's really exciting. But the thing that has made the NCAAs so popular is that the teams are from across America. Everybody's got a team in there and someone to root for. And the tension builds and builds. I thought the 64-team field would be unwieldy. Yet all those teams have added a dimension to make it rated up there with the Super Bowl and the World Series. It creates great national attention in America. When I played in it, the field was the four regional champs in the West and the four regional champs in the East. The Ivy League had representation.

Packer—When you played in the tournament in 1941, no one could have envisioned its growth over 50 years.

Yet you probably had as much insight as anybody. At least you asked ABC to get involved in it.

Gowdy—Yes, I did. I used to pound away at that. I used to make speeches: "You want a real bargain day in America? Go see the semifinals of the college basketball championship. WHERE? Right here in America. In no other major sport can you get the four best teams together in one day in one arena. Then the color of it all, and the bands. I watched it this year as a spectator in New Orleans. I left there, and my wife, who's not a big sports fan, said, "That was a great week down there, really exciting."

I've seen this thing grow. It started in '39, and I played in it in '41, so I've been in it since it's birth. And I broadcast I think 14 finals on TV and four on radio, so I've done 18 in some form. I've seen it advance and advance, and I don't think anybody thought it would get this big. I think now it's at the stage where it could become a national high school tournament. When I say high school I'm talking about the excitement, where a Marion, Indiana, could win three in a row, where a small town could beat a big town. All that human drama's packed into it now. Unknown teams knock off the big boys. Teams you've never heard of suddenly come out, and you see what great players they are. All that human element has made it what it is.

The human element and the great games. I think of the Louisville-UCLA game you and I did together in 1975. Another of the great games was the Runnin' Rebs of Las Vegas against Dean Smith's North Carolina team in the '77 semis. I'd never seen this Vegas team play. I thought, "What is this, a bunch of smokers running up and down the court and shooting?" They played baseline-to-baseline defense and baseline-to-baseline offense, and they missed a shot right at the end that hit the hoop and bounced away. North Carolina played Marquette for the national title, and Dean Smith went into the four corners. I think he is the greatest coach that ever lived. They were behind at the half, caught up, tied Marquette, went up a point or two, then went into that stall. I think it cost him the game. I bet Dean still thinks about that. In a championship, one of the worst things you can do is get your team's momentum up, then go into a stall too early. But he put that four corners on them, and Marquette beat him. I will never forget that game.

My next connection with the Final Four was the '46 championship game at Madison Square Garden. I was a broadcaster for Oklahoma A&M, now Oklahoma State. We had about a 50-station network throughout the state of Oklahoma. The game was Carolina's Bones McKinney against A&M's Bob Kurland. I did that game, and the Aggies won the national title. So that was the first championship game I did in the NCAA tournament. Apparently they had 18,000 packed in there. It was a good game.

Ducks, Firs and Such

The NCAA tournament was born in 1939 during the days of the two-handed set shot, an era of lower scores and shorter players . Black-leather high tops were the going shoe, and slam dunks were almost unheard of.

The NCAA was a meek sister in those early years. The National Invitational Tournament, couched in the big crowds and big publicity of Madison Square Garden, had been launched a year earlier, 1938, and met with almost instant success. After seeing their first college game at the Garden in 1934 (between New York University and Notre Dame) New Yorkers were hungry for sports entertainment, and they delighted in the NIT.

The NCAA tournament, on the other hand, matured slowly, existing in an embryo of small college gyms and sparse crowds. Yet the college coaches and administrators who formed it took heart in the idea that it was a national tournament, its early rounds staged in university communities across the heartland.

The tournament's original format divided the country into eight districts from which one team would be selected for the eight-team field. This initial format lasted for the first 12 years of the tournament.

The eight teams were picked by selection committees from each region. In that first year, it became apparent that the NIT would take many of its teams from the pool of independent schools, while most of the NCAA's entries were affiliated with conferences.

In that first year, the field included Brown with a 17-3 record, Villanova at 19-4, Ohio State at 14-6, Oklahoma at 11-8, Texas at 19-4, Wake Forest at 18-5, and Utah State from the old Skyline Conference. Oregon entered with a 26-5 record, having played what for those times was a monstrous 31-game schedule.

The four eastern division teams met March 17 at the Palestra in Philadelphia, where it was noted that the inclusion of Villanova helped draw a crowd. With only 3,000 spectators, the western divisions began three days later in San Francisco.

The Oregon Ducks were something of an early trendsetter, playing an ambitious schedule and using a dominant inside game. Coach Howard "Hobby" Hobson's team was tall by 1939 standards, with 6-foot-8 Slim Wintermute at center, and two 6-foot-4 1/2 forwards—Laddie Gale and John Dick—on either side. Their fans nicknamed them "The Tall Firs."

With their height and the experience their schedule brought them, the Firs flexed their power game in the West and moved past Texas, 56-41, and Oklahoma, 55-37.

In the East, Ohio State was anything but a favorite. Through the regular season, Coach Harold Olsen's Buckeyes hadn't shown much offensive flair. Only four times in a 20-game schedule had they scored more than 50 points. Yet they awakened offensively in the tournament and outdistanced Wake Forest 64-52 in the first round, as guard Dick Baker scored 25 points, then a Palestra record. With the outburst, Ohio State broke the Palestra's team-scoring record of 52 points, which is a good indication of the tempo of the game in the 1930s.

Baker's teammate and State's captain, Jim Hull, took over in the second round and quickly broke his teammate's new record by scoring 28 points as the Buckeyes eliminated Villanova, 53-36.

Patton Gym at Northwestern University in Evanston, Illinois, was the site of the championship that Friday, March 27. About 5,000 spectators were attracted to the event, where they watched 5-foot-8 guard Bobby Anet, the shortest of the Firs, push Oregon to the first NCAA championship. The Ducks led 21-16 at the half, then used their inside advantage to win, 46-33. Dick scored 15 for the winners; Hull paced Ohio State with 12.

TOURNAMENT NOTES: The championship trophy was broken during the game when Oregon's Anet crashed into the trophy table going after a loose ball. The NCAA netted a $2,531 loss on its first tournament, the only deficit in the history of the event.

Opposite—Oregon Coach Howard Hobson was elected to the Hall of Fame in 1965. Bottom left—Front: (L-R) Wally Johansen, Slim Wintermute, Bobby Anet, Coach Howard Hobson, Laddie Gale, John Dick; Back (L-R): Bob Hardy, Red McNeely, Jay Langston, Ford Mullen, Matt Pavalunas, Trainer Bob Officer, Ted Sarpola, Earl Sandness. Above left—Big Ten Commissioner John Griffith presents the NCAA championship trophy to Bobby Anet of Oregon. Ohio State center James Hall is in the center. Above right—Oregon's Lauren "Laddie" Gale was elected to the Hall of Fame in 1976.

1939

Oregon	fg	ft-fta	pf	tp
Gale	2	4- 5	1	8
Dick	5	5- 5	3	15
Wintermute	2	0- 1	1	4
Anet	4	2- 3	3	10
Johansen	4	1- 2	1	9
Mullen	0	0- 0	0	0
Pavalunas	0	0- 0	0	0
Totals	17	12-16	9	46

Ohio State	fg	ft-fta	pf	tp
Hull	5	2- 2	2	12
Baker	0	0- 1	0	0
Schick	1	0- 0	1	2
Dawson	1	0- 0	4	2
Lynch	3	1- 3	3	7
Maag	0	0- 0	0	0
Scott	0	1- 1	1	1
Boughner	1	0- 0	0	2
Sattler	3	1- 2	0	7
Mickelson	0	0- 0	2	0
Stafford	0	0- 0	0	0
Totals	14	5- 9	13	33

Half time: Oregon 21-16. Officials: Getchell and Clarno.

Hoosiers, Ho!

History marked the 1939-40 college basketball season with a neat crease, folding one era while ushering in another. Dr. James Naismith, who had founded basketball in 1891, died on November 28, 1939. While his passing marked an end to the formative years of the game, the modern era was born quietly three months later on February 28, 1940, when a New York station, W2XBS (it would later evolve into WNBC), offered the first televised broadcast of a college basketball game, a doubleheader from Madison Square Garden matching Pitt against Fordham and NYU against Georgetown.

As for the second edition of the NCAA tournament, its competition was stronger. Even better, the 1940 tournament produced some surprises. It was the year that legend laid its framework in the finals meeting between Indiana, coached by Branch McCracken, and Kansas, coached by Dr. Forrest "Phog" Allen.

For all their later years of glory, both teams were Cinderellas in 1940. Indiana finished second in the Big Ten behind Purdue, despite two wins over the Boilermakers. When Purdue declined the invitation to the NCAA tournament, the Hoosiers were only happy to take their place in history.

Kansas, meanwhile, had won a playoff from Oklahoma and Missouri to take the Big Six title, but the Jayhawks weren't considered prime contenders. The top team in the country was thought to be Southern Cal with Ralph Vaughn and a 19-2 record. The Trojans had ended Long Island's 34-game winning streak during the regular season, then had hammered Oregon State, 62-26, in the Pacific Coast playoff. In the first round of the NCAA West, Southern Cal defeated another favorite, Colorado, which had won the NIT just days earlier and accepted a bid to the NCAA.

Despite the Trojans' momentum, Kansas stopped them in the West semifinals, 43-42. USC led by a point with 17 seconds to play, but Howard Engleman scored to give Kansas the upset. Ralph Miller, who would go on to coaching greatness at Oregon State, scored 10 points for Kansas.

In the East, Indiana's fast-break offense ran a weave drill through the competition. First the Hoosiers dispatched little Springfield College, 48-24. Then they eliminated Duquesne, a team that had lost to Colorado in the NIT finals earlier in the year.

The Finals were held in Kansas City's Municipal Auditorium, meaning a home crowd advantage for the Jayhawks, whose campus was an hour away. The crowd was estimated at a little over 9,000, near capacity for the 10,000-seat auditorium. But the game was dominated by Indiana, 60-42. Marv Huffman scored 12 for the Hoosiers and was named the the tournament's most valuable player, the first selected by the NCAA. Huffman and teammates Jay McCreary and Bill Menke were selected to the first all-tournament team, along with Engleman and Bob Allen of Kansas.

TOURNAMENT NOTES: The second NCAA tournament made a profit of $9,590. The two schools in the championship each received $750.

Indiana Coach Branch McCracken.

Team photo above—The Indiana Hoosiers National Champions 1939-40: Front (L-R) Jim Gridley, Herm Schaefer, Bob Dro, Marv Huffman, Jay McCreary, Curley Armstrong, Ralph Dorsey. Back (L-R) Coach Branch McCracken, Chet Francis, Bill Menke, Andy Zimmer, Bob Menke, Ralph Graham. Bottom—Dr. James Naismith, inventor of basketball, died as the 1939-40 season began. Bottom right—Indiana's Marv Huffman was named tournament MVP.

1940

Indiana	fg	ft-fta	pf	tp
Schaefer	4	1- 1	1	9
McCreary	6	0- 0	2	12
W. Menke	2	1- 2	3	5
Huffman	5	2- 3	4	12
Dro	3	1- 1	4	7
Armstrong	4	2- 3	3	10
Gridley	0	0- 0	0	0
R. Menke	0	0- 0	0	0
Zimmer	2	1- 1	1	5
Dorsey	0	0- 0	0	0
Francis	0	0- 0	1	0
Totals	26	8-11	19	60

Kansas	fg	ft-fta	pf	tp
Ebling	1	2- 5	0	4
Engleman	5	2- 3	3	12
Allen	5	3- 4	3	13
Miller	0	2- 2	4	2
Harp	2	1- 3	1	5
Hunter	0	1- 1	0	1
Hogben	2	0- 0	0	4
Kline	0	0- 0	0	0
Voran	0	1- 2	0	1
Sands	0	0- 0	0	0
Johnson	0	0- 0	0	0
Totals	15	12-20	11	42

Half time: Indiana 32-19. Officials: O'Sullivan and McDonald.

Badgered

The University of Wisconsin Badgers had suffered through a ninth-place finish in the Big Ten for the 1940 season. But then Coach Harold "Bud" Foster's players found their identity in his methodical offense and shoved Indiana aside for the conference championship in 1941.

That March, the Badgers found themselves with a 12-game winning streak and a home-court advantage heading into the first round of the NCAA tournament. Even that almost wasn't enough to survive.

Wisconsin's first-round opponent was Dartmouth, with All-American Gus Broberg. Although the game was played in Wisconsin's gym, Broberg scored 20 points and kept Dartmouth ahead until the last minute, when Wis-

consin sophomore John Kotz hit two free throws to allow the Badgers to advance, 51-50. All-American center Gene Englund scored 18 points for Wisconsin.

The Badgers' opponent in the East semifinals was Pittsburgh, another methodical team that had eased past North Carolina, 26-20. In a match of methodology, Foster's team worked its precision game to a 36-30 win before 14,000 screaming fans (NCAA officials noted the enthusiasm and revenue a home crowd could generate). For the third year in a row, the Big Ten had a team in the finals.

In the West, a fast-breaking Washington State team had beaten Stanford in the Pacific Coast playoffs and kept that pace through the NCAA opening rounds. Led by 6-foot-7 center Paul Lindeman, State beat Creighton, 48-39, in the first round and faced Arkansas, the tournament favorite, in the West semifinals at the Kansas City Municipal auditorium.

The Razorbacks were considered heavy favorites to win the third NCAA championship with high-scoring guard Johnny Adams. Adams kept up the heat during the tournament, averaging 24 points over two games, but Washington State's fast break rolled to the win, 64-53.

The Badgers took their leather knee pads, striped socks and quaint control offense to Kansas City, where sportswriters were predicting that Washington State's fast break would blow by Wisconsin.

But Foster's cautious offense and stifling defense turned the game into a battle of centers. Englund overpowered the taller Lindeman, as State's offense went through a nine-minute scoreless stretch in the first half. When State's offense again struggled in the second half, Wisconsin's plodding attack settled the issue, 39-34.

TOURNAMENT NOTES: Wisconsin sophomore John Kotz scored 12 points in the final and was named the tournament MVP. North Carolina's prolific scorer George Glamack (he had scored 45 points during a regular-season game), knocked in 31 points during the tournament's first consolation game, setting an NCAA playoff scoring record that would last almost a decade.

Left—Wisconsin's John Kotz was MVP of the 1941 tournament.
Above right—Wisconsin's Charles Epperson rebounds against Washington State's Kirk Gebert. The Badgers celebrate by carrying Coach H.E. "Bud" Foster off the floor.
The Wisconsin five join hands at bottom right (L-R)—Ted Starin, Gene Englund, Charles Epperson John Kotz and Fred Rehm.

1941				
Wisconsin	fg	ft-fta	pf	tp
Epperson	2	0- 0	3	4
Schrage	0	0- 0	1	0
Kotz	5	2- 3	2	12
Englund	5	3- 4	2	13
Timmerman	1	0- 0	1	2
Rehm	2	0- 1	2	4
Strain	0	2- 2	1	2
Alwin	1	0- 0	0	2
Totals	16	7-10	12	39
Washington State	fg	ft-fta	pf	tp
Gentry	0	1- 2	1	1
Gilberg	1	0- 2	1	2
Butts	1	1- 1	1	3
Lindeman	0	3- 4	1	3
Zimmerman	0	0- 0	0	0
Gebert	10	1- 2	1	21
Hunt	0	0- 0	0	0
Sundquist	2	0- 1	3	4
Hooper	0	0- 0	0	0
Totals	14	6-12	8	34

Half time: Wisconsin 21-17. Officials: Haarlow and Cameron.

Stanford's Run

The 1941-42 college basketball season was marked by the eeriness of Pearl Harbor and America's gathering of forces to fight World War II. As much as possible, however, the NCAA tournament maintained a business-as-usual atmosphere. The competition brought together a collection of first-rate college teams: Once-beaten Colorado and young-but-talented Stanford from the West; in the East, sportswriters were raving over the Illinois Whiz Kids and Dartmouth with George Munroe.

And a grand tradition was born as Adolph Rupp's Kentucky Wildcats made their first appearance in the tournament. They would make the field 30 more times over the next 44 years, winning five championships. Their role in the '42 tournament was that of spoiler. In the East first round, played in New Orleans before only 3,000 spectators, Kentucky ended the season of sophomore All-American Andy Phillip and the Illinois Whiz Kids, 46-44. For the first time in the tournament's short history, there would be no Big Ten team in the finals.

With the Illini finished, Dartmouth and Munroe charged to the top in the East and whacked Rupp's team in the semifinals, 47-28.

In the West, Everett Dean's Stanford team had compiled a 25-4 regular-season record, but the Indians struggled in their opening round game against Rice. After building a substantial first-half lead, they floundered in the second half and fell behind late. Finally, they regained their footing on the strength of freshman forward Jim Pollard's 26 points and defeated Rice, 53-47.

A classic confrontation was anticipated in the West semifinal match-up between Stanford and Colorado. Traveling on the talent of Bob Doll and Leason McCloud, Colorado had put together a string of wins against the country's top teams, losing only to Wyoming, 40-39.

But the Buffalo's magic came unglued against Stanford. Pollard scored 17 points, and the Indians advanced easily to the finals, 46-35.

Dean, who had coached at Indiana for 14 years before leaving for Stanford in 1938, was poised to claim the championship when bad luck struck. Pollard was diagnosed as having the flu and was unable to play in the final. Suddenly the scoring burden shifted to substitutes Jack Dana and Fred Linari. Dana scored 14 points and Linari six. Howard Dallmar led Stanford with a game-high 15 points as the Indians downed Dartmouth in a walk, 53-38.

TOURNAMENT NOTES: Dallmar was named the tournament MVP, as Stanford used its one and only appearance in the NCAA tournament to claim the championship. Stanford remains the only school in tournament history with a perfect record, 4-0.

Team photo below—Stanford's 1942 NCAA champions (L-R): Bill Cowden, Howie Dallmar, Ed Voss, Jim Pollard, Don Burness, and Coach Dean.

1942				
Stanford	fg	ft-fta	pf	tp
Dana	7	0- 0	0	14
Eikelman	0	0- 0	0	0
Burness	0	0- 0	0	0
Linari	3	0- 0	0	6
Voss	6	1- 1	2	13
Madden	0	0- 0	0	0
Cowden	2	1- 2	3	5
McCaffrey	0	0- 0	0	0
Dallmar	6	3- 5	0	15
Oliver	0	0- 0	0	0
Totals	24	5- 8	5	53
Dartmouth	fg	ft-fta	pf	tp
Meyers	4	0- 1	1	8
Parmer	1	0- 0	0	2
Munroe	5	2- 2	1	12
Shaw	0	0- 0	0	0
Olsen	4	0- 0	0	8
Pogue	0	0- 0	0	0
Pearson	2	2- 2	3	6
McKernan	0	0- 0	0	0
Skaug	1	0- 0	2	2
Briggs	0	0- 0	0	0
Totals	17	4- 5	7	38

Half time: Stanford 24-22. Officials: Curtis and Adams.

An Interview With Jim Pollard

As a sophomore, Jim Pollard helped Stanford win the 1942 NCAA championship. After college, he teamed up with the great George Mikan to give the Minneapolis Lakers a string of five NBA championships in six years.

Packer—You played two great games in the 1942 NCAA tournament, leading Stanford right up to the finals. But you missed the championship game. What happened?

Pollard—I missed the final game. I was really crying. I was an 18-year-old sophomore, and I was playing the best ball I had played in my life. I got out of bed one morning with a really bad case of sinus. That was the days before penicillin so I was given sulfa drugs and had a bad reaction to the sulfa. I got out of bed about 7:30 to go to the game on Saturday night at 8:00. I had to bundle up; the doctor was with me. I had to put a towel over my head or he wouldn't let me go. As soon as the game was over I had to go back to the hotel.

Packer—You sat on the bench?

Pollard—No, they wouldn't even let me sit on the bench. I had to sit in a special place with some of the good alumni. And as soon as the game was over the doctor made me go right back to the hotel. I could only watch it.

Packer—That had to be a heartbreak for you because you had played well.

Pollard—Yeah, it was a big time. I had made 43 points in two games. I broke all the scoring records at that time. So I was ready. I was in great shape. The guys on the team were in great shape except for our forward Don Burness (who had sprained an ankle). How I got ill I have no idea. I just got hit with it and was down on my back with a fever of 104 for about three days in a row.

Packer—Being held out must have been very emotional for an 18-year-old on the brink of becoming a star.

Pollard—Oh, it was a crushing defeat as far as I was personally concerned because we had had all our reports from coach Everett Dean, and I thought I was ready to break every record again. I felt I was in a good streak; the team was in good shape; and we had a tremendous amount of confidence in ourselves. To miss out on the big, number one game of the year was crushing.

Packer—With you and Don Burness out, how did Stanford win the championship?

Pollard—The guy who really came through and won most valuable player was Howie Dallmar. Dallmar was a great ball player, and he just stepped forward. Everett Dean knew how to motivate players. I don't know how he

Jim Pollard was elected to the Hall of Fame in 1977.

did it, but before the earlier games he had talked to me about picking up the scoring slack. Before my big games in the early rounds, I was so excited that I didn't go to sleep until 4:30 the next morning. I think he did the same thing with Howie before the championship.

Packer—In those early years of the NCAA, the hotbed of basketball was thought to be the East, particularly New York City. How did Stanford put together a championship team?

Pollard—Well, we had a unique team. First of all, the first seven guys on our ball club had all played center in high school. We were all local. There were three from San Francisco and the rest from the Oakland area. The whole team was very familiar with one another because most of us had played against each other in high school. But at Stanford, we changed positions. Coach Dean converted three of us to forwards and two of us to guards. And we didn't have any trouble adjusting because in the games, as soon as we found we had a small man playing against us, we would post up and play the pivot again. As a team, a lot of times we would play the double pivot. We had a marvelous coach in Everett Dean, one of my all-time favorite gentlemen, who would sit down and patiently talk with us and convince us that what he was doing was right. He made me a forward and Howie Dallmar, who was a great ball player, a guard. Our guards were 6-foot and 6-foot-4, which was unusual in those days. We were all pretty good ball handlers because we had played the center where we need to be able to pass all the time. So we got along very well. Our rebounding was the best in the country, I think. And yet in my memory we had only one team that could outrun us, as big as we were. We had two guys at 6-foot-3, one at 6-foot-4, one at 6-5 and one at 6-6. In 1942 that was great height.

Packer—Everett Dean came to Stanford from Indiana in 1938. Did he bring the running game with him, or was it something he had to adjust to in West Coast play?

Pollard—I think he brought a little bit, and he also adjusted to California play. When I went to Stanford, he made me drop everything that I shot and shoot the one-hander, which was much better suited to the running game than the set shot.

Packer—You were a two-handed shooter at that time?

Pollard—Yeah, either that or I played the pivot. Or I did a lot of hook shooting or follow up. My high school coach did not like the one-handed shot, and I was not allowed to shoot it. When I got to Stanford, I wasn't supposed to shoot the two-handed, which was terrible anyway. I became a one-handed shooter. I think Everett adjusted some of his style from Indiana, which was a running style, into our particular offense, where all of us were one-handed shooters. We didn't have any two-handed shooters on the club.

Packer—Fans and basketball observers seem to think

there's a lot of new strategy in modern basketball. But Stanford played a match-up zone in your day, plus a lot of different defensive looks.

Pollard—In the 1942 final against Dartmouth in the NCAA we played a three-man zone and a two-man, man-to-man. Bill Cowden, who was our defensive guard, simply played their big man man-to-man the whole time and never switched off. We played that frequently that year.

Packer—In 1938 Hank Luisetti finished a four-year career at Stanford by scoring 1,596 points, which was then a collegiate record. He was known for his one-handed "Wild West" shot. When he played in the East, it was suggested that his style was freakish and fundamentally unsound. Did he have an influence on West Coast players?

Pollard—Oh, tremendously. Really he was not the first one-handed shooter. But he popularized it, and he was one of the greatest ball players and he had great style. He was a great guy to watch. He had that charisma about him that everybody liked. And I think that because he was such a graceful ball player and such a great one that everybody tried to copy the greatness he had. But Hank was not primarily a scorer. He was a great defensive ball player and an excellent passer. Everybody gives him credit for popularizing the one-hander, which he did. I admit I freely copied it because he was my hero when I was a kid.

Packer—What was the first time you ever saw Luisetti play?

Pollard—When I was a sophomore in high school. He was at Stanford. I lived in Oakland, and we used to go to the ball games because my playground coach in the summer played guard on the Cal team and every once in a while he could sneak us into a ball game. He'd take two or three of us good kids, sneak us in, and tell us to sit way up at the top and get lost someplace. But I got to see Hank play a number of times and played against him frequently in the service for a couple of years. Then when I got out of the service we were going to play together in the Oakland area. I was dying to play with him. He had been hurt during the war when he got spinal meningitis. We scrimmaged about 10 minutes one day. Hank and I took the next three best ball players and scrimmaged against them and just wiped them. Hank was marvelous. But that was the only time in my knowledge that he walked on the floor and shot the ball. He walked off the floor just like he was drunk. He was weaving; he'd lost his sense of balance. I don't think he ever got on the court again to play.

Packer—Did Coach Dean change your shot during your freshman year?

Pollard—We were not eligible as freshman. Dean and his assistant, H.B.Lee, who played with Hank Luisetti at Stanford, used to come out right after practice to work with me individually. He would always get me and for maybe 15 to 20 minutes every day we would go down to an empty basket and pass the ball. Shoot right, shoot left, fake right, fake left, go right, double fake, fake, come back and shoot the one-hander. He made me learn all the moves that the forwards play. I did that every day religiously after practice. He would say, "Well, this is the position you're going to play next year, and you've got to learn to play it well."

Packer—Jim, where did you develop the fluid style you had when I first saw you play with the great Minneapolis Lakers team. Fans today think of great agile forwards such as Dr. J. But you were really the first guy who had a flair at that position, who had an ability to put the ball on the floor, drive to the hoop, shoot the jumper, play at your size with a flair. Where did that come from?

Pollard—I don't know. I think a guy who really helped me was my high school coach. I still love the old man. I go out to see him every couple of months now. He still lives in Oakland. In the old days, frontcourt players seldom ever dribbled. I can remember when I was a senior in high school I made 29 points in a game. The scoring record was 30, and I got hungry. I wanted the 31 points and took a wild shot. And he benched me with three minutes to go in the game. I must have come out crying like the dickens, like a spoiled 17-year-old. Coach said, "No, Jim, this is a five-man game. You will get your place back because you're the best ball player, for no other reason."

And so finally I went back. I missed two free throws, I missed a layup, and I missed a tip shot. And to this day he has never given me one bit of sympathy. I think he helped me a lot because he thought I was poor dribbling left-handed. I went to practice one day, and the manager met me there and he said, "Jim don't get mad at me but the coach has orders. You are to take this ball and dribble up and down the side of the court left-handed until he calls for you."

I did that for 10 minutes every day for about two weeks. Finally I got in a ball game and I got out in a forward spot and I faked the guy and I put the ball on the floor right-handed and flipped the ball over to the left hand and dribbled in and made a layup and I ran right to the coach and yelled and screamed at him: "It works, it works!" From then on I never had a moment's hesitation dribbling left-handed.

When I got with Everett Dean at Stanford he preached team play. He used to practice a lot on rebounding skills. He allowed me to rebound with one hand, which a lot of coaches used to look down on. But I felt I could jump a little higher and reach an inch or more, and sometimes jumping against a guy 6-10 or 6-11 I needed that one-inch advantage. I did most of my rebounding one-handed. Both my high school and college coaches stressed passing. A lot of the things you do in basketball come naturally

or are learned from playground ball. But many other key ingredients were stressed by coaches. Those things helped me a tremendous amount.

Packer—Today when a team wins the NCAA tournament, the players and coaches receive great ticker-tape parades and TV accolades. What happened when Stanford won in 1942 and had a long trip home to California from Kansas City?

Pollard—The very next day we had to catch a train for a three-day trip back. If I remember right, Everett Dean told me one time finally after all the money had been counted we made ninety three dollars and some cents. And no one was there at the train depot to welcome us back. There were a couple of alumni to cheer us off when we left and then we had the trip back to Stanford and except for a few close friends or fraternity brothers, we didn't have any fans there at all. The San Francisco Chronicle gave us a great write-up and told us we had done a great job and mentioned the national fame we brought to Stanford. But otherwise, it all blew over fairly quickly.

Packer—Right after the championship you left school and later went into the service. If there had not been a war, could Stanford have repeated as champions?

Pollard—Well, we would have lost two very valuable guys—Bill Cowden, our top defensive guard, and Donnie Burness. The rest of us would have returned. We had returning players in four of the five positions. Actually, we had the guard situation well taken care of with Howie Dallmar. And we had three excellent forwards. We could have used a backup center and a backup guard, but it could have happened because we were good competitors. I know Dallmar got to be better, I got to be better, our center was a guy who improved more than anybody. We had three key positions that were improving. It could have happened.

Cowboys In The Garden

World war leaned heavily on college basketball in 1943, as it did all of American society. The country's need for military manpower siphoned off many of the game's bright young players. With wartime travel restrictions, most schools played games closer to home. Cross-country and intersectional rivalries were put on hold and replaced by games with nearby YMCAs and amateur athletic association teams. More than anything, the war seemed to give fate an even larger role in the outcome of competition, if that's possible.

Many of the country's best teams formed at military bases, where college athletes were sent for training after being drafted. Some colleges benefitted from the upheaval. Those who prospered had military training programs on their campuses or with bases nearby, meaning a new talent pool. Dick McGuire had starred at St. John's, but after he went in the service, he suddenly appeared at Dartmouth, where he was undergoing military training. His presence helped the New Hampshire school to an NCAA appearance in 1944.

The war also placed a premium on good players, mostly freshmen and sophomores, who were too young to be drafted. At DePaul, 6-foot-10 freshman center George Mikan was too tall to be drafted and led Coach Ray Meyer's first team to the NCAA semifinals.

The Whiz Kids at the University of Illinois with Andy Phillip were back again, dominating the Big Ten and earning plaudits as the best team in the nation. Yet when the season came to a close, school officials declined an invitation to the NCAA tournament.

That move meant that for the first time the Big Ten would not be represented. It also created a rare opportunity for any other Midwest team to receive an invitation. Meyer's DePaul team was selected.

With George Mikan scoring 20, the Blue Demons from Chicago dispatched Dartmouth, 45-35, in the first round of the East Regionals. In the other bracket, John Mahnken led the Georgetown Hoyas over New York University, 55-36.

Eyeing the financial success of the NIT in Madison Square Garden, the NCAA tournament directors had decided to move their East Regionals and the national championship game to the Garden in 1943. The invitation to NYU, the first New York school to appear in the NCAA tournament, was an apparent attempt to draw the city crowd to the Garden. A crowd of 16,500 showed up for the March 24 opening of the East Regional, only to see NYU's offense fizzle in a 55-36 loss to freshman center John

DePaul's George Mikan.

Mahnken andthe Georgetown Hoyas.

The East Regional final in the Garden was a faceoff of freshman centers - DePaul's Mikan and - Georgetown's Mahnken. Mikan would go on to greatness in the NBA, but for a night in the NCAA tournament Mahnken prevailed, scoring 17 points to Mikan's 11, as Georgetown

Wyoming Coach Ev Shelton celebrates the 1943 championship with his Cowboys.

came from behind and won, 53-49.

In the West, the University of Texas with All-American guard John Hargis had the power, but Wyoming and Kenny Sailors had the magic. In the opening round in Kansas City, Hargis set a new tournament record by scoring 30 as the Longhorns eased by Washington, 59-55.

Wyoming faced Oklahoma in the other West opener and trailed until the fourth quarter when center Milo Komenich led the Cowboys to a 53-50 comeback win. Komenich finished with 22 points. In the West finals, Wyoming again fell behind early, as Hargis scored another 29 points. But the Texas star got into foul trouble late, allowing the Cowboys to sneak into the national championship game, 58-54. Komenich again led Wyoming with 17 points.

With no home team in the championship, the Madison Square Garden crowd dwindled to 13,000 for the NCAA finals. That, however, was still much larger than the crowds the event had drawn in Kansas City in previous years.

The Cowboys resumed their familiar pattern in the championship game against Georgetown. The Garden chilled both teams into a low-scoring first half (Wyoming led, 18-16, at intermission). Georgetown took a five point lead in the third quarter. The Cowboys caught up, and the game remained close until the last 90 seconds, when Wyoming scored nine straight points to claim the championship, 46-34.

TOURNAMENT NOTES: Kenny Sailors scored 16 points in the championship to be named the game's MVP. Hargis of Texas had scored 59 points in two games, an NCAA record. After the NCAA tournament, Wyoming played the NIT champion, St. John's, in the Red Cross Classic, a war-effort benefit. The Cowboys won, 52-47, giving the NCAA an edge in bragging rights.

1943

Wyoming	fg	ft-fta	pf	tp
Sailors	6	4- 5	2	16
Collins	4	0- 0	1	8
Weir	2	1- 3	2	5
Waite	0	0- 0	0	0
Komenich	4	1- 4	2	9
Volker	2	1- 2	3	5
Roney	0	1- 2	1	1
Reese	1	0- 0	0	2
Totals	19	8-16	11	46
Georgetown	**fg**	**ft-fta**	**pf**	**tp**
Reilly	1	0- 0	0	2
Potolicchio	1	2- 3	1	4
Gabbianelli	1	2- 3	3	4
Hyde	0	0- 0	0	0
Mahnken	2	2- 3	2	6
Hassett	3	0- 3	4	6
Finnerty	0	0- 0	0	0
Kraus	2	0- 1	3	4
Fenney	4	0- 0	1	8
Duffey	0	0- 0	0	0
Totals	14	6-13	14	34

Half time: Wyoming 18-16. Officials: Kennedy and Begovich.

Utah's Train Ride

Easily, 1944 qualifies as college basketball's strangest season. The path of the champion, the University of Utah, was circuitous and fateful. But then, in retrospect, so was the rest of the season.

NCAA officials faced the ultimate challenge of keeping competition alive amid the homefront chaos created by the American war effort. As a result, the tournament field was a hodgepodge.

Region 7 sent no representative to the tournament because the Skyline Conference had suspended play. So the Big Six Conference sent two schools, Iowa State and Missouri, a team with a 9-8 record. With an impressive 26-6 record, Washington won the northern division of the Pacific Coast Conference, and California, at 7-3, won the southern. But travel restrictions meant the two divisions couldn't have a playoff. Instead, the committee selected Pepperdine, 21-11.

To round out the West field, the NCAA offered a bid to Utah, but Coach Vadal Peterson and his Utes declined, electing instead to go to the NIT. In their place, the NCAA invited Arkansas.

In the East bracket, the Region 4 selection committee opted to send an inferior Big Ten team, Ohio State with 14 wins and six losses. Ray Meyer's DePaul team with George Mikan was overlooked with a 20-3 record that included a win over Ohio State. Region 2 sent Temple with a 13-8 record.

Somehow, the Region 3 committee chose little Catholic University in Washington, D.C., which Dartmouth promptly dismissed, 63-38, in the first round. Over four years, Dartmouth had blossomed into a New Hampshire powerhouse with a 74-10 record. By 1944, the Indians had prospered by having a military training camp on campus and picked up several stars from other colleges, including Dick McGuire, the top player in New York City from St. John's; Harry Leggat from NYU; and Cornell veteran Bob Gale.

In the other East first-round game, Ohio State and star Arnie Risen brushed aside Temple, 57-47. The Buckeyes, however, were no match for All-American McGuire and Dartmouth in the regional finals. Dartmouth center and team captain, Audley Brindley, scored 28 points as the Indians advanced to the championship game, 60-53.

The West Regional, meanwhile, had been thrown into chaos when the University of Arkansas team was involved in an automobile accident while driving to the tournament in Kansas City. Two players were injured, forcing the Razorbacks to withdraw.

Desperate for a replacement, tournament officials looked around and found Utah, which had just been dumped by Kentucky, 46-38, in the first round of the NIT. The Utes had to pass through Kansas City on their train ride home to Salt Lake City, so they agreed to stop over and play in the tournament. Perhaps fate has played stranger games, but not in the NCAA tournament.

With only nine players, including a starting five that averaged 18 years of age, the Utes sliced through the West Regionals, ousting Missouri, 45-35, then Iowa State, 40-31. Suddenly Peterson's team was headed back to New York on the train to play for the championship.

If anything, the tournament brought out the best of the war-weary New Yorkers. One of the Utes was 5-foot-7 guard, Wat Misaka, a Japanese-American, whose hustling made him a favorite of the 15,000 spectators. But it was the 6-foot-3, silky-smooth freshman, Arnie Ferrin, who led Utah to the championship. He scored 18 points in regulation to give the Utes what appeared to be a 36-34 victory, until Dartmouth's Dick McGuire hit a bankshot from half court just before the buzzer to give the NCAA its first overtime championship game.

Ferrin's teammate, Herb Wilkinson, pitched up a one-hander from the top of the key at the close of overtime to give Utah the title, 42-40. Flushed out of the NIT, the Utes had found new life in the NCAAs. A week later, they played NIT champion St. John's in the Red Cross benefit and won, 43-36, thus making their storybook comeback and their championship season complete.

1944				
Utah	fg	ft-fta	pf	tp
Ferrin	8	6- 7	0	22
Smuin	0	0- 0	2	0
Sheffield	1	0- 0	1	2
Misaka	2	0- 0	1	4
Wilkinson	3	1- 4	0	7
Lewis	2	3- 3	2	7
Totals	16	10-14	6	42
Dartmouth	fg	ft-fta	pf	tp
Gale	5	0- 2	1	10
Mercer	0	1- 1	3	1
Leggat	4	0- 0	1	8
Nordstrom	0	0- 0	0	0
Brindley	5	1- 1	3	11
McGuire	3	0- 1	3	6
Murphy	0	0- 0	0	0
Vancisin	2	0- 0	3	4
Goering	0	0- 0	0	0
Totals	19	2- 5	14	40
Half time: Dartmouth 18-17. Regulation Score: 36-36. Officials: Osborne and Menton.				

TOUR-NAMENT NOTES: Ferrin, with 22 points in the final, was named the MVP.

An Interview With Arnie Ferrin

Arnie Ferrin, an 18-year-old freshman, was named MVP of the 1944 tournament. He scored 22 points in the final to lead Utah to the championship.

Packer—The lineup Utah had in 1944 averaged 18 years old. How was that national championship lineup assembled?

Ferrin—In 1944, our coach, Vadal Peterson, didn't recruit. The nine fellows on the traveling squad—and we only had nine because it was a war year—elected to go to the University of Utah by their choice. I'd been an All-State player every year in high school and I just went up and knocked on the coach's door, introduced myself, and asked if I could try out for the team.

Packer—Did he know who you were?

Ferrin—I don't know, but I had a letter of introduction from the Dean of Boys at my high school, so I had some credentials. I had brought along my own equipment, and I asked if I could be on the basketball team.

Packer—You started school in September, and six months later you had won a national championship. Did the other guys on the team know who you were?

Ferrin—Nine of the fellows were from Utah, and I knew them all. Wat Misaka and I lived the farthest from the university, 35 miles for me. It was wartime, and if you played ball then, you were either 4-F, you were a freshman, or you were in medical, or dental, or engineering school. They were the only people still in school. During the year, some players got drafted, and by tournament time we were down to nine players.

Packer—Did anybody have a scholarship?

Ferrin—Fred Sheffield may have. Besides being an excellent basketball player, he was the NCAA high-jump champion. We were all freshmen and sophomores, and it was kind of fun. We started three or four freshmen, and that was unique in itself because I don't think there has ever been another team that won the championship with that many freshmen starters.

Packer—I didn't realize it before, but you weren't exactly in a league. You only played three games that year against college opponents, so most of your opponents were industry and army teams.

Ferrin—The first year of the war a lot of conferences disbanded, not knowing what the war would do. An interesting thing though, we played against a number of professional players. And we played two military teams, Fort Warren and Salt Lake Air Base, and both had members of the Globetrotters playing for them. So the teams

Utah's Arnie Ferrin.

we played might have been better than normal college teams because they were a composite of the good athletes the military bases could put together. Dartmouth was a Navy/Marine school, and Dick McGuire was playing for them. He had played for St. John's before going into the service, and then he played for Dartmouth while undergoing training. Joe Vancisin also played for that Dartmouth team, and Joe, I believe, had previously played at Michigan. Each of the teams we played was a composite of the good college players who had found a school where they could play basketball and get Army, Navy, or Marine training.

Packer—Where in the world did you nine Utah kids learn the skills to be so good so quickly?

Ferrin—You can attribute some of that to the Mormon Church, because in every area there's a basketball court, and that's where people go after school and on Saturdays. The Church probably had the largest tournament in the world; every ward had a team. Certainly Latter-day Saints players had played a lot of church basketball by the time they got to college. As a result of that influence, there was a basket in front of every barn or garage. Basketball was very popular in Utah back then.

Packer—At tournament time in 1944, the Utah players

Utah's 1944 National champions top row: (L-R) Wat Misaka, Roy Kingston, Arnie Ferrin; Bottom Row (L-R) Fred Lewis, Jim Nance, Bob Lewis, Coach Vadal Peterson, Fred Sheffield, Dick Smuin and Herb Wilkinson.

had a choice—NIT or the NCAA. What strange events led you to choose the NIT, but yet, a few days later, wind up as the NCAA champions?

Ferrin—Playing in the NIT was the result of a very simple choice made by the nine players and the two coaches and graduate manager. The choice was this: "How many people have been to New York City?" Of the 12, only two had been to New York. The choice was not which tournament to play in but which city to visit, Kansas City or New York City, and that really wasn't a hard choice. It was a matter of everybody wanting to go to New York City, so we picked the NIT.

Packer—So you're off on a long train ride to New York City and your first opponent is Kentucky. What did you know about Kentucky from your scouting reports?

Ferrin—That's an insightful question because the scouting report of Kentucky was the first scouting report the University of Utah basketball team ever had. David Peterson payed $25 for it. Someone came up and said that he'd scouted Kentucky and that he'd be willing to sell the scouting report for $25. David thought it was a major purchase, but he bought it. One of the things I remember vividly was that the scouting report said their guards didn't shoot well. In our game, one of them scored 24 or 25 points; we left him alone and he killed us. But we didn't know anything about them, really; didn't scout them

personally; really didn't know the players. We had read a little bit about them in national publications, but the press coverage was minimal. On the other hand, they didn't know much about us either.

Packer—So you're in New York, and you open the tournament with Kentucky, and you lose the game, and everybody is disappointed. Or being freshmen, did you just say we had a good time anyway?

Ferrin—I think we were disappointed because we felt we were a pretty good basketball team. When we received the phone call to replace Arkansas in the NCAA tournament, some of the people who had never been to New York thought we should stay and see New York. Others thought we should go to Kansas City and play. The coach said, "We can go play in the NCAA tournament or we can spend two or three more days in the city." The attitude of some of us was, "Why don't we go and play in the NCAA and then come back to New York?" That year, the NCAA finals were being held in New York City, so we thought we could win our way back and spend the whole week in New York.

Packer—The reason you're in the NCAA tournament is because Arkansas can't accept its bid to play, and you are asked to replace them. Why couldn't Arkansas accept the bid?

Ferrin—Arkansas was on the way to the tournament

and they were in an automobile wreck. One of their players was killed and several were hurt. So, all of a sudden, the NCAA has a tournament starting in two days and they're a team short. Our team had received an invitation to the NCAA earlier, and when we were out of the NIT, the NCAA called again and asked us if we would come and play.

Packer—So you climb on the train again and travel halfway back across the country to Kansas City, roughly a two-day trip. You don't have time to practice, and you start the tournament against Missouri.

Ferrin—Didn't practice; didn't have a scouting report; no preparation. We just started playing. One thing some of the old coaches will remember is that during timeouts you could not go to the bench. When you took a timeout, the players sat down on the floor and talked about what was happening and made the decision right there. You saw the coach before the game and at halftime. If he had a message for you during the game, he'd send in a substitute so you could take a timeout.

Packer—You play Missouri in the opening round and beat them by 10 points, a relatively comfortable win for a team that was the underdog. In the game, you end up with 12 points. Next you go against Iowa State. In that ball game, you didn't score a lot, but again your club won comfortably, 40-31. You win that trip back to New York City for the NCAA Final Four and you play Dartmouth, which won the East Regionals by beating Ohio State.

Ferrin—We knew that Dartmouth had accumulated all the good players on the East Coast, or at least a number of them. They had a Navy/Marine program up there. One of the things I remember is that after the tournament there was going to be a Red Cross benefit game between the winner of the NCAA and the winner of the NIT. Before we played Dartmouth, the Dartmouth players told us that their off-campus passes had expired, and if they won the NCAA title, they would not be able to stay off-campus any longer and play in the benefit game. They'd have to go back to school, and we'd have to take their place and play the winner of the NIT as losers. That was a little incentive. How'd you like to stay and play that game as a loser?

Packer—You guys win the game in overtime, 42-40. You end up with 22 points in the game and the MVP award. Anything particular about the game or the Dartmouth club that you remember?

Ferrin—I remember that Dartmouth's McGuire was running down the left sideline around midcourt and threw the ball in to put it into overtime.

Packer—How far out was he?

Ferrin—He was just inside halfcourt. It was a left-handed shot, and he banked it off the board. It was hard to have somebody do that to you when you think you've got the game won .

Packer—But you won in overtime, outscoring them six to four.

Ferrin — I made four free throws, and the game was tied with a few seconds left when Herb Wilkinson kicked one in from the top of the key, and we did win it 42-40.

Packer—One of the things that intrigued me was that the game was played in Madison Square Garden. You had played there in the opening round of the NIT, and I understand there were 15,000 people there, which was the largest crowd ever to see a tournament game. Then, a few nights later you turned around and played the Red Cross game and had 18,000 fans. At that time, the seating capacity of the Garden was only 12,500. The Red Cross game must have been a bigger deal then the NCAA championship.

Ferrin—We played St. John's in the Red Cross game. St. Johns was a local team, so the difference in the crowd was that Dartmouth really didn't have the New York City fans that St. John's had. St. John's had won the NIT and New York people wanted to see their team play the winner of the NCAA. So it really was a dream game.

Packer—So a team that was assembled in September with a bunch of guys introducing themselves to the coach became the national champions, and it was the first time that a team participated in both the NCAA and the NIT.

Ferrin—That's right. One of the more interesting stories about our team that I don't think anybody ever talked about is that one of our key players, Wat Misaka, was a Japanese/American. Of course, we were at war with Japan. Wat hustled and tried so hard, and he became a favorite with the fans. I think that's a real tribute to the people of our country. Here was a Japanese-American born in Ogden, Utah; whose mother fixed hair on probably the toughest street in the West, and he is playing basketball in New York City, and he becomes the darling of the crowd.

Packer—Everybody thinks that basketball is an eastern sport, but in '42 Stanford won the national championship with Jim Pollard and Harry Dallmar. In '43, Wyoming won with Kenny Sailors, and the first NCAA tournament was won by Oregon. Was there any connection between those great western teams? Did you see any of them play?

Ferrin—Wyoming was in our conference, but I had not seen Stanford or Oregon play. But if you want to identify a reason for their early success, my opinion would be that New York was too heavy into the set shot. We played more wide open and used the one-handed jump shot. Our game a faster, more productive game because of our style. That was a very obvious difference between eastern and western basketball.

Iba and Kurland

The 1944-45 basketball season brought the maturing of the game's two dominating young big men, DePaul's George Mikan and Oklahoma A&M's Bob Kurland; both of them hovering at 6-foot-10, both of them eager to prove that tall boys could play the game, if not with grace, at least with guile and power. Their defensive domination, particularly that of Kurland, led to a rewriting of the goaltending rule. When they entered college in 1942, basketball was still the domain of the little man. The primary offensive weapons were the dashing, driving guards, the 5-11 set shooters. After watching Kurland and Mikan for four years, coaches across the country realized that the sport had seen its future.

With "Foothills" Kurland at center, the Oklahoma A&M (later to become Oklahoma State) Aggies of Coach Henry Iba would win back-to-back NCAA championships in the 1945 and '46 seasons. For Mikan and DePaul, locked out of the NCAA by the Big Ten, the 1945 season would bring an NIT championship. Twice the country's top college scorer, Mikan would add to his legend when he joined the Minneapolis Lakers of the NBA and led them to five league titles in six years. Kurland, on the other hand, turned down substantial pro offers to remain an amateur after college. He played with the Phillips Petroleum Company team in Amateur Athletic Union competition and represented the United States in the 1948 and '52 Olympics, the only American basketball player to ever compete on two Olympic teams.

After the 1944 season, Kurland's sophomore year, the NCAA had changed its goaltending rule and no longer allowed players to knock away shots when the ball was on its downward arc to the basket. To balance that measure, the rules committee also decided that players should be allowed five fouls, instead of four, before fouling out.

Many observers mistakenly thought the goaltending rule change would diminish Kurland's presence in the game. Instead, the last two years of his college career were a study in domination, especially the 1945 season. Fast-break basketball took the college game by storm in the 1940s, as coach after coach became enamored of the running one-handed shot. But Hank Iba's teams played a plodding, methodical game that featured Kurland's height as its strength. With that mindset, the Aggies ground out 23 wins against four losses during the 1944-45 regular season.

Their first round opponent in the West regional that year was defending champion Utah, which had lost Arnie Ferrin and Fred Sheffield to a draft notice before the tournament. Accordingly, A&M pounded the Utes in the first round, 62-37, as Kurland scored 28.

In the other West bracket, Oregon returned to the NCAAs after winning 29 games in a monstrous 41-game, regular-season schedule. The Ducks racehorse match-up with Arkansas was a tournament classic. The Razorbacks outran Oregon, 79-76, setting an NCAA record for the most points scored in a game. The Arkansas pace, however, slowed considerably in the West finals against Kurland and the Aggies. Iba's control game did just that as A&M advanced easily, 68-41. Kurland scored only 15, but teammate Cecil Hankins knocked in 22.

Howard Cann's New York University team emerged in the East, blasting by Tufts, 59-44, in the first round to the delight of the Garden crowd. NYU featured high-scoring forward Sid Tannenbaum and freshman Dolph Schayes at center.

In the other bracket, Ohio State beat Kentucky, 45-37, setting up another golden game in the East finals. The hometown Violets brought the first capacity crowd—18,500—to the Garden in NCAA tournament history. But the noise quieted when NYU fell behind by 10 with two minutes left. Then Cann used a trick that N.C. State's Jim Valvano worked successfully in 1983. NYU fouled repeatedly, and although Ohio State had a choice in those days of taking the ball out of bounds or the free throws, Coach Harold Olsen took the shots. After the Buckeyes missed several times at the line, NYU's Don Forman hit a set shot to tie the score at 62, sending the game into overtime. Once there, NYU found its footing and prevailed, 70-65.

For the first time, the NCAA had a final in the Garden featuring a New York team. Cann's Violets played A&M a tight game, but Kurland scored 22 points and Iba claimed his first NCAA championship, 49-45. The outcome set up the meeting the basketball world had been waiting for: Kurland and A&M versus Mikan and DePaul, the NIT champions, in the Red Cross benefit game. Unfortunately, both big men were held down by foul troubles (Mikan was disqualified with only 14 minutes gone in the game). Kurland scored 14, Mikan 9, as A&M won, 52-44.

The 1945-46 season offered fans much promise, then failed to deliver it, as Kurland and Mikan never had the opportunity for a rematch. Mikan's only crown for his senior season was the collegiate scoring race, which he won with a little better than 23 points a game.

Kurland, on the other hand, was the centerpiece in Iba's grand defensive machine. He averaged 19 points at the heart of A&M's controlled offense. Only in the last regu-

Team photo above—Tug Wilson, NCAA commissioner, presents Oklahoma A&M's Coach Hank Iba the 1945 national championship cup in Madison Square Garden. Front row(L-R): York, Kern Parks, Parrack, Wylie. Back row (L-R) Johnson, Halbert, Kurland, Williams, Hankins, Millikan. Below: Dolph Schayes of NYU was elected to the Hall of Fame in 1972.

1945

Oklahoma A&M	fg	ft-fta	pf	tp
Hankins	6	3- 6	3	15
Parks	0	0- 0	3	0
Kern	3	0- 4	3	6
Wylie	0	0- 0	0	0
Kurland	10	2- 3	3	22
Parrack	2	0- 1	3	4
Williams	1	0- 1	1	2
Totals	22	5-15	16	49

New York University	fg	ft-fta	pf	tp
Grenart	5	2- 3	3	12
Forman	5	1- 2	1	11
Goldstein	0	2- 2	2	2
Schayes	2	2- 6	2	6
Walsh	0	0- 0	2	0
Tanenbaum	2	0- 0	2	4
Mangiapane	2	2- 4	3	6
Most	1	2- 3	2	4
Totals	17	11-20	17	45

Officials: Curtis and Adams.

1946

Oklahoma A&M	fg	ft-fta	pf	tp
Aubrey	0	1- 2	1	1
Bennett	3	0- 0	4	6
Kern	3	1- 3	2	7
Bradley	1	1- 2	1	3
Kurland	9	5- 9	5	23
Halbert	0	0- 0	0	0
Williams	0	2- 4	2	2
Bell	0	1- 1	1	1
Parks	0	0- 0	0	0
Totals	16	11-21	18	43

North Carolina	fg	ft-fta	pf	tp
Dillon	5	6- 6	5	16
Anderson	3	2- 3	3	8
Paxton	2	0- 0	4	4
McKinney	2	1- 3	5	5
White	0	1- 1	0	1
Thorne	1	0- 0	2	2
Jordan	0	4- 8	3	4
Totals	13	14-21	22	40

Officials: Kennedy and Collins.

Above left: Coach Hank Iba captured NCAA titles in 1945 and 1946. He coached the U.S. Olympic Team in 1964, 1968 and 1972 Top Right:New York University Coach Howard Cann brought his team to the 1945 NCAA finals. He was elected to the Hall of Fame in 1967. Bottom right:Coach Ben Carnevale directed North Carolina to the 1946 NCAA finals. He was elected to the Hall of Fame in 1969.

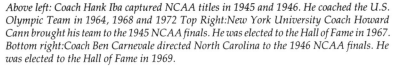

lar game of the season, against St. Louis University in Kurland's hometown, did Iba turn his center loose offensively. Kurland gave the basketball world a brief glimpse at his potential by scoring 58 points.

With a 28-2 record, the Aggies entered the tournament as the favorite and did nothing to damage their reputation. Kurland scored 20 in the first round as A&M strode past Baylor, 44-29. In the second round, he powered in 29 more in a relatively easy 52-35 victory over California.

In the East, the script didn't run so smoothly. The Madison Square Garden fans saw their NYU favorites downed by North Carolina, 57-49, in the first round. The Tar Heels were led by forward John Dillon and a skinny, talkative center, a 27-year-old ex-serviceman, Horace "Bones" McKinney.

For the third year in a row, the Garden fans were treated to an overtime, which again featured Ohio State and again resulted in a Buckeye defeat. With a 60-57 win,

Carolina gained the finals against A&M. "I had to save some of my strength for Kurland," McKinney told reporters in the locker room after the Ohio State game. Perhaps the 6-foot-6 McKinney should have held a bit more in reserve. As it was, the Tar Heels almost upset Iba's masterpiece. After dogging Kurland much of the game, McKinney fouled out in the second half with five points. Kurland followed him to the sidelines minutes later after scoring 23. The game came down to a frantic final moment, when the Aggies, ahead 41-40, had to inbound the ball against the pressing Carolina defense. A&M was successful and scored to claim a second championship, 43-40.

TOURNAMENT NOTES: Kurland had scored 72 points in three games and was named the MVP for the second consecutive year. John Dillon led the Tar Heels with 16 points in the final.

An Interview With Bob Kurland

Bob Kurland, one of the game's early great big men, was named most valuable player of the tournament in 1945 and 1946.

Packer—Bob, what was your most competitive game as a college player?

Kurland—Our Oklahoma State team, which was then called Oklahoma A&M, played the 1945 Red Cross benefit game against DePaul University in Madison Square Garden. We had won the NCAA, and DePaul with George Mikan had won the NIT. Mikan and I, I guess, were the two big men in the game in those days. We had played off and on against one another. It was billed as a real shootout. We filled the Garden. I guess we had 18,500 people and smoke to the rafters. The old Garden was a great place to play because the people would sit on the edge of the floor, and in those days there were a lot of things going on in the stands that I didn't understand. A lot of fingers went up and down behind those big black cigars. But the New York fans were the greatest fans in the world because they appreciated a good performance. If it was a bad performance, they told you. If it was a good performance, they told you. But it was tough, playing in the old Madison Square Garden, on a parquet floor that was not very level and had soft spots in it. It was a tough place to play. Fat? Kennedy was the referee; he was a colorful guy. To me, that was the game as far as a my college career. It was he epitome of a challenge.

Packer—You had several match-ups with Mikan.

Kurland—We had played, as I recall, Mikan before in Chicago and in Stillwater, and in the 1944 NCAA tournament in New York. DePaul beat us that year. We were sophomores that year, and George and I stumbled around the floor together. He outstumbled us that particular night. I think the series with Mikan—the game in Chicago, the ones in Stillwater, the ones in New York—was one of the greatest challenges, as far as I was concerned.

Packer—At that time, the champion of champions game, the Red Cross benefit pitting the NCAA champion against the NIT champion, would have been bigger than the NCAA championship?

Kurland—Yes, and to my knowledge, Billy, that Red Cross benefit has never been done since 1945, when the war ended. The NCAA grew in stature, and as the tournament base expanded they were able to include more teams. In those days we had, I think, eight teams selected. Today's tournament is a better tournament because it gives more opportunity to a greater number of schools; it

Bob Kurland.

gives more exposure.

The quarterfinals were played regionally. The West teams played the semifinals in Kansas City. We rode a train for two-and-a-half days and came to New York and played the finals, a little bit different than getting on a jet airplane and riding three hours and getting off. It was a little tougher in those days, particularly for a guy my size who slept in a short bunk.

Packer—How were the Midwest and the far West able to develop so rapidly in basketball in those early days?

Kurland—Basketball had been founded in Springfield, Massachusetts, and the old pro league was the thing that the Easterners cut their teeth on. But basketball was well established in the West, both in the universities and colleges and in Amateur Athletic Union circles. The pro league was in the East, but we had some very good players in the Midwest and the West. California, because of transportation and communication problems from East to West in the early days, was not recognized. Hank Luisetti was at Stanford in the thirties, but other great West players competed in obscurity. And the other thing was that there were not very many fans in the West. The game had its foundation in the East. The East had the papers; they had a way of informing people. The news of games in the West never seemed to get to the East fans, and often times they were surprised when a team like the Oklahoma Aggies in those days could come out of the Midwest and shellac them in New York.

Packer—In 1945 your Oklahoma A&M team did exactly that. You faced NYU, which had to be the pride of New York City, for the NCAA championship.

Kurland—They were tough. I was very distressed to hear about a man whom we played against, who was shot in New York City this past year, Sidney Tannenbaum, as I think about that particular game. They were tough kids, not big kids, but tough kids, usually of Italian or Jewish descent. They were tough neighborhood kids who usually played on the playground, and they would run right through you. They were great at driving, and we would discipline ourselves under Coach Henry Iba to expect that. We had a strategy laid out for the eastern style of playing. It consisted of diving in the middle and knocking them down.

Packer—You mentioned the travel problem in those days. How about scouting? If there was no TV, how did you get your information about the teams?

Kurland—Well, I think there was an exchange of information between coaches. Coaching was a little bit different then. We talked about coaches that appear on benches today and the business of motivation and the loyalty of the players to the coach and the relationship. I look at TV today, and I see the coach talk to three people before he talks to the player. He has a conference of assistant coaches before he talks to the player. Our coach, Hank Iba, got the scouting reports, probably from radio announcers or from fellow coaches. Films were very scarce in those days. Many times you would walk on the court and get a surprise that would require a major adjustment. In my opinion, we never had the best athletic material. But what we had was a number of plans and strategies that were applicable against the stars of the games we were playing, and I think in a matter of five minutes Coach Iba could adjust our game plan to any circumstance we ran into. Many times we discovered if the guy was right or left handed after he had thrown in two or three, and we adjusted quickly. We didn't have scouting reports. We would go generally prepared. We knew how the eastern teams played. Coaches knew one another's strategies and plans and styles pretty well, and they would adjust their players to a particular strategy. You play against strategies and you adjust to individuals.

Packer—As a young player in 1944, were you excited about playing in the NCAA tournament?

Kurland—I first heard of the NCAA tournament in 1944 when we played in the NIT. We had looked hopefully to the NCAA because Henry Iba liked the structure of the tournament. He felt we would feel more comfortable playing in it. We got invited to the NIT that year and got fourth place in it (after losing to Mikan and DePaul in

the semifinals). We were aware that the other tournament was going on because Utah had played in the NIT and had been knocked out by Kentucky but had gone on and won the NCAA with Arnie Ferrin. So we were aware there was another tournament, and as we began the NIT, we thought even if we get licked maybe we can get into the NCAA because we had a pretty good club.

But the NCAA today, compared to what it was then, is entirely different. Today, they talk about millions of dollars. I would estimate if Oklahoma State took home a few thousand dollars from the NCAA in 1944 it would have been a great benefit to a struggling athletic program.

Packer—You played in NCAA championship games. How do those games compare, with your being the defending champions the second year? Did the tournament grow from year to year?

Kurland—The first year, 1945, we came into the tournament not knowing what the objective was. I think it was more exciting the first time. It seemed something was exploding every game for us as we got closer and closer. We really didn't know what was coming in the next game. The second year we were a little more cold-blooded about it because we had set our sights early in the season. Our objective the second time was to win the NCAA, and we thought about it, thought about it, thought about it. In 1946 we looked forward to the finals, and you could just relax.

We played under Henry Iba. One thing he told us early in the scheme of things—and this was the great thing about him—he said, "You guys are going to have all the wins. I'm going to take all the losses, but we'll do it my way."

Old Iba was known for being a volatile man with a loud voice on the bench. At half time he was anything but that. It was cold, calculated logic in terms of our strategy. We had guys who kept shot charts, but we didn't have 14 advisors and assistant coaches and all that. Henry would come in after standing in the hall and thinking about it and would say, "Here's your problems." We had complete confidence in what he told us. There was never a deviation from the strategy and the style and the tactics that he developed. We were good mechanics, not great athletes. We knew the game, we knew where everyone was on the floor at all times, we knew the tempo of the game, and what the strategy was.

Earlier tonight, Billy, you commented that Bobby Knight's 1987 Indiana champions didn't have to take the time outs because they knew what was going on. We had a team like that. We very rarely got rattled or upset, and we played our game the best we knew how. If we won, we won. And if we lost, we lost. This may sound a little bit corny, but great teachers have that ability. You go back and look at our culture and look at our religious history. We had one guy who said, "You do it my way. I'll take all the blame for the trouble you get into, but I'll forgive you

After battling with Kurland in college, DePaul's Mikan went on to a stellar pro career.

for it." He was a great teacher, and it influenced our culture. Great coaches do the same thing. You do it my way, you execute the way I tell you. You can have all the wins, and I'll take all the losses and that takes the pressure off you. That's the difference between Henry Iba and many coaches today. You take all the wins, I'll take the losses—It's fundamentally right in many teaching situations.

Packer—Let's talk about his teaching. You came to Oklahoma A&M, but no one expected you to lead the Aggies to two NCAA championships.

Kurland—No, the only thing I was leading to was a college education. We had just come through the Depression. I was in St. Louis, and I wanted to be an engineer. Oklahoma A&M had a good engineering school. Henry Iba was a man whose reputation and integrity had been established. I guess I've had my nose pinned a few times by being too idealistic in many ways. But I needed - because of being, as Phog Allen classified me, "a glandular goon" - I needed something to tie on to. I remember sitting in Henry Iba's office. He said, "I don't know if you can play college-level basketball or not. But I'll make you this promise: If you'll go to school, if you'll practice every day, I will see that you will have the opportunity to have your room, board, tuition, books, and get an education." And that was our deal. And that's the way we took it. I still

have the correspondence from him. I'm going to send it to the Tulsa sports editor with the idea that he can make a story out of it, as to what went on in the way of recruiting in those days and what goes on today.

Packer—How about your teammates? Certainly this ball club has to go down in history of the Final Four as one of the great clubs that ever played in its period. How did it ever get assembled?

Kurland—When I was a freshman at Oklahoma State there were 132 guys who came out for basketball. Henry Iba never cut a guy off the team. He never said, "You can't play." But after two weeks or three weeks they kind of weeded themselves out after four-hour practice sessions every day. And those that stayed, played. We look at the 1945 team here, and I think baloney. But they were good basketball players. Cecil Hankins was a great athlete. He could dunk the ball and was probably 5-foot-11. Dunking in those days was exceptional. John Wylie was slow. Doyle Parrack was excitable. This kid was the toughest kid I ever saw, J.L. Parks. He didn't have fingers, he had fists when he dribbled the ball. He was the quickest starting - he could break faster then any kid I ever saw. Weldon Kern, he was not a great basketball player. Bill Johnson was slow. Halbert played because his brother played at West Texas, and Joe was the guy that was my meat man in practice. Blake Williams had a bad heart. And this is a fact, Billy. There were times in major games when we'd have to break and call time out and his heart would "fibrillate," and he'd have to lay down before his heart would come back in rhythm. Never happened in a championship game but I remember it happening once in Chicago.

Packer—Playing basketball in the middle of the war years must have been stressful.

Kurland—That was very difficult. I started school in '42 when college athletics was still organized. But many schools had decided to discontinue their athletic programs. After we had, by Iba's standards, a bad season,14 and 12, (it was my freshman year) he called us all in and said,"This is the worst basketball season I've ever had." He said, "But I'll never have another team like this. But I'll tell you this: You boys are going to war, and I want everyone of you to know if you come back here, and you want your scholarship, you've got your college education."

This was before the days of the veterans' program. He didn't tell them, "Boys, you may or may not come back." He told them, and he meant it. He said, "You tried, and I know you're upset about the circumstances of your going to war." And most of these kids were in the ROTC, and they were going to war. He said, "But I guarantee you've got your college education waiting for you." And that's a hell of a coach.

But it was very disruptive. The soldiers came in and took over the gym. They threw us out of the cafeteria. We didn't have any training table. We ate out in the chili bowls and old restaurants. And I told Henry Iba, "I'll never play for you again."

He said, "What do you mean you'll never play for me?"

And I said, "Henry, we didn't get enough to eat." (Laughs.)

Packer—How about the game next year? You played against the University of North Carolina. Did you know anything about that ball team?

Kurland—We knew they had Bones McKinney, who had been in service and was a good ball player. I think he was 27 at the time. And a guy named Hook Dillon and other people. We were probably better prepared in terms of their abilities, and Dillon was a great player inside about the top of the free throw circle. McKinney was supposed to be the rebounding power. They were a well-balanced team, and Carnevale was a good coach. But we came to them better prepared than we were with New York University.

Packer—I understand McKinney had a lot to say to you before that game, or at least was very talkative during the course of that game.

Kurland—I made it a practice to never listen to anybody during a game but Henry Iba. Iba had a saying that, "By God, boys, if your ears are in the stands, you're not going to play."

I don't know what McKinney said. He still talks of the fact that he got his fanny beat and I take some consolation for that.

Packer—I read somewhere that Coach Iba said you were not a natural shooter. What was meant by that?

Kurland—That depends on what he called a natural shooter. The accurate term is "natural scorer." I've often said that playing for Iba was very difficult in that he had his own style of play. You have to remember that Iba had never had - there were almost no coaches who'd ever had - people as tall as I was. So the early coaches really were pioneers in discovering skills that were required in playing a post type of game in those days. I think that Iba probably helped me develop physically by making me jump rope and teaching me to develop movement, particularly in defense, which I took great pride in. But offensively, I look back and I think I learned as much from a man named Floyd Burdette,who happened to be in the Air Corps training program, who was a captain, came back and re-enrolled in Oklahoma State in 1943 was on the team. Floyd, in spite of the fact that he was in the Air Force, was 6-5 or 6-6. Floyd was 28, and he taught me the business of how to hook a guy inside with your elbow, or put your elbow on his hip, or roll on him, and to really develop the kind of shot, a quick little jump-push shot. Mikan had what I call the sweeping hook shot, but I never had that type of strength Mikan had.

Packer—When you entered as a freshman, how tall were you and how much did you weigh?

Kurland—I was 6-9 and weighed 175 pounds.

Packer—When you left, you were what?

Kurland—I was 6-10 1/2 and weighed 225. But we had no weight program. Our total training room consisted of a big jar of vitamin pills, a tape box and a great big bottle of Merthiolate. That's all we had.

Packer—So you just didn't get hurt?

Kurland—I played one season with a broken toe and another with a broken hand.

Packer—Explain the goaltending rules and controversy of your day.

Kurland—Goaltending involves striking the ball on its downward flight or while it is in the cylinder of the basket. There were other people who could goaltend, but we were the first team to sit down and deliberately devise a strategy and to play a defense that included goaltending as its central theme. The first time we tried it was against Oklahoma University when I was a freshman. Oklahoma had beaten us down at Norman. They had a good team. Later they were beaten up by Wyoming in the NCAA tournament. We had no way to beat them except by coming up with something unique. I had jumped rope that whole year and by this time I could put part of my arm well above the rim. We only practiced three days on this defense. Bruce Drake and the Oklahoma team came into Stillwater, which is a mad house to play in, and they took the first shot. I knocked it down, and they took the second shot and I knocked it down. Alva Paine and Gerald Tucker (Oklahoma stars), God, they went crazy. They called a time out, and they didn't know what the heck to do. That was the last game of the season.

Iba thought about it, and we started off the next year with a rinky dink team because most of the guys had gone to war. We had a pick-up team, and we had to find something that was different. So we developed a technique where it was literally a zone defense with me knocking the ball down. We were very effective at it. But goal tending is really psychological. If a player is ready to shoot, for instance, and he has to jerk and think about shooting, then he's probably going to jerk his shot the next time he shoots.

That's what happened with the goaltending deal. You had a distinct psychological advantage if you'd knock down the first two or three shots. People in many cases would beat themselves psychologically, and that was a bad thing for the game. But it was a way of winning, and it was within the rules. Iba was one of those that advocated discontinuing goaltending. Oklahoma Coach Bruce Drake, because his team was the first one to be injured by it, was against allowing goaltending.

Opposite page—North Carolina's Bones McKinney led the Tar Heels to the NCAA title game in 1946.

He was chairman on the NCAA rules committee at the time. He had a guy named St. Clair, who came down to Norman when we played them as a sophomore. He had a chair built on top of the backboard, and Mr. St. Clair sat up there all night seeing whether my hand was in the so-called cylinder of the basket. Iba said, "Bob, knock down two or three and then don't touch it." We never goaltended that night, and he sat up there waiting for us to do it.

Packer—According to the rules of the day, a defensive player could hit or catch a shot on its downward flight to the basket, but you could not interfere with the ball once it was in the cylinder of the basket. Of course, today, a defensive player can only hit a shot on its upward flight.

Kurland—That's correct. Now the rule says that you cannot strike the ball on the downward arc. In those days, your hand had to be outside the rim. That's what St.Clair was sitting up behind the basket looking for. It was very difficult in those days to see if your hand went through that cylinder or not.

Packer—Did you have any drills for your "goaltending defense?"

Kurland—Just my jumping drills. But the remainder of the team was set up in zones to cover the floor. It was a specific defense planned around the other four players. I was supposed to patrol this zone in the free-throw lane and on either side of the basket. We devised a zone defense that was built around goaltending. It was a difficult thing.

Packer—Coach Iba's image was that of deep belief in the man-to-man.

Kurland—Billy, that's why Iba was hard to play for in one sense. We became good mechanics of the game. All of us could play every position on the court. Despite the fact that I was almost 7-feet tall, we had an offense where I rotated to the guard position. All of us knew exactly where everyone was on the floor at all times. We had three or four offenses against the man-to-man defense. We had a tight man-to-man and three zone defenses, and each one required personal discipline as to the position you played on the court. Pete Maravich made an observation when we were playing in Oklahoma City. I asked him, "What do you think the big difference in game is, Pete?"

He said, "Nobody knows what the other positions are. They all play their own spot, and they have no conception of what the other guy is doing." The main thing that makes Larry Bird great today, in my judgment—he has no great foot speed, and I can relate to this because I didn't have foot speed; he's not a great jumper and I was not a great jumper in terms of leaping ability —is that he is initially quick, and he knows every position on the floor and knows where everybody is all the time. And that was the difference in our team with less athletic ability. We didn't have to look. We knew he would be there, or we knew if

something else was happening where, we were supposed to be defensively.

If you look at the records, you'll find that Oklahoma State, which was supposed to be a slow-running team, was probably one of the highest-scoring teams during the years we won the championships. Iba played what he called "the percentages." He took his abilities, his players and what he taught, and he maximized the things he had to work with. Again it comes back to the fact that he was a teacher. He was a terrible recruiter. He would not recruit. He was a mentor, and he expected people to come to him because he was a teacher. As a result, he took on a double chore: Trying to teach people with less physical ability. That is why he was such a great coach.

Packer—Were people across the nation excited about the National Championship in those days?

Kurland—I can't judge that. I know that they were always excited to have the entertainment in New York, particularly basketball in '45 and '46. The war was over. People were adjusting to the post-war years. Sports were a great outlet, but certainly they were not the religion they've become today.

Packer—Is that healthy? Which way do you think was better, the low-key approach or today's big business?

Kurland—I think sports have reached a point today where there should be a lot of re-evaluation as to what sports needs. I have a story I like to think about as to what heros are, why they were invented, and what heroes should be. I believe in heroes. I have always had heroes. I think heroes are necessary because all of us recognize we are human, and we know we can't be gods. So we invented heroes, which are between humans and the gods. They are people of great strength, great courage, who have had a long-lasting effect in what they've been involved in, whether it's politics or religion or so forth. My problem today is - whether it's the media, I don't think it's the individual - somehow we create heroes who are not really heroes in my evaluation. We need to pick out those people who are genuine for the adoration they receive. I think America's a sucker for heroes.

I think all the values have to be re-examined. We're going through a very difficult time in this country in terms of all the hypocrisy. I think sports is a tremendous outlet for tension that exists in our society today. Many people use it as an escape, and I have no problem with that. I think it's healthy. But I think in terms of the values that are established, the "media" - whatever that might be - should be very careful as to how they create heroes.

Packer—Talking about heroes, you were one at the time. What was it like coming back to Oklahoma A&M with the championship? How was the campus as compared to now with the Final Four hoopla, the heroes' welcome home, the ticker-tape parades and all that?

Kurland—We got off the train in Perry, Oklahoma, and

Madison Square Garden in New York was the thriving center of college basketball in the 1940s. Here the crowd moves through the turnstiles for the 1946 NCAA title game.

some of the assistant coaches were there with their cars. And a couple of days later the student council asked the president if they could have a pep rally over at the auditorium in the theater. We came over, and everybody got up on the stage and the kids clapped and we all went back to class.

Packer—As you were walking back to the classroom, if all of a sudden I could transport you forward in time to see the celebration at Indiana in 1987 when that club came back home after winning the championship - could you have imagined such changes?

Kurland—No, because the whole idea of the consequences of our winning that tournament were not there. It wasn't within our thinking that there would be a follow-up on it. When I was a senior and the pro leagues had started to form, I was looking at the possibility of getting a job. But the rest of the players knew that this was the end of their athletic career. It was not going to lead to something else. So it was natural to say, "This is over. We set it down and we go on about our lives."

It wasn't the idea that we planned every action with the idea that we had to be careful that the consequences were going to have a result a year away or six months away. It was much simpler in those days. We played, as I said in the beginning, to get a college education.

These were our friends, these were the guys we lived and died with as far as athletics were concerned. And these were not kids. In '45 and '46 we had guys that were in the war and had been shot at. Some of them had been in Iwo Jima and Italy, and these were not boys. These were guys that didn't rattle. These were men playing a boys' game.

Packer—If you could take that ball club and put it into today's game, what would happen?

Kurland—I think that they wouldn't get past the first round. The reason is that the game has changed so much. Today you have men my size who at 11 or 12 years of age go into programs that discipline them for the next seven years. We didn't have a weight room. When the semester was over, I got back on the bus went back to St. Louis, and started looking for a job. I didn't pick up a basketball until the next September. We were not physically prepared. But I'll say this, from the standpoint of the mechanics of the game, we executed, lost the ball fewer times, had a better percentage of shooting than many of the teams do today. But we did not have the physical skills that they have come on with today. If I take pride in anything, as far as basketball is concerned in my relationship to the game, it is first that I have great admiration for men like Henry Iba and Ray Meyer, who were brave enough to take odd people or strange giants like myself and had the courage to put their careers on the line in trying to teach us how to play. You can't measure our performance to today's performance or tomorrow's performance. That's foolish. But the other thing I take pride in is, we opened the door and caused people to think that a good big man properly trained in the old axiom will always beat the good little man. That's true in boxing, football, anything you get into. That's what I take pride in today, that we've opened the door to the idea that the big man could play the game, which in our day was, by eastern standards, played by guys 5-10, 5-11, who were quick, took the set shot and so forth; that we opened the door for what the game is today, played by magnificent athletes who are just performing geniuses.

Kaftan and the Crusaders

In 1946-47, the Holy Cross Crusaders didn't have a home gym, and they didn't have a starter over 6-foot-4 (center George Kaftan was just that height). But they did have Doggie Julian as a coach, and they had a whiz-bang, fast-break weave drill as their offense. And when the season was over, they had an NCAA championship.

The Crusaders achieved their feat in a season that marked the return of normalcy to college basketball after the upheaval of World War II. The foremost sign of this normalcy was the return of war-seasoned players to the lineups: Arnie Ferrin at Utah, John Hargis at Texas, Andy Phillip at Illinois, Kenny Sailors and Milo Komenich at Wyoming, and Danny Kraus at Georgetown.

The faces in college basketball weren't all veteran. Young Bob Cousy was a reserve guard on the Holy Cross bench, but he wasn't the big story in '47. The headlines belonged to Kaftan, a ball of rebounding and inside-scoring brilliance. On the strength of his play, Holy Cross entered the tournament with a 24-3 record, despite having played those games on the road or in Boston Garden. Nursing a 20-game winning streak at tournament time, the Crusaders were considered something of a favorite in the East.

Their first-round opponent was Navy, coached by Ben Carnevale, who had led North Carolina to the finals the year before. With little trouble, Kaftan and company doused Carnevale's dreams of reaching the finals a sec-

ond year, 55-47. The second round opponent was the favorite of the Garden crowd, City College of New York, coached by the great Nat Holman. The Crusaders fell behind the Beavers in the first half, but surged in the second. Kaftan scored 30, and Holy Cross won in a walk, 60-45.

In the West, the first round featured a shootout of veterans in which Hargis and Texas outlasted Sailors and Wyoming, 42-40. In the other bracket, Oklahoma and center Gerry Tucker survived the first of two squeakers, 56-54 , over Oregon State. At 22-6, the Sooners had entered the tournament with the Big 6 championship. Their West finals matchup with favored Texas stirred the usually dormant basketball fever across the Southwest. The methodical, powerful Tucker led the Sooners with 15 points, but it was role player Ken Pryor who lofted a long set shot with 10 seconds left in overtime for a 55-54 win to give Oklahoma its first trip to New York and the Finals.

At the Garden, Tucker scored 22 as Oklahoma stayed at the heels of the Crusaders. With three minutes left, Holy Cross led, 48-45, but then exploded to win the championship, 58-47.

TOURNAMENT NOTES: George Kaftan with 18 points in the finals was named MVP. Texas beat CCNY, 54-50, in the consolation game.

George Kaftan of Holy Cross rebounds and looks to start the fast break in the 1947 NCAA title game against Oklahoma.

1947				
Holy Cross	fg	ft-fta	pf	tp
Kaftan	7	4- 9	4	18
O'Connell	7	2- 4	3	16
Oftring	6	2- 3	5	14
Mullaney	0	0- 0	2	0
Haggerty	0	0- 0	0	0
Laska	0	0- 0	0	0
Curran	0	0- 1	2	0
Reilly	0	0- 0	1	0
McMullin	2	4- 4	0	8
Cousy	0	2- 2	1	2
Bollinger	0	0- 0	0	0
Graver	0	0- 0	0	0
Totals	22	14-23	18	58
Oklahoma	fg	ft-fta	pf	tp
Reich	3	2- 2	3	8
Courty	3	2- 3	4	8
Tucker	6	10-12	3	22
Paine	2	2- 2	0	6
Landon	1	0- 1	4	2
Waters	0	0- 0	0	0
Day	0	0- 0	0	0
Pryor	0	1- 1	2	1
Merchant	0	0- 0	1	0
Totals	15	17-21	17	47
Half time: Oklahoma 31-28. Officials: Andersen and Kennedy.				

Above, the Madison Square Garden marquee touts the 1947 NCAA tournament. Right: Oklahoma's Gerry Tucker (33) reaches over Holy Cross's Kaftan for a rebound in the final.

Kentucky's Rise and Fall

Center Alex Groza was one of a trio of All-Americans leading Kentucky in 1948 and 1949. Later, however, it would be revealed that he was involved in point-shaving. Opposite page—Kentucky basketball coach Adolph Rupp is pictured in 1946 with then-Kentucky football coach Paul "Bear" Bryant.

Coach Adolph Rupp's University of Kentucky Wildcats emerged as the superior team in post-war America, reeling through a blur of victories and championships that mesmerized their fans in the Bluegrass. At the top of their game, Rupp's teams of 1948 and '49 stirred the grand ego of Kentucky basketball. Yet for all their accomplishments, their fame was fleeting. The real chord they struck was scandal. And, for the most part, that is how history remembers them: as point shavers.

A man of overbearing pride, Rupp had begun coaching basketball at the school in 1930 and by March 1948, his trophy case lacked only an NCAA championship. His teams had won five straight Southeastern Conference Championships since 1944. The Wildcats' first national post-season acclaim came with a one-point victory over Rhode Island for the 1946 NIT Championship. Kentucky returned to the NIT finals in '47, only to lose to Arnie Ferrin and Utah.

For the 1947-48 team, Rupp had three potential All Americans in greyhound guard Ralph Beard, 6-foot-7 power center Alex Groza and forward Wallace "Wah Wah" Jones. Beyond those three, Kentucky was deep in talent with Cliff Barker, Dale Barnstable, Jim Line and Ken Rollins. Rupp had recruited Groza as a skinny high school senior in 1945. The younger brother of pro football player Lou, Groza appeared briefly in Kentucky uniform before going into the service his freshman year. Two years later, he returned to the Wildcats as a mature physical specimen well on his way to becoming an imposing inside player.

The forte of those late forties Wildcats was offense. They regularly ran up 70 points or more in an era when most games were settled with scores in the 50s. Their regular-season record in 1947-48 was 29-2, the two being one-point losses to Notre Dame and Temple. The Kentucky starters - Beard, Jones, Groza, Barker and Rollins - came to be known as the Fabulous Five, despite the fact they were backed up by a bench of All Americans who played often and well. By NCAA tournament time, most sportswriters figured the only team capable of beating them was defending champion Holy Cross.

Kentucky sliced up Columbia, 76-53, in the first round of the East Regionals. In their next game, against Holy Cross in the East finals, the Wildcats shut down Bob Cousy and advanced, 60-52. In the West, Baylor had eased by Kansas State and Washington. But it made no difference. Kentucky rapped the Bears in the NCAA finals, 58-42, and Rupp had his championship. Groza was awarded

the MVP trophy.

From there, the dream continued to the '48 Olympics, played in London, where the Kentucky squad was combined with Bob Kurland and the Phillips Petroleum amateur squad to form the U.S. team. With Groza and Kurland in the same lineup, the Americans easily outclassed the world competition for the gold medal.

For the 1948-49 season, the Associated Press introduced its nationwide poll, and as expected, the Wildcats ruled it. An early-season loss to St. Louis in the Sugar Bowl tournament convinced the Baron that his team needed to concentrate on getting the ball to Groza. With that adjustment, the Kentucky inside game was dominant, until the team entered the NIT, where it was upset by Loyola of Chicago in the quarterfinals, 61-56. Two years later, it would be revealed that the Wildcats lost the game while trying to shave points. But those developments were known only to the players and a small circle of gamblers in late 1949. Kentucky entered the NCAA tournament and made quick work of the opposition. Villanova fell first, 85-72, in the East opener. Then the Cats humiliated a strong Illinois team, 76-47, in the East finals.

In the West, Hank Iba had another Oklahoma A&M team moving through his brand of controlled paces. The Aggies nipped Wyoming, 40-39, then powered past Oregon State, 55-30. The 1949 finals had been shifted to Seattle, giving Rupp's team the discomfort of a 3,000-mile train ride from the East Regionals at Madison Square Garden. That, however, didn't seem to deter them as they gave "the Baron in the brown suit" his second NCAA championship, 46-36.

TOURNAMENT NOTES: Groza scored 25 of his team's 46 points in the final and was again named the MVP. Groza, Beard and Jones were named first-team All-Americans by United Press International. After the season, the three would form the nucleus of a new pro team, the Indianapolis Olympians. With stock ownership in the team, the wealth and fame of the three young Kentuckians would grow, until 1951 when it was revealed Groza and Beard had accepted bribes during college to shave points. They were subsequently banned for life from the NBA, and their team eventually folded as a result of the negative publicity.

Above—Kentucky's All-American forward, Wallace "Wah Wah" Jones. Opposite page—All-American guard Ralph Beard was known for his quickness.

1948

Kentucky	fg	ft	tp
Jones	4	1	9
Barker	2	1	5
Groza	6	2	14
Beard	4	4	12
Rollins	3	3	9
Line	3	1	7
Holland	1	0	2
Barnstable	0	0	0
Totals	23	12	58

Baylor	fg	ft	tp
Owens	2	1	5
DeWitt	3	2	8
Heathington	3	2	8
Johnson	3	4	10
Robinson	3	2	8
Pulley	0	1	1
Hickman	1	0	2
Preston	0	0	0
Srack	0	0	0
Totals	15	12	42

Officials: Haarlow and MacDonald.

1949

Kentucky	fg	ft	pf	tp
Jones	1	1	3	3
Line	2	1	3	5
Groza	9	7	5	25
Beard	1	1	4	3
Barker	1	3	4	5
Barnstable	1	1	1	3
Hirsch	1	0	1	2
Totals	16	14	21	46

Oklahoma A&M	fg	ft	pf	tp
Yates	1	0	1	2
Shelton	3	6	4	12
Harris	3	1	5	7
Bradley	0	3	3	3
Parks	2	3	5	7
Jaquet	0	1	0	1
McArthur	0	2	1	2
Pilgrim	0	2	1	2
Smith	0	0	1	0
Totals	9	18	21	36

Officials: Ogden and Curtis.

Triumph, Then Tragedy

Nat Holman had what you might call the complete basketball experience. As a playmaking guard, he was a key member of pro basketball's original Celtics. In the years after his retirement from playing, he became the coach at City College of New York. There, in 1950, his team achieved what no other had ever done: It won both the NIT and NCAA tournaments. But from the height of that tremendous accomplishment, Holman suffered a swift and very steep fall, when it was discovered eight months later that his players had accepted bribes from gamblers.

CCNY's storybook season had an improbable beginning in that Holman had only one veteran, Irwin Dambrot, among his starting five. The rest of the team was comprised of sophomores. The Beavers finished the regular season 17-5, a modestly successful record, enough to get a bid to the NIT, but certainly not representative of the world beaters they were about to become. In the first round, they drew defending champion San Francisco and made short work of the Dons, 65-46. In the second round, they faced NCAA defending champion Kentucky and issued Adolph Rupp's team its worst tail-kicking in his 42

years of coaching, 89-50. Afterward, Rupp predicted the Beavers would take the title.

CCNY's scoring outburst was enough to get the attention of the press, and the interest increased when the Beavers outlasted Duquesne, 62-52, in the tournament's third round. But the opponent in the championship was top-ranked Bradley, and the sportswriters predicted that midnight would strike on CCNY's "Cinderella," which, by the way, appears to have been the first usage of that term in describing an upset winner on a roll in the tournament.

As the AP's top team, the Braves had three All-American candidates in forward Paul Unruh and guards Gene Melchiorre and Bill Mann. However, the Beavers' Ed Warner usurped the all-star attention by scoring 87 points in four NIT games, including 16 in the final, to earn MVP honors. In the process, he led CCNY to the upset championship, 69-61.

Fate then worked a neat little trick, as the same teams played to the finals of the NCAA, also held in the Garden, CCNY got there by edging Ohio State and North Carolina State in the East Regionals. Bradley advanced through the

Below: Front row (L—R) Mike Wittlin, Ed Roman, Joe Galiber, Coach Nat Holman, Irwin Dambrot, Norman Mager and Seymour Levey. Second row (L—R) —Floyd Layne, Arnold Smith, Ed Warner, Al Roth, and Herb Cohen. Third row (L—R)—Ronald Nadell, Arthur Glass, LeRoy Watkins, Ed Chenetz and Larry Meyer. Fourth row (L—R)—Mgr. Al Ragusa, Asst. Coach Bobby Sand.

West with victories over UCLA and Baylor. But the Braves found there was no change in the script for the finals. In the closing moments with CCNY leading by a point, Dambrot blocked a Melchiorre shot, giving the Beavers an easy layup and a 71-68 championship.

The celebration was long and loud, the jubilation carrying right through to the next February, when abruptly several CCNY players were arrested for their part in point shaving. The investigation into gambling in college athletics revealed that between 1946 and 1950, 86 games in 23 cities had been fixed by 37 players. The players represented 22 colleges, but it was widely believed that the probe could have pinpointed dozens of others.

The 1951 gambling scandal brought an end to NCAA games in the Garden, as critics blamed the atmosphere there for fomenting the corruption. Rupp of Kentucky had claimed that gamblers couldn't touch his players with a 10-foot pole, yet only weeks later, the investigation revealed that, in fact, Rupp's great players from 1948-49 had accepted bribes. The scandal also dampened enthusiasm for college basketball in New York City, a setback from which programs such as Long Island University and NYU never fully recovered.

As for CCNY, the investigation revealed that grade records had been falsified to allow its talented basketball recruits admission to the university.

TOURNAMENT NOTES: Dambrot was named MVP. In the quarterfinals, NC State had beaten Holy Cross, 87-74, setting a new tournament record for points scored in a game.

Bottom left—CCNY's Ed Roman battles NC State on the boards in the 1950 semifinals. Below right—CCNY Coach Nat Holman.

1950				
CCNY	fg-fga	ft-fta	pf	tp
Dambrot	7-14	1- 2	0	15
Roman	6-17	0- 2	5	12
Warner	4- 9	6-14	2	14
Roth	2- 7	1- 5	2	5
Mager	4-10	6- 6	3	14
Galiber	0- 0	0- 0	1	0
Layne	3- 7	5- 6	3	11
Nadell	0- 0	0- 0	1	0
Totals	26-64	19-35	17	71
Bradley	fg-fga	ft-fta	pf	tp
Grover	0-10	2- 3	3	2
Schlictman	0- 3	0- 0	2	0
Unruh	4- 9	0- 0	5	8
Behnke	3-10	3- 3	4	9
Kelly	0- 1	0- 2	0	0
Mann	2- 7	5- 5	5	9
Preece	6-11	0- 0	5	12
D. Melchiorre	0- 0	0- 0	0	0
G. Melchiorre	7-16	2- 4	4	16
Chianakas	5- 7	1- 3	4	11
Stowell	0- 0	1- 1	0	1
Totals	27-74	14-21	32	68

Half time: CCNY 39-32. Officials: Eisenstein and Gibbs.

Goodbye To The Garden

If anything, the 1950-51 college basketball season was eventful. The NCAA tournament expanded its field to 16 teams. And Adolph Rupp's Kentucky Wildcats won their third championship, making Kentucky the first school and Rupp the first coach to capture three titles. But those tarts lost their sweetness in an atmosphere of uncertainty, as each day through the spring of 1951 newspaper headlines told of the expanding investigation of game fixing.

Again Rupp had dug into his supply of All-Americans and come up with a young team seemingly poised at the edge of a dynasty. Two freshmen—Cliff Hagan and Frank Ramsey—emerged as top-flight talents. At the heart of the team was 7-foot junior center Bill Spivey, who led the Wildcats to the '51 championship.

Yet the Kentucky dream ended there. Spivey became embroiled in the gambling scandal and was indicted for perjury. He maintained his innocence, and the case resulted in a hung jury. But Spivey's college career was ended.

With the embarrassment of scandal, the NCAA ended its relationship with Madison Square Garden and selected Minneapolis, Minnesota, as the site of the 1951 finals. With its 16-team format, the tournament headed off in a new direction. Under the new rules, the selection committee would take the teams with the best won-lost percentages in the 10 major conferences. In addition, six teams would be tapped with at-large bids.

The draw of that first 16-game tournament laid the groundwork for tradition. Kentucky met cross-state rival Louisville in the opening round of the East. The Cards successfully shut down Spivey, but forward Shelby Linville scored 23 points, a career best, and the Wildcats advanced, 79-68.

In the second round, Rupp's team faced St. John's, the only New York school not implicated in the scandal. The Redmen featured a competitive little guard by the name of Al McGuire, younger brother of Dick. Al, of course, would make his presence known years later in the Final Four. But on this night in 1951, he scored five points and watched his Redmen go down, 59-43.

Kentucky's real test in the tournament came in the East finals against Illinois and forward Don Sunderlage.

The Illini led by seven at the half, 39-32, but Spivey fell into an offensive trance in the second half and seemed poised to pull Kentucky to the finals, until he fouled out with 28 points and 16 rebounds. The game tightened, then with 10 seconds left Shelby Linville hit a 10-footer to give the Cats a 76-74 lead. Sunderlage's last hook shot missed

at the buzzer, and once again Rupp was in the finals.

In the West, Kansas State-coached by Jack Gardner-emerged from the pack. A balanced team with a deep bench, State had defeated NIT champion Brigham Young on the way to the finals. The team balance was enough to help Gardner's team to a two-point lead at the half, but Kansas State went through an eight-minute stretch of the second half without scoring. That was enough for Kentucky to dominate and win going away, 68-58.

TOURNAMENT NOTES: Spivey scored 22 points with 21 rebounds for the final, yet NCAA officials decided not to select an MVP.

Opposite page—Big Bill Spivey, a 7-footer, led Kentucky in 1951 , but his college career was interrupted when he was implicated in the point-shaving investigation of 1951. Above right—Kentucky All-American Cliff Hagan shoots a hook shot against Georgia. Below—Coach Rupp admires his teams' collection of trophies.

1951					
Kentucky	fg-fga	ft-fta	rb	pf	tp
Whitaker	4- 5	1- 1	2	2	9
Linville	2- 7	4- 8	8	5	8
Spivey	9-29	4- 6	21	2	22
Ramsey	4-10	1- 3	4	5	9
Watson	3- 8	2- 4	3	3	8
Hagan	5- 6	0- 2	4	5	10
Tsioropoulos	1- 4	0- 0	3	1	2
Newton	0- 0	0- 0	0	0	0
Totals	28-69	12-24	45	23	68
Kansas State	fg-fga	ft-fta	rb	pf	tp
Head	3-11	2- 2	3	2	8
Stone	3- 8	6- 8	6	2	12
Hitch	6-15	1- 1	9	3	13
Barrett	2-12	0- 2	3	1	4
Iverson	3-12	1- 2	0	3	7
Rousey	2-10	0- 0	2	3	4
Gibson	0- 2	1- 1	1	5	1
Upson	0- 1	0- 0	2	1	0
Knostman	1- 4	1- 2	3	1	3
Peck	2- 3	0- 1	0	0	4
Schuyler	1- 2	0- 1	1	2	2
Totals	23-80	12-20	30	23	58
Half time: Kansas State 29-27.					

Back To Tradition

Caught in controversy and turmoil, college basketball tapped the connection to its deepest tradition in 1952, and in the process, seemed to regain a sense of its beginnings. That connection to tradition was Dr. Forrest "Phog" Allen, coach of the University of Kansas and direct descendent of basketball's bloodline. Allen had graduated in 1905 from Kansas, where he had played for Dr. James Naismith, the game's founder.

Allen had coached the Jayhawks since 1920, but in 32 years, the NCAA championship had eluded him. An outspoken and opinionated man, Allen had been particularly critical of the "sinful" atmosphere of college basketball in Madison Square Garden. With the scandal having run its course and taken its toll, Allen's Kansas team moved to the fore in college basketball. The main reason for the Jayhawks' advancement was Allen's 6-foot-9 center, Clyde Lovellette. A senior, Lovellette played a beefy inside game that made him college basketball's most accomplished performer. It also brought Allen his much desired NCAA championship.

Lovellette finished his senior year by setting the all-time NCAA scoring record, 1,888 points. His last two points of the season, in the NCAA finals against St. John's, allowed him to ease past the record of 1,886 points, set just days earlier by Dick Groat of Duke.

Lovellette weighed more than 270 pounds by the close of his college career, leading the newspapers to dub him "Man Mountain." Allen saw in this early version of the "Round Mound of Rebound" the opportunity to dominate opponents. So the Kansas coach designed an offense around the star and encouraged him to shoot freely and often. "He is closer to the basket than anyone else on the floor," Allen explained to reporters at the time, "so I'd rather see him go for it than anyone else."

After a long career in the NBA, Lovellette returned to his hometown of Terra Haute, Indiana, where he was elected sheriff. Actually his career in "enforcement" was begun a decade earlier in the NCAA tournament. In the opening round game of the 1952 Midwest Regional, he scored 31 points against TCU. In the second round against St. Louis, Lovellette shattered the NCAA single-game scoring record with 44 points. On the strength of that

Above opposite—Dr. F.C. "Phog" Allen, Kansas' legendary coach, surveys the action from the bench. Bottom opposite—Clyde Lovellette, Kansas star and MVP of the 1952 NCAA tournament.

scoring, Kansas strode to the finals in Seattle.

For all of Allen's disdain for the New York basketball culture, it was a "City" team that opened the door for Kansas to win the championship. St. John's ousted top-ranked Kentucky in the second round of the East Regionals, 64-57, then dumped second-ranked Illinois and star center Johnny "Red" Kerr in the national semifinals, 61-59.

In the national championship game in Seattle, the Redmen were carried by center Bob Zawoluk, who scored 20 points. But St. John's was no match for Lovellette's inside mastery. He muscled in 33 points as the Jayhawks prevailed easily, 80-63.

TOURNAMENT NOTES: For the first time since 1939, the NCAA selected an all-tournament team: Lovellette, Zawoluk, Kerr, Ron MacGilvray of St. John's and Dean Kelley of Kansas. Lovellette was named MVP after setting tournament records for points (141) and rebounds (69). Kansas had its connections to the past in Naismith and Allen, but the Jayhawks' bloodline also ran to the future of the game in a little-used substitute on that championship team, guard Dean Smith.

1952

Kansas	fg-fga	ft-fta	rb	pf	tp
Kenney	4-11	4- 6	4	2	12
Keller	1- 1	0- 0	4	2	2
Lovellette	12-25	9-11	17	4	33
Lienhard	5- 8	2- 2	4	4	12
D. Kelley	2- 5	3- 6	3	5	7
Hoag	2- 6	5- 7	4	5	9
Houghland	2- 5	1- 3	6	2	5
Davenport	0- 0	0- 0	0	1	0
Heitholt	0- 0	0- 0	0	0	0
Born	0- 0	0- 0	0	0	0
A. Kelley	0- 0	0- 0	0	1	0
Totals	28-63	24-35	42	25	80
St. John's, N.Y.	fg-fga	ft-fta	rb	pf	tp
McMahon	6-12	1- 4	2	4	13
Davis	1- 4	2- 3	2	4	4
Zawoluk	7-12	6-11	9	5	20
Duckett	2- 5	2- 2	2	4	6
MacGilvray	3- 8	2- 5	10	3	8
Walsh	3- 6	0- 0	4	3	6
Walker	0- 2	0- 0	2	4	0
McMorrow	1- 3	0- 0	0	3	2
Sagona	2- 2	0- 0	0	5	4
Giancontieri	0- 0	0- 2	1	0	0
Peterson	0- 1	0- 0	0	0	0
Totals	25-55	13-27	32	35	63

Half time: Kansas 41-27. Officials: Eisenstein and Ogden. Attendance: 11,302.

Kansas City Shootout

The 1952-53 season brought an offensive explosion to college basketball, as more and more teams adopted fast-paced offensive schemes. Another major reason for the outburst was the NCAA's tampering with the free-throw shooting rules in an attempt to cut down on excessive fouling. The rule changes had just the opposite effect, and the number of free-throw shots per game ballooned. It was not uncommon for a team to have 25 to 40 foul calls per game. Game scores soared with the changes, from the 60s to the 80s, 90s, even beyond 100.

As a result, the 1953 NCAA tournament became a shootout with most major scoring records falling. Also, the tournament again expanded, this time to 22 teams with the addition of two more conference and four at-large bids. The format required that six schools - from conferences with strong records in NCAA play - receive first-round byes.

The assault on the scoreboard began with the opening whistle, with Seattle guard Johnny O'Brien scoring 42 points in a first-round victory over Idaho State. In the next round, Bob Houbregs of Washington wiped out Clyde Lovellette's single-game scoring record of 44 points with a 45-point performance against Seattle. Meanwhile, Louisiana State sophomore Bob Pettit was making his showing in the first two games with a measly 28 and 29 points.

When the smoke cleared, two traditional powers were left standing: Indiana in the East, Kansas in the West.

Branch McCracken's Hoosiers faced Phog Allen's Jayhawks in a rematch of the 1940 final between their teams. Fittingly, tournament officials had returned the finals to the Kansas City Auditorium, site of the earlier game. Still, the 1953 championship was anything but a reprint of Indiana's 60-42 blowout in 1940. Instead, it was a classic, a one-point nail-biter that took Allen and McCracken to the edge of their competitiveness.

Both teams had received first-round byes. Kansas was the defending champion but had lost Lovellette to graduation. His replacement was B.H. Born, who quickly established his own identity as a scorer. Teamed with Dean Kelley and Harold Patterson, Born scored consistently throughout the tournament.

The Hoosiers pinned their hopes on All-American guard Bob Leonard and 6-foot-10 sophomore center, Don Schlundt. Both were up to the task. Leonard scored 23 to help Indiana past DePaul, 82-80, in the opening game. Then Schlundt came alive in the next round, ramming in

41 points in a 79-66 win over Notre Dame. In the semifinals against LSU, the two combined, Schlundt scoring 29 and Leonard adding 22, more than enough to offset a 29-point game by Pettit, as Indiana advanced, 80-67.

The championship was the tightest in tournament history, as the teams went the distance with barely a basket separating them. The outcome hinged on Born's fouling out late in the game. The score was tied at 68 with about 30 seconds left when Kansas fouled Leonard. Usually a proficient free-throw shooter, Leonard missed his first but made the second, leaving the Hoosiers playing defense with a one-point lead. Kansas struggled on offense and had to settle for a late shot by substitute Jerry Alberts. It missed, and the celebration began in Bloomington.

TOURNAMENT NOTES: Schlundt had scored 30 points in Indiana's winning effort, but in a controversial move the NCAA named Born of Kansas as MVP, the first time a player for a losing team had received the award. Joining Schlundt and Born on the all-tournament team were Houbregs, Leonard and Kelley.

Opposite—Indiana Coach Branch McCracken. Above—The Hoosiers and their fans do a little celebrating in 1953. Right—B.H. Born of Kansas was named the tourney MVP in '53.

1953

Indiana	fg	ft-fta	pf	tp
Kraak	5	7-10	5	17
DeaKyne	0	0- 0	1	0
Farley	1	0- 0	5	2
Schlundt	11	8-11	3	30
White	1	0- 0	2	2
Leonard	5	2- 4	2	12
Poff	0	0- 0	0	0
Scott	2	2- 3	3	6
Byers	0	0- 0	1	0
Totals	25	19-28	22	69

Kansas	fg	ft-fta	pf	tp
Patterson	1	7- 8	3	9
A. Kelley	7	6- 8	3	20
Davenport	0	0- 0	0	0
Born	8	10-12	5	26
Smith	0	1- 1	1	1
Alberts	0	0- 0	1	0
D. Kelley	3	2- 4	2	8
Reich	2	0- 0	2	4
Totals	21	26-33	17	68

Half time: 41-41. Officials: Lightner and Shaw.

LaSalle and Gola

The gambling probe had led to more woes at the University of Kentucky in 1953. Subsequent investigations turned up additional charges of illegal payments to athletes, academic irregularities, and recruiting violations. As punishment, the NCAA and Southeastern Conference suspended the Wildcats, so they played no games during the '53 season, choosing instead to practice and play intrasquad scrimmages.

When Rupp's players returned to competition in 1954, they did so with a vengeance, turning their high-scoring machine loose on opponents. The Wildcats racked up 25 wins against no losses, and their prizes included a 13-point victory over defending NIT LaSalle and Tom Gola in the finals of their own Kentucky Invitational at Christmas.

Kentucky blasted Pettit and LSU in an SEC playoff, and just as Rupp was poised to take what some thought was his greatest team into NCAA competition, he suffered another setback. The NCAA declared that stars Frank Ramsey, Cliff Hagan and Lou Tsiropoulas were ineligible because they had earned enough credits to graduate.

As a result, the Wildcats never entered the tournament and basketball fans were never given the satisfaction of seeing a rematch with Gola and LaSalle. The Philadelphia school struggled only once in the tournament, in the opening round against Fordham. Down by a bucket with four seconds left, Gola took an inbounds pass and drew a crowd of defenders. Instead of forcing a shot, Gola rifled a pass to teammate Fran O'Malley under the basket for a score at the buzzer to send the game into overtime. Once there the team from Philadelphia prevailed, 76-74. Gola finished with 28 points, but he was just getting started.

The next round brought an 88-81 win over NC State, a tally high enough for a new NCAA record for total points scored in a game. Gola had 26 rebounds to go with his 26 points. Navy was the next victim, 64-48, as Gola turned in 24 rebounds and 22 points. He slowed somewhat in the national semifinals at Kansas City with only 19 points against Penn State, but LaSalle had little trouble with the Nittany Lions.

The championship became a matter of unranked teams. Bradley had snaked through the West, defeating Oklahoma City, Colorado, Oklahoma A&M, and Southern Cal in turn. Gola and LaSalle struggled in the first half and trailed 43-42 at intermission. But in the second half, Coach Ken Loeffler shifted from his man-to-man defense

to a zone, and LaSalle claimed the championship easily, 92-76.

TOURNAMENT NOTES: Gola, a consensus All-American, was named the tournament MVP. However, the outcome of the NCAA tournament had little effect on the Associated Press voters, who named Kentucky the top team.

LaSalle Coach Kenneth D. Loeffler.

1954

La Salle	fg	ft-fta	pf	tp
Singley	8	7-10	4	23
Greenberg	2	1- 2	1	5
Maples	2	0- 0	4	4
Blatcher	11	1- 2	4	23
Gola	7	5- 5	5	19
O'Malley	5	1- 1	4	11
Yodsnukis	0	0- 0	5	0
O'Hara	2	3- 4	1	7
Totals	37	18-24	28	92
Bradley	fg	ft-fta	pf	tp
Petersen	4	2- 2	2	10
Babetch	0-	0- 0	0	0
King	3	6- 7	4	12
Gower	0	1- 2	1	1
Estergard	3	11-12	1	17
Carney	3	11-17	4	17
Utt	0	0- 0	1	0
Kent	8	0- 2	2	16
Riley	1	1- 2	1	3
Totals	22	32-44	16	76

Half time: Bradley 43-42. Officials: Anderson and Dean.

An Interview With Tom Gola

Packer—Tom, can you remember the first time you ever heard of a Final Four?

Gola—Back in 1951, when I was at LaSalle College, now LaSalle University, the biggest tournament in the country was the NIT. In '52, LaSalle went to the NIT and won it. In 1953, we also played in the NIT, although we lost to St. John's in the first round. In 1954, it became mandatory that any team that won its conference had to participate in the NCAA tournament. We won the Mid-Atlantic Conference, so we went to the NCAA tournament. We made it to the Final Four and won the tournament.

Packer—Because you were an easterner from Philadelphia, I guess you thought of the NIT, Madison Square Garden, and the New York City Holiday Festival as the premier events in basketball?

Gola—That's right. Everybody on the East Coast went to the Garden, and, of course, the New York teams were very strong in those days. Manhattan, Seton Hall, and St. John's were the powerhouses, and the West Coast teams were not really big factors in basketball in those days. When we went to the NCAA, it wasn't like it is today. I don't believe the first game was televised, at least not nationwide. In 1955, we went back to the NCAA and played San Francisco, with Bill Russell and K.C. Jones, in the finals. They won, and I believe that was the first game that was televised nationally.

Packer—You had won Most Valuable Player in the NIT when you were a sophomore. Your team, which was outstanding, got knocked off. You really didn't have a lot of those guys coming back in 1954, your junior year, so it was really a different ball club, wasn't it?

Gola—After my sophomore year, academics entered the picture. There were three fellows who were declared ineligible because they didn't have the grades. My junior season, we had one senior, and the rest of the team was sophomores. We won the NCAA, but we were lucky to have won the Fordham game, which we won in the last second.

Packer—Take me through the Fordham game.

Gola—We were down by two points with only four seconds left on the clock. We had the ball at midcourt, and the inbounds pass came to me at the foul line. Fran O'Malley cut toward the basket from my right side. I happened to see him , and I bounced the ball to him and he made the layup to tie the game. In the overtime, it was nip and tuck, and we had a two point lead with six seconds left. Fordham's Eddie Thomas put up a shot at the buzzer that almost went in, but fortunately it missed.

Packer—Who did you play in your Final Four opener?

Gola—We played Penn State with Jesse Arnelle and Jack Sherry, and we beat them to advance to the final game with Bradley.

Packer—Bradley was a team that had over-achieved that year. Did you know anything about Bradley?

Gola—Bradley was a midwest team. There was a kid on the Bradley team named John Kent, and John Kent and I played together on an all-star team in high school in Paducah, Kentucky.

Packer—It was a small world even back in those days. Your coach, Kenny Loeffler, was one of the great disciples of the zone defense. Did using the zone give you an advantage, since most teams played man-to-man?

Gola—Well, it's funny, because Kenny Loeffler stressed man-to-man. He said if you couldn't play man-to-man, you couldn't play a zone. What he did was to fall back on a zone for a change of pace, for a surprise defensively, or if I was in foul trouble. So the zone really wasn't our strength. We were good man-to-man.

Packer—You beat Bradley 92-76 in your first national championship? Anything you remember about that game?

Gola—We were dragging most of the game, and at halftime we were behind. All of a sudden, we started to click, and we went on a scoring tear in the second half. I think that was the highest scoring championship game up to that time.

Packer—You head back to Philadelphia having won the NCAA title. How did that compare to winning the NIT a couple years before?

Gola—When we won the NIT, we had a big parade waiting for us, and we marched up Broad Street and back to campus. In '54, when we won the NCAA, the president of city council presented us a proclamation and the city gave us awards. Anytime you win anything, the campus is where it's at. We had a parade, they carry you on their shoulders. We had a super time both when we won the NIT and when we won the NCAA .

Packer—What was the first Final Four you ever heard of as a kid?

Gola—The teams I really followed were CCNY and Bradley. Unfortunately, they were involved in a scandal, but I watched those two teams when Melchiorre and Unruh were there.

Packer—What was the makeup of your team the next year. Did you think you could repeat as national champions?

Gola—I was the captain and a senior. We had mostly juniors and one sophomore, a very talented individual named Alonzo Lewis. That season, we won a lot of ball games, and I guess we had four or five losses. Going into the NCAA tournament, I don't think we were the favor-

ites, although, at the time, nobody had heard of Bill Russell.

Packer—It's hard for me to believe that there could have been a guy like Russell and a team as good as San Francisco and you had not heard of them in Philadelphia.

Gola—The West Coast was not a prominent factor in NCAA basketball. People aren't going to believe me, but Bill Russell was not a big name on the East Coast until they beat us in that tournament. Of course, the next year they went undefeated because Russell and K.C. Jones went right through everybody. But the year that I went out there in '54, Russell didn't know me and I didn't know him.

Packer—Had you ever seen him?

Gola—No, I had not seen Bill Russell until we met in the lobby of the hotel. He was coming in and I was going out. When we got into the game, I didn't play Russell nor did he play me. K.C. Jones played me, and we stayed in a zone the whole game.

Packer—What did your scouting reports say about Russell and K.C. Jones?

Gola—It's funny how people talk about scouting reports today. There are films, and high technology, and people planning ahead and watching a team for three or four games. We didn't know anything about Bill Russell or K.C. Jones or San Francisco. A guy from the team's public relations office used to go out and scout teams, and Loeffler would give him 10 or 20 bucks. Today, you have professional scouts and you buy these high-tech scouting reports, but then it was all amateurish.

Packer—After your semifinal game, did you guys hang around to watch Russell play?

Gola—Yes.

Packer—This was your first look at the team. What was your opinion?

Gola—Well, I'll be honest with you. I've always said that Bill Russell is a great athlete. But in those days, I didn't think he could shoot, and I don't think he shot that well in the pros except for that little hook shot. But he had defensive ability that nobody could match. In those days, there was no such a thing as offensive goaltending, so when somebody took a shot, he could jump up and guide it into the basket. He would get maybe 20 points a game just steering in all the shots. The guy who hurt us that night was K.C. Jones, with 20-some points, and K.C. was not known for his shooting ability. Russell guarded Alonzo Lewis and also sagged off back into the pivot on me. Alonzo just couldn't hit his shots. If he had, it would have been nip-and tuck all the way. But that was one of those things.

Packer—As a collegiate player, was K.C. as good a player as you have seen?

Gola—Oh yeah. There's always a guy on the team who sacrifices, who plays good defense, who moves the ball, and that was K.C. He was the catalyst for San Francisco. On our team, we had Frank O'Malley, who only scored 14 or 15 points a game, but he was a general out there. He kept everything going, and he was a good defensive ball player. And K.C. was the same way. Today everybody is offense-minded, but there are certain guys who have to do the dirty job—take the ball out of bounds, play some defense. When I was in college, I played around the basket, but we had a five-man team so everybody handled the ball and everybody was equal. Nobody had to worry about getting the ball and everybody scored. When I got to the pros, we had great scorers, and I went into the back court. I played in the back court for 10 years and never had the opportunity to play the forward position. I think I could have scored a lot more in the forward position, but I ended up in the back court because of my defensive ability. I ended up playing Sharman, Oscar Robertson, Jerry West, Hal Greer, and I mean I ran for 10 years.

Packer—Against San Francisco, the dream of winning two national championships ends. At that point, did you envision what kind of pro careers you and guys like Russell and K.C would have? Could you have imagined that San Francisco would be undefeated the next year? Were they that awesome?

Gola—No, they weren't awesome. We had a bad night. Nobody could predict what would happen when we went into the pros. Bill Russell was just the player the Boston Celtics needed. Cousey, Sharman, "Easy Ed" Macauley—all these guys were great offensively, but they had no defense. Russell was the catalyst that made that club go, and I don't care if anybody else raises his hand and takes the credit. Bill Russell provided defense to the Boston team, and that made them champions.

Packer—How would that San Francisco team stack up against today's teams?

Gola—Oh, nobody could touch Russell.

Packer—Is that right? Would he be just as effective playing today?

Gola—That's right. I was up in Springfield for the opener of the Peach Bowl Festival with Navy playing North Carolina State. David Robinson was there and I thought, "That guy is Bill Russell exactly, except that Bill Russell couldn't shoot."

Packer—Tom, your junior year you were the MVP in the championship game. You had 19 points and 19 rebounds. Anything particular you remember about winning the MVP?

Gola—No, what I remember about the NCAA was during my second year. George Mikan was at the NCAA that year and he was talking to me about going into the pros. When we won that championship, he came to me and asked me to go into the pros. The AAU was offering $5,400 a year, which was big money in those days. I signed

my first contract in the pros for $11,500, plus a bonus. If you look at that salary compared to today's, I expect the ball boy makes more.

Packer—Probably. Bobby Knight got fined $10,000 dollars for hitting the score board.

Gola—But the school made a million dollars.

Packer—Do you have any idea what LaSalle brought home from the NCAA tournament?

Gola—I don't know. There was no TV at the time.

Packer—You got into foul trouble in that game with San Francisco. Did that force you to play differently?

Gola—I don't remember if I got in foul trouble or not because I very rarely fouled out. When I did get into foul trouble, we usually bounced back into a zone.

Packer—You played in two Final Fours and two NITs. Was there ever a time in 1955 when you envisioned a Final Four like we know it today?

Gola—Never thought about it in those days. The NCAA championship is probably the best event on TV today. I think it beats anything around, whether it's football, horse racing, or baseball.

Packer—One last question. You were a highly regarded high school player. How did you end up at LaSalle?

Gola—In 1951, LaSalle High School and LaSalle College were on the same campus. LaSalle College had an enrollment of fewer than 1,000 students. The basketball powers at the time were Kentucky and NC State, and I leaned that way. I went down to Kentucky and met Adolph Rupp. That's when he had "Wah Wah" Jones, Ralph Beard, and Rollins. I also went to NC State. I loved the campus, and I was close to going to State. But it just happened that there were three alumni who approached me with different pictures, and I got a little nervous. My coach was with me and, in the final analysis, I decided to go to LaSalle. I never regretted it. My two brothers also got scholarships. I guess the statute of limitations has run out and the NCAA won't be after me, but my two brothers and I got a college education. And that was great for my father, a Philadelphia policeman who raised seven kids and couldn't afford to send any of them to college. So all

The Dons Of A New Age

When K.C. Jones and Bill Russell graduated from high school on the West Coast in the early 1950s, there was no rush of scholarship offers for them to play basketball in college. That, in itself, is a prime argument against the vast ignorance of racial segregation. Black players had begun breaking the color barrier at some colleges in the 1940s, but by 1952, when Russell finished high school in Oakland, opportunities remained limited.

At the urging of an alumnus, University of San Francisco Coach Phil Woolpert gave Russell a try out and, subsequently, a scholarship. K.C. Jones had joined the Dons a year earlier. Before four years were up, the two of them would lead basketball into a new age.

A 6-foot-1 guard, Jones was a serious student of the game. The Dons might have reached their championship pitch before the '55 season had Jones not suffered a severe appendicitis attack that almost killed him early in the '54 season. With Jones out , the Dons struggled while Russell worked to improve his unpolished basketball skills.

The young 6-foot-9 center was fueled by a natural high-octane intensity that made him a great rebounder and shot-blocker. During his early years at San Francisco, offensive goaltending was within the rules, and Russell often used his jumping ability to "guide" errant shots into the basket. Still, his mindset was all defense.

Nothing could have been more pleasing for Woolpert, a coach who spent most of his practices working on defense. "It just isn't good basketball," Woolpert once remarked of the running, fastbreak game. "I wouldn't know how to go about coaching it. You can't expect to execute scoring plays when you're running up and down the court like madmen."

Jones returned to the lineup for the '55 season, and the little-known Dons wasted no time in showing the basketball world their defensive prowess. Early in the season they lost a road game, 47-40, to eighth-ranked UCLA with Willie Naulls. They wouldn't taste defeat again during the remainder of Russell's college career. With a 23-1 regular season record, USF entered the West Regionals and sliced up West Texas State, 89-66, and Utah, 78-59. Only in the regional final were they tested, when Oregon State and 7-foot-3 center Swede Holbrook pushed them to the final whistle before falling, 57-56.

At the Final Four in Kansas City, Russell scored 24 as San Francisco beat Colorado, 62-50. Third-ranked LaSalle and Tom Gola were the opponents in the finals, having returned there by thrashing West Virginia, Princeton, and Canisius in the East, before edging Iowa in the national semis.

The national championship was tight for a half, as both teams performed in a trance. But while the newspaper hype had pitted Russell against Gola, Woolpert assigned Jones to cover the 6-foot-6 forward, leaving Russell free to dominate the paint. In the second half that strategy began to pay off as the Dons steadily outdistanced LaSalle to win, 77-63. Jones had 24 points, and Russell, who was named MVP, had 23.

Playmaker Hal Perry returned with Russell and Jones for the 1955-56 season, and scorers Gene Brown and Mike Farmer joined the Dons' rotation. The only drawback was Jones' eligibility. Because of appendicitis, he had been granted an extra year of play, but his eligibility extended only through the regular season. He would be unable to play in the tournament. By tournament time, their winning streak was 51 games, and it continued there.

Left—San Francisco Coach Phil Woolpert. Right—K.C. Jones of San Francisco drives against California in 1956.

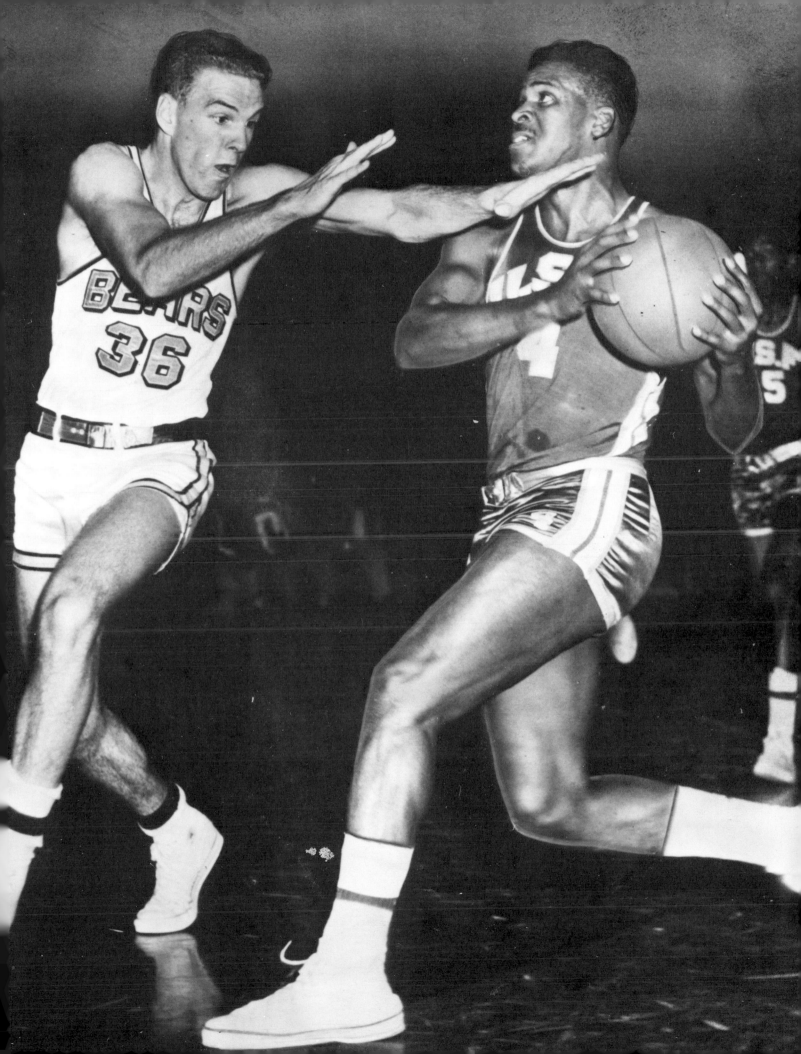

In order, San Francisco turned aside John Wooden's UCLA team, and Utah in the West Regional, and Southern Methodist in the national semis, with Russell scoring 22 in each game.

The national championship, played in Northwestern University's new arena in Evanston, Illinois, brought San Francisco face-to-face with fourth-ranked Iowa and All-American Carl "Sugar" Cain. The Hawkeyes had left tournament victims Morehead State, Kentucky and Temple in their wake, but they were no match for Russell and company. San Francisco claimed its second championship, 83-71, and with it a $12,500 winner's share from the NCAA.

TOURNAMENT NOTES: Russell scored 26 points in the final but wasn't named MVP. That award went to Temple's Hal Lear, who broke the tournament's single-game scoring record with a 48-point performance in the consolation game against Southern Methodist. San Francisco ended the season with a 55-game winning streak, the longest in NCAA history. The Dons extended their number of wins to 60 straight into the 1956-57 season before losing to Illinois, 62-33. Russell and Jones, of course, went on to greatness with the Boston Celtics.

Above—California Coach Pete Newell with San Francisco's Bill Russell and K.C. Jones at ceremonies honoring both players as All-Americans. Right—Hal Lear of Temple was named the 1956 MVP. Opposite— Russell's hook shot.

1955

San Francisco	fg	ft-fta	pf	tp
Mullen	4	2- 5	5	10
Buchanan	3	2- 2	1	8
Russell	9	5- 7	1	23
Jones	10	4- 4	2	24
Perry	1	2- 2	4	4
Wiebusch	2	0- 0	0	4
Zannini	1	0- 0	0	2
Lawless	1	0- 0	0	2
Kirby	0	0- 0	1	0
Totals	31	15-20	14	77

La Salle	ft	ft-fta	pf	tp
O'Malley	4	2- 3	1	10
Singley	8	4- 4	1	20
Gola	6	4- 5	4	16
Lewis	1	4- 9	1	6
Greenberg	1	1- 2	4	3
Blatcher	4	0- 0	1	8
Maples	0	0- 0	0	0
Fredericks	0	0- 0	0	0
Totals	24	15-23	12	63

Half time: San Francisco 35-24.

1956

San Francisco	fg	ft-fta	pf	tp
Boldt	7	2- 2	4	16
Farmer	0	0- 0	2	0
Preaseau	3	1- 2	3	7
Russell	11	4- 5	2	26
Nelson	0	0- 0	0	0
Perry	6	2- 2	2	14
Brown	6	4- 4	0	16
Baxter	2	0- 0	0	4
Totals	35	13-15	13	83

Iowa	ft	ft-fta	pf	tp
Cain	7	3- 4	1	17
Schoof	5	4- 4	3	14
Logan	5	2- 2	3	12
George	0	0- 0	0	0
Scheuerman	4	3- 4	2	11
Seaberg	5	7-10	1	17
Martel	0	0- 0	0	0
McConnell	0	0- 0	0	0
Totals	26	19-24	10	71

Half time: San Francisco 38-33.

Nothing Finer Than Carolina

The University of North Carolina Tar Heels found a magic rhythm in the 1956-57 Final Four. The cadence to their championship march was triple overtime. They survived three extra periods against Michigan State in the national semis. Then, for good measure, they ran another three overtimes in the finals against Wilt Chamberlain and Kansas to claim their first trophy.

When it was over, Frank McGuire's Tar Heels had completed the perfect season, 32-0, the most wins ever crammed into an undefeated NCAA championship season. It was the season that stirred the coals in Carolina's hot bed of fierce regional basketball pride.

McGuire had come to Carolina in 1952 after compiling a 106-36 record at St. John's. His presence immediately opened a recruiting conduit to New York's playground talent, the first major signee being 6-foot-5 Lennie Rosenbluth, a willowy Jewish kid with a clear-shooting conscience.

The next year McGuire added another talent transfusion from the North in Joe Quigg, Bob Cunningham, Pete Brennan and Tommy Kearns. McGuire dressed them in blazers, schooled them in his basketball, and turned them loose on the Atlantic Coast Conference. By 1956, they had found a footing and finished the regular season 17-4, only to lose to Wake Forest in the ACC semifinals.

Although they won early, the 1957 team showed signs of being mired in dissension. Finally, McGuire ordered a players' meeting, where the demons were exorcised. From that point the Heels snaked their way through the season with three close wins over Wake Forest and a double-overtime escape at Maryland.

The East Regional went smoothly enough with comfortable wins over Yale, Canisius and Syracuse. Carolina arrived at the Final Four in Kansas City's Municipal Auditorium with a 30-0 record and the top ranking in both the AP and UPI polls. The newspapers were gleeful over what appeared to be an impending collision with second-ranked Kansas, led by 7-foot-2 sophomore Wilt Chamberlain. Just about everybody figured the Jayhawks and their agile young giant would dash Carolina's dreams.

But that's getting a bit ahead of the story. Carolina still had to get past seventh-ranked Michigan State and Johnny Green in the semifinals. From a 29-29 tie at the half, the game moved to a 58-58 close at regulation. With 11 seconds left in the first overtime, the Spartans held a 64-62 lead and a chance to win at the free-throw line. But Brennan rebounded the missed shot, drove the length of the floor and scored to send the game into its second extra period. After both teams managed two points, the third overtime began at 66-all. Finally, Rosenbluth hit two shots, and Kearns added two free throws, enough to outlast Michigan State, 74-70. In less than 24 hours, they would meet Kansas for the title.

"Phog" Allen, the great recruiter, had been denied the pleasure of coaching his greatest recruit, Chamberlain, when before the season he was forced to retire at age 70. Dick Harp, Allen's assistant, took over and guided Kansas through a grand season. Chamberlain had averaged nearly 30 points, and the Jayhawks had lost only once, an upset to Iowa State. After a first-round bye, their trip through the Midwest Regional had carried them past Southern Methodist and Oklahoma City, as "Wilt the Stilt" scored 36 and 30 points.

They were more than happy to take a homecourt advantage in Kansas City, and eliminated San Francisco (Russell and Jones had graduated) by a whopping 80-56, as Chamberlain scored 32.

For the championship, McGuire sent 5-foot-10 Tommy Kearns out to jump center against Chamberlain. After disconcerting the Kansas center with comedy, the Heels followed up by surrounding him with a stifling zone. That worked well enough as Carolina ended the first half with a 29-22 lead. But in the second, Chamberlain shook loose from the zone, and the Jayhawks moved into position to claim the title. Harp went to the stall with a three-point lead and 10 minutes left. With 1:45 left in regulation, Rosenbluth fouled out having scored 20. Only a late basket by senior Bob Young allowed the Heels to tie it at the end of regulation, 46-all. The first overtime produced a single basket by each team, and the second overtime was scoreless.

With under 10 seconds left in the third overtime and Kansas holding a 53-52 lead, Carolina's Quigg was fouled in the act of shooting and awarded two shots. After McGuire called timeout, Quigg calmly made both, then sealed the championship, 54-53, by slapping away the Jayhawks' inbounds pass as time expired.

TOURNAMENT NOTES: Chamberlain was named the tournament MVP but would never make another visit to the Final Four. Kansas didn't reach the tournament his junior year, and he played with the Harlem Globetrotters his senior year. As for the Heels, they returned to Raleigh-Durham Airport and found a crowd of 10,000 waiting to celebrate.

Opposite—Kansas sophomore Wilt Chamberlain in 1957.

1957

North Carolina	fg-fga	ft-fta	rb	pf	tp
Rosenbluth	8-15	4- 4	5	5	20
Cunningham	0- 3	0- 1	5	4	0
Brennan	4- 8	3- 7	11	3	11
Kearns	4- 8	3- 7	1	4	11
Quigg	4-10	2- 3	9	4	10
Lotz	0- 0	0- 0	2	0	0
Young	1- 1	0- 3	3	1	2
Team			6		
Totals	21-45	12-22	42	21	54

Kansas	fg-fga	ft-fta	rb	pf	tp
Chamberlain	6-13	11-16	14	3	23
King	3-12	5- 6	4	4	11
Elstun	4-12	3- 6	4	2	11
Parker	2- 4	0- 0	0	0	4
Loneski	0- 5	2- 3	3	2	2
L. Johnson	0- 1	2- 2	0	1	2
Billings	0- 0	0- 0	0	2	0
Team			3		
Totals	15-47	23-33	28	14	53

Half time: North Carolina 29-22. Regulation Score: 46-46. First Overtime: 48-48; Second Overtime: 48-48. Officials: Conway and Anderson.

An Interview With Lennie Rosenbluth

Lennie Rosenbluth scored 20 points in North Carolina's 1957 championship battle with Kansas.

Packer—Lenny, you fouled out of the championship game against Kansas. Is that right?

Rosenbluth—Yes, that really hurt. I fouled out with a minute and 50 seconds to go in regulation. I really felt frustrated sitting on the bench. All I could do was root for the players, "Let's go, let's go." It's a lot harder sitting on the bench than it is playing the ball game. But the way things turned out we won the game, so maybe it happened for the best.

Packer—You were an unusual player, not only in your style of play, but you were the first guy Frank McGuire brought down to North Carolina as he assembled one of basketball's greatest teams.

Rosenbluth—I was going to NC State. Everett Case had recruited me heavily in New York, and I went down to State to look at the campus and see everybody, and before I know it, it's a tryout. Back in those days, you were allowed to bring kids in from all over the country for tryouts for the varsity. But I didn't realize it was a tryout because I was in tremendously bad shape, and Everett Case had said the scholarships were no longer open. So I went back to New York.

Meanwhile, McGuire contacted me and said, "I want you to come with me, but I will not be at St. John's. I'm going somewhere else." I knew Frank McGuire and McGuire knew me. We had had a big testimonial dinner in New York for Frank in '52, the year he took St. John's to the Final Four. He told me he was going one of two places—either Alabama or the University of North Carolina. Of course, he ended up at UNC and so did I, although I had to go to prep school for a year to pick up some of the subjects I needed.

Packer—If it hadn't been for Frank McGuire, North Carolina would have been the furthest thing from your mind as the school you wanted to attend?

Rosenbluth—I was going with Frank. I told Frank, "Wherever you're going, I'm going. If you stay at St. John's, I'm staying with you at St. John's. If you're going to Alabama, I'm going."

Packer—As a kid growing up in New York City, the NIT was a bigger deal to a guy like you than the NCAA. When was the first time you ever heard about NCAA championships?

Rosenbluth—I believe it was in '51 when the betting scandals hit in New York. Before that, almost every New

York kid wanted to play at City College, NYU, or Long Island University. LIU was the power back then, and it was the dream of every kid in New York City to play for LIU. They were always in the Top Ten. City College won the NIT and the NCAA in '50, and then this scandal hit. A lot of schools dropped their programs. LIU never re-established its program and neither did City College.

NYU had a couple of good years, but then everyone started to leave the city. When I was a kid, the NIT was the first choice of the colleges. Then came the NCAA. But after the scandals, city players started going to out-of-state schools and the NCAA became the leading tournament.

Packer—Tommy Kearns mentioned to us that four Catholic kids went down to North Carolina acting as missionaries. You think of integration and how long that took in the ACC and other southern schools. For you it wasn't easy as one of the few Jewish players to go south. Was that a tough move for you and were you accepted in most places?

Rosenbluth—In some places, some of the players might say something to me. But I ignored it because in New York I had played in the church leagues and I played at the YMCA, the only white kid in an all-black YMCA. So that didn't bother me. I think it bothered the other players, but I just felt like putting points on the board and winning. Like Frank McGuire said, "All you have to do is stay ahead of the teams and that hushes the crowd and hushes the players." Basically, that's what I tried to do.

Packer—I've seen films of the celebration that the fans in Carolina gave you when you returned home after winning the NCAA tournament. Was that anything you could have envisioned when you first started playing there?

Rosenbluth—No, and that's one of the saddest parts of my Carolina experience. I did not get to go back on the plane. Frank McGuire and I flew to New York to be on the Ed Sullivan Show. There are two things that I regret: Missing that homecoming, which is a once-in-a-lifetime thing, and the Olympic games held in '56 in Australia. I couldn't get there to compete, and I think it would have been a tremendous thrill to represent the United States. And I guess if I go all the way back to my freshman year, there was another disappointment. I remember my first freshman game. We couldn't get into the gym. The gym was locked, and we had to get the custodians to open the doors so we could go out and play. The stands were completely empty. Maybe 100 people showed up. However, by our senior year the gym wasn't big enough to hold everybody.

When I first went to Carolina, basketball was the furthest thing from people's minds. Frank McGuire's basketball office was behind an old ticket window, and you had to walk sideways to get in. It's changed, and I guess I was lucky enough to be there right from the beginning as Frank McGuire was building the program that has become one of the greatest programs in the United States.

Packer—Compared to what we see now in the Final Four, did you think in 1957 that the tournament would ever become a national event like it is today?

North Carolina Coach Frank McGuire.

Rosenbluth—No, not really. When we played back in '57, I don't think Carolina even put it on TV, and it wasn't even on radio nationwide. I know my father couldn't pick it up on a Florida station. He had to go out to the car to try and pick up a Charlotte station. Of course, today, it is just built up to one of the greatest sporting events in the United States. I think it's fantastic.

Packer—The 1957 finals must have been some championship game, a player of your caliber on a team that is undefeated going up against a team like Kansas with Wilt Chamberlain. Had you ever seen him play prior to the time you played against him?

Rosenbluth—Most of us were playing in the Catskill Mountains during the summer, and we played against Chamberlain when he was in high school, so we were not awed by his back-dunks or by how big he was. As we got ready for the game, we tried to remember that no matter if he dunked the ball over his head or whatever, it was still just two points. It counts the same as hitting a little jump shot from 10 feet out, so we tried not to be awed. We put a man in front of him, behind him, and on either side of him and said, "Hey, go ahead and do," and I think we held him to a fairly low score. Plus, I don't think he got that many rebounds. You mentioned Tommy jumping center against Wilt. We all had a little chuckle, and it just took all the tension out of the game.

An Interview With Tom Kearns

Tommy Kearns was a sparkplug guard on North Carolina's 1957 national championship team.

Packer—Tommy, one of the great scenes of all times in the NCAA championship was the center jump to start the championship game in '57. What in the world were you doing, a 6-foot guy jumping against the 7-foot Chamberlain?

Kearns—Frank McGuire's assistant coach had seen the play at the YMCA in the early '30s. I really didn't know anything about the plan for me to jump center against Wilt until Coach McGuire said something to me five minutes before the game. I just passed it off, however. After the player introductions, we sat on the bench and he said, "Tommy, you're going out to jump against Wilt." I was just as surprised as anybody.

Packer—What was the outcome of the tap?

Kearns—Well, of course I got it! But I think Wilt was taken aback, as I think the whole team was. It set a tone for the game, and we jumped off to a very big lead as a result. I think it was a a daring move by Coach McGuire, and it had an awful lot to do with us winning the game.

Packer—In the championship game against Kansas, you went to triple-overtime. You should have been used to it by then, because you all were the cardiac kids that year.

Kearns—And don't forget that in the '50s we played the tournament games on consecutive nights, Fridays and Saturdays, instead of on Saturday and Monday like it is today. In the semifinals, we played Michigan State and that game was three overtimes, and then we played Kansas in the finals for three overtimes. We played six overtimes in two days. That was like playing three-and-a-half games in two days. We only had 10 players and I think only seven played over the last 17 or 18 games, so we all played virtually the whole game every game. For the last 21 or 22 games, I played every minute of every game.

Packer—You fellows on that '57 team were all northern guys. How did you all end up on a team in North Carolina? In those days, recruiting was basically regionalized.

Kearns—That was the doing of Frank McGuire. Frank was persuaded to go to Chapel Hill by Jerry Carmichael. I think there was a lot of heat on in Chapel Hill because Everett Case was at NC State, and he was doing a lot of good things. And Duke was always a power in basketball, and I think one day Mr. Carmichael decided the University of North Carolina should be on the same level as State

and Duke. Coincidentally, Frank's son, Frankie Jr., had some physical problems, and it was comforting to Frank to be in Chapel Hill near the hospital. When Frank went there, he just kept that New York connection. It didn't matter if Frank were in Omaha, or Tulsa, or Chapel Hill, he was going to recruit New York kids.

Packer—But you fellows were born and bred for New York City basketball in New York City schools. Why did you want to go down south?

Kearns—Well, it was Frank.

Packer—In other words, he could have told you to come to Hong Kong and you would have gone?

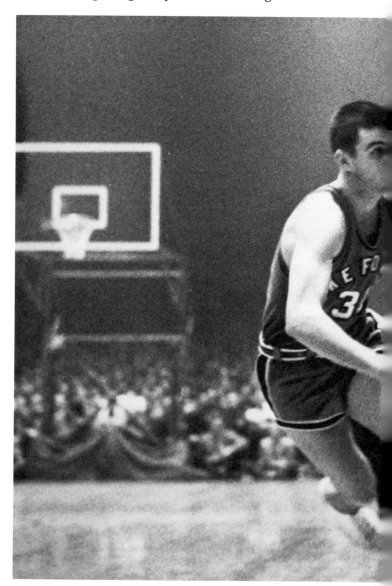

Kearns—Hong Kong or Taiwan or wherever. Of the five New York players, four of us had gone to Catholic boys' schools. We had problems with the high school Catholic principals sending our grades down to a southern Baptist-type school. The lines were more clearly drawn back then than they are now. It was fairly difficult to make a commitment to a non-Catholic southern school. It was a major concern for our parents. I remember very clearly when Coach McGuire came to my house to recruit me. He came with Bill Berony, one of his good friends, who lived fairly close to our family. Coach McGuire had a theme. We were going to go down south as missionaries. So now we were athletes and missionaries, and Catholicism was going to march through North and South Carolina. Frank was just a very charismatic guy.

Below—Kearns driving against ACC opponent Wake Forest.

Kentucky Fiddlesticks

For the 1957-58 season, college basketball was stocked with a wealth of future NBA stars. Oscar Robertson, a Cincinnati sophomore, led the nation in scoring with a 35.1 average. Elgin Baylor, also averaging more than 30 points per game, carried the University of Seattle to the national championship game. Jerry West was the firepower in West Virginia's arsenal, shooting the Mountaineers to the top ranking in both the UPI and AP polls, but his team was again upset in the first round of the NCAA tournament. Wilt Chamberlain, a junior center for Kansas, also scored better than 30 per game, yet the Jayhawks were bounced out of championship competition by cross-state rival, Kansas State.

For all their ability, none of the above players could find a path to take their teams to the national title. Instead, the limelight was taken once again by the Baron in the brown suit, Kentucky's Adolph Rupp, who guided a collection of unheralded players to the school's fourth NCAA championship.

His team was ranked ninth in the AP poll, but the UPI poll, voted by Rupp's fellow coaches, made no mention of the Wildcats. "I know I have plenty of enemies," he told reporters, "but I'd rather be the most-hated winning coach in the country than the most-popular losing one."

Whereas Rupp's powerhouse 1949 team had been called the "Fabulous Five," he took to calling the '58 unit the "Fiddlin' Five," sometimes with affection, sometimes not. With a string of undefeated Southeastern Conference seasons in his wake, Rupp and his followers considered a 12-2 finish nothing more than ho-hum.

But in the Mideast Regional, played on Kentucky's home floor, the Wildcats bullied Miami of Ohio, 94-70, and a good Notre Dame team, 89-56. Suddenly, the press began to recognize that Kentucky's Vern Hatton and John Cox weren't such bad players after all. But it was the team's special sixth man—a continued "home-court advantage"—that made the difference in the Final Four. The championship was played in Louisville's Freedom Hall, where Kentucky basketball mania ruled the proceedings.

The national semifinal against Temple and All-American guard Guy Rodgers was the thriller. Kentucky and the Owls had met once during the regular season, a match that took three overtimes before Kentucky won on a 47-foot shot by Hatton at the buzzer. The NCAA confrontation was just as tight. Temple led 60-59 with 15 seconds left, but Rodgers missed a free throw for Temple and Hatton made a layup seconds later for a 61-60 win. The

Kentucky's Vernon Hatton.

Left—Temple All-American guard Guy Rodgers drives against Kentucky's Johnny Cox in the 1958 Final Four thriller, won by Kentucky, 61-60. Right—Johnny Cox.

Baron's boys were advancing to yet another national championship game.

In the other bracket, Seattle and Elgin Baylor, who had transferred from Idaho, beat Kansas State, 73-51. The championship pairing was tantalizing: Baylor, a great player with an unknown team, against Rupp's dynasty, albeit a "fiddlin'" edition of that dynasty. A record NCAA crowd, 18,803, squeezed into Freedom Hall for the game, and the Kentuckians present weren't disappointed.

Rupp outwitted Seattle's John Castellani, who had assigned Baylor to guard Kentucky forward John Crigler. The Baron simply directed that the ball go to Crigler and that Crigler drive against Baylor. The Seattle star was called for three personal fouls in the first 10 minutes of play. Despite that, Seattle led by three at the half. And with Baylor showing a superhuman mixture of caution and grace, the Chieftains showed a 61-60 lead midway through the second half. But then Hatton and Cox cut on the booster rockets and blasted to the title, 84-72. Rupp had his fourth championship in 11 seasons.

TOURNAMENT NOTES: Baylor scored 25 points in the championship (he made only nine of 32 attempts from the floor) and was named MVP. Oscar Roberston had scored 56 points, an NCAA record, in a regional consolation game against Arkansas.

1958

Kentucky	fg-fga	ft-fta	rb	pf	tp
Cox	10-23	4- 4	16	3	24
Crigler	5-12	4- 7	14	4	14
Beck	0- 1	0- 1	3	4	0
Mills	4- 9	1- 4	5	3	9
Hatton	9-20	12-15	3	3	30
Smith	2- 8	3- 5	6	4	7
Team			8		
Totals	30-73	24-36	55	21	84
Seattle	**fg-fga**	**ft-fta**	**rb**	**pf**	**tp**
Frizzell	4- 6	8-11	5	3	16
Ogorek	4- 7	2- 2	11	5	10
Baylor	9-32	7- 9	19	4	25
Harney	2- 5	0- 1	1	1	4
Brown	6-17	5- 7	5	5	17
Saunders	0- 2	0- 0	2	3	0
Piasecki	0- 0	0- 0	0	0	0
Team			3		
Totals	25-69	22-30	46	21	72

Half time: Seattle 39-36. Attendance: 18,803.

Smarter Than The Average Bears

College basketball's superstars—Oscar Robertson of Cincinnati and Jerry West of West Virginia—finally carried their teams to the Final Four in 1959, but the championship trophy was claimed by California, a team of modest talent but superior coaching.

Coach Pete Newell armed his California Bears with a clawing, pressure defense. That, and a steady, controlled offense were enough to overcome first Robertson, then West, two of the all-time great basketball talents.

With the level of play obviously improving, the 1959 season saw the NCAA tournament heading off into its third decade. Television had yet to balloon the popularity of the game, but there were signs of steady growth. More than 15 million people had paid to see college games in 1958 and 1959. Big college programs and tournament committees across the country began looking for larger arenas to accommodate the crowds.

The '59 finals were again held in Louisville's Freedom Hall, and the pressure for tickets was even greater because the University of Louisville Cardinals were surprise participants in the Final Four after beating Eastern Kentucky, second-ranked Kentucky and third-ranked Michigan State to claim the Mideast Regional crown.

However, the real story of the '59 season was California's successive dismissals of Cincinnati and West Virginia.

As a junior, Oscar Roberston had again won the national scoring title (32.6 points per game) while leading Cincinnati through the Midwest Regional. He performed all chores - ball handling, scoring, rebounding - as Coach George Smith's Bearcats sat poised at the edge of a dynasty. Cincinnati would make five consecutive appearances in the Final Four. But for all his greatness, Robertson would never enjoy a college championship.

Jerry West played much the same role for West Virginia, a do-it-all superman of rebounding, scoring and ball handling. Incredibly, the 6-foot-3 West played forward for the Moutaineers. In 1958, 6-foot-10 center Lloyd Sharrar had helped West Virginia to a top ranking in the polls. But Sharrar had graduated, and the burden fell on West for '59. He responded with an incredible feat in the East Regionals.

West Virginia beat Dartmouth, 82-68, in the first round, but then fell into deep trouble against St. Joseph's in a second round game in Charlotte, North Carolina. With 13 minutes to go in the game, St. Joseph's led, 67-49, only to watch West score 21 points in nine minutes. When the smoke cleared, West had 36 points in carrying the Mountaineers to a 95-92 miracle win. Reaching once more into their bag of dreams, they stretched past Boston University in the East finals, 86-82, to earn their first trip to the Final Four. There, they doused the hopes of hometown favorite Louisville, 94-79, and waited for the Cincinnati/California survivor.

The Bears featured 6-foot-10 Darrall Imhoff at center and flanked him with defensive specialists Bob Dalton and Jack Grout. Newell's pressure worked perfectly, as Cal's defense held Robertson to 19 points and Imhoff's hook shot anchored the offense for a 64-58 win.

The Bears used that same steadiness in the final to take a 12-point lead against West Virginia in the second half, but once again West turned on his magic. The Mountaineers raced back, but ran out of time. They never regained the lead, losing 71-70.

TOURNAMENT NOTES: West, who had scored 160 points in five games, was named MVP. He had scored 28 in the final, but California allowed West Virginia to take only 55 shots.

1959

West Virginia	fg-fga	ft-fta	rb	pf	tp
West	10-21	8-12	11	4	28
Akers	5- 8	0- 1	6	0	10
Clousson	4- 7	2- 3	4	4	10
Smith	2- 5	1- 1	2	3	5
Bolyard	1- 4	4- 4	3	4	6
Retton	0- 0	2- 2	0	0	2
Ritchie	1- 4	2- 2	4	0	4
Patrone	2- 6	1- 2	4	1	5
Team			7		
Totals	25-55	20-27	41	16	70
California	fg-fga	ft-fta	rb	pf	tp
McClintock	4-13	0- 1	10	1	8
Dalton	6-11	3- 4	2	4	15
Imhoff	4-13	2- 2	9	3	10
Buch	0- 4	2- 2	2	3	2
Fitzpatrick	8-13	4- 7	2	1	20
Simpson	0- 1	0- 0	2	2	0
Grout	4- 5	2- 2	3	1	10
Doughty	3- 6	0- 0	1	3	6
Team			7		
Totals	29-66	13-18	38	18	71

Half time: California 39-33.

An Interview With Pete Newell

Pete Newell won the NCAA championship in 1959, then took his California team to the finals again the next year. He is considered one of the all-time great coaches.

Packer—With California coming off two straight national championship appearances, you have nobody on the All-Pac Ten team. How did that happen?

Newell—Darrall Imhoff, the center, never lettered in high school. He broke his foot his freshman year at Cal, and I don't think he ever scored in double figures until he was a junior. So he was certainly not predicted to be much of a player his senior year, but he turned out to be a fine player. Another of our players was Bill McClintock, a junior college transfer who was a good steady player, but he wasn't flashy and he was kind of overlooked. My gosh, we had really good players because we won the national championship, but they weren't flashy. They complemented each other, they played solid defense, they handled the ball well, but they didn't score enough points to impress the people who pick all-star teams. It was a bunch of players who merged their individual skills into a team effort.

Packer—Pete, in regard to West Coast basketball, who influenced the development of your system?

Newell—I played for Jimmy Needles, and he gave me a great college basketball background. I still think he was one of the most forward-thinking men I've ever run into in basketball. He was far ahead of his time. He was talking about transition basketball when no one even knew what the word meant. And he was a great defensive coach. All my defensive schemes came from my exposure to him.

Packer—One of the things that amazes me is that, although you didn't lose a game after mid-January, you still went into the Final Four not ranked in the Top Ten.

Newell—West Coast basketball has always lagged in national recognition. We don't like it but we accept it. Yet, when you look at the NCAAs, we've had more NCAA champions than any other part of the country.

Packer—When you were playing against Oscar Robertson, you waited until the last moment to assign somebody to guard him. Tell us that story.

Newell—I had a player named Rob Dalton. He was about 6'3," and he looked like the results of an X-ray. On a clear day, you could see right through him, but he was really a competitive kid. As a 16-year-old, he was a national doubles champion in tennis. Really an excellent athlete, but he didn't have a very imposing physique. We

California's Pete Newell on the bench.

always played man-to-man defense and, before a game, I might ask one of my guards how he would play the center or ask a center how he would play the small forward. They might get switched to another player on defense, and I wanted them to be aware of that. Anyway, just before the game I went over the assignments and the last player was Oscar. Well, Oscar was *the* player in college basketball. He was in every magazine that had anything to do with sports, and he had set all kinds of records and was truly one of our all-time great players. I called Rob "Thunderbird," because he was the only kid I knew rich enough to own a Thunderbird. So I said, "Thunderbird, I'm going to give you Oscar." And I can see him tense up; this is what he wanted. So we get out before the game, and you know how players shake hands and introduce themselves. Well, Bobby walked up to Oscar before the game and put his hand out and said, "My name is Dalton, what's yours?" A year later, when I was in Rome with Oscar, he says to me, "You know that guy you had guarding me in Louisville? He knew what my name was, didn't he?"

Packer—You had to go against Oscar twice in the Final Four, and you also had to go against Jerry West. Then you coached those fellows in the Olympics. When did you first see Jerry play?

Newell—It was the Friday night in the semifinals when West Virginia played Louisville. I was out on the West Coast, and I hadn't had the opportunity to see West Virginia play before. We didn't have TV like now, when you can see every top team in the country four or five times just by flipping a few dials.

Packer—Who was the tougher player on the college-level, Oscar or Jerry?

Newell—I think Oscar was probably tougher. Because they are considered two of the best pro guards of all time, a lot of people don't know that they both played forward in college. But Oscar handled the ball more. Oscar played forward more like Larry Bird plays forward. He was such a great passer. He brought the ball up even though he was playing forward. Jerry was more strictly a forward. He was so tough when he got the ball. It was a little easier to play Jerry without the ball. Oscar would go down and get it. Then they'd clear for him, and he'd just take it on his own. There was no way you could stop Oscar one-on-one from penetrating and getting his shot. Later, when Jerry became a guard, he really improved his game and he was like Oscar. You couldn't stop either one of them one-on-one. But, in college, I'd say Oscar was a little harder to defend because of his ability to go out and get the ball.

Packer—You guys had to travel all the way from the West Coast to Louisville for the Final Four. Louisville was at its home base, West Virginia was only 100 miles away, and Cincinnati was right up the road. Was that a disadvantage for you?

Newell—We felt it was an advantage for us because we came in there without anybody paying any attention to us. We didn't have any alumni at the game like the other teams. The only thing we had going for us was the Cal Straw Hat Band. They were worth their weight in gold because they started off the festivities by playing *My Old Kentucky Home*, and all the Kentucky people adopted us and rooted for us. Even though we didn't have any California people, we had a lot of Kentucky rooters and a lot of Kentucky support. And I credit our band with that. I didn't feel we had any disadvantage about anything, not the court or the officials. I just didn't believe in thinking about the negative. I tried to look for the positives and I think that's why we were a good team. We were always thinking about what we could do, not what the other team could do.

Packer—Cincinnati was ahead 33-29 at halftime. They were six-point favorites, but you came back to win 64-58. What was the key in that game?

Newell—I thought we played excellent defense. We made Oscar work like the dickens for the ball. We made him bring the ball up, and we did really a good job of defensive rotation. We tried to deny Oscar the ball. If were going to get beat, we wanted those other guys to beat us. We were a very difficult team to fast-break on

because we pressured the rebounder.

Packer—Jerry West had 38 points against Louisville to put West Virginia in the finals against you. You guys are down 23-13, but you come back and lead at halftime.

Newell—We were getting unbelievably easy shots. The shots were so easy that we were losing the tempo of the game. I put in a new center, forward, and guard to try to create some movement of the ball. We had to have the tempo. They were a fast-breaking team and they could really run. We were not comfortable with the pace, but we were kind of trapped into it. So I wanted to reverse the tempo. We ended up going down five straight times and scoring, and we got control of the game and ended up at the half in very good shape.

Packer—West had 15 at the half, but you guys had built up a good lead, 57-44. How do they come back on this patient Pete Newell team that didn't allow many comebacks?

Newell—We were really good at holding leads, but I'll tell you what happened. They played a really good side-court-trap press, and that was something we had not seen. I'd heard about it, but we really didn't have a chance to practice for it. We'd played side-traps before, but not as good as this one. I had a problem getting my center to come up higher. I feel that anytime you have a trap on the side, the center has to read it and come out at least 3 feet farther to create the passing lane. Anyway, they got back in the game, and Jerry was such an electric player anyway, he made two or three hoops in a row, and our 13-point lead's down to about five.

Packer—What was your greatest elation as a coach?

Newell—I was tremendously proud and happy at Cal. We didn't have a program like other people, with the alumni involved. We had the kind of a program where kids worked for their scholarships. They had to put in 30 hours a month on some kind of job; that was all part of their scholarship. All our kids graduated. The two guards on that NCAA championship team are both tremendously successful in business; one president of a savings and loan; the other an owner of one of the top tire companies in the West.

Packer—The next year everybody knows about California, and you work your way back to the Final Four. Of all the people you've got to face, it's Oscar again. And Cincinnati is a much better ball club, right?

Newell—Well I guess it was better. They had Paul Hogue playing center. He was a number one draft choice, a big strong kid.

Packer—Cincinnati never won an NCAA championship with Oscar. You beat them both times you faced them.

Newell—We beat them both times. It's conceivable they could have won five NCAAs in a row. We beat them because we just happened to have the style to handle their club. One of their assistants had said the year before, "All that slow West Coast basketball, we'll bury them early." He happened to say it with a lot of our people and friends around; that it wasn't going to be much of a battle. They were worried about West Virginia. The next year they said we surprised them, that they weren't ready for that kind of ball, and the word to the media was, "We're ready this year." But the result was the same. The next two years they played position basketball and went from a 85-or-90-point a game team to a 60-or-70 point team, and they won two NCAA titles and should have won a third. I took that as a compliment to our style of play.

Packer—In the two games Oscar played against you, he got 18 and 19 points. But in the second game, he went 4-for-16. What plan did you have to defense him?

Newell—We rotated on him. Everywhere he went, we would throw a second guy at him. They were worried about our press, but we really just faked the press because we wanted Oscar to bring the ball up the court. There was no way we could steal the ball from Oscar, but we pecked at him in what I call our "coward press." We looked like we were pressing, but mostly we were making them worry. When Oscar got to midcourt, he'd give up the ball to the guard and move to the forward's spot. Then we denied him the return pass.

Packer—In 1960, you come to the Final Four ranked number one. Cincinnati is ranked number two and Ohio State is number three. Ohio State had very young team that year. What did you know about that club?

Newell—I don't know if you've ever heard this story, but it was chronicled by *Sports Illustrated*. In the summer right after we had won the NCAA, I was a lecturer in Minnesota. Out west, we head coaches and assistants used to have a lot of basketball discussions, but we didn't look at the pedigree of the guy we were talking with as long as he was a basketball coach. Anyway, Freddie Taylor had taken over the year before at Ohio State, and they have the worst defensive record in the history of the Big 10. He comes to my clinic and says, "Pete, I really want to talk to you. I'd like to pick your brain on defense. Will you help us?" I said fine. So I spend about three hours every afternoon going over defense with Fred.

I'm playing against Jerry West's team in the LA Classic in December the next year. It was 1960, and Fred's assistant comes to me and says he's got to talk to me. He's got a list of questions a foot long that he says Fred needs answers to. I answer all his questions, and later in the season he meets me somewhere, and he's got a few more. What do you think happens? I end up playing Ohio State in the NCAA finals and he beats me with some of the defensive things we talked about. He told the story and SI asks me if this is true. The next obvious question is, "Would I do it again?" Hell yes, I'd do it again. And I would because so many coaches helped me along the

Cal's Darrall Imhoff scores against West Virginia in the 1959 Final Four. Number 44 in the background for West Virginia is Jerry West.

way. I'ved always been accessible to any college or high school coach to talk basketball. I want to help them to repay people for helping me.

Packer—In the tournament, Ohio State came out strong with Jerry Lucas, Havlicek, and Siegfried shooting the lights out. I guess there was no way to come back against them.

Newell—We got it back to eight, but they hit 16-of-19 the first half. Believe it or not, we had a defensive plan, but they beat us with their quickness, especially Mel Nowell. This was the only time I felt our defense was a step slow.

Packer—What was the greatest individual performance you ever saw in the Final Four?

Newell—Well, Bill Bradley had a fantastic game in a consolation game, but Bill Walton's feat of 21-of-22 against Memphis State was probably the greatest single performance.

The Buckeye Bunch

Jerry West and Bob Cousy have said Oscar Robertson was the greatest player they ever saw. Robertson's talent encompassed all of the game, from playground razzle-dazzle to team strategy. He seemed to see everything on the court and understand it. After two years of missing the national championship, he and his Cincinnati teammates appeared close to claiming the prize in March 1960.

The Bearcats headed into the NCAA tournament with a 26-1 record and the top ranking in the Associated Press poll. With wins over DePaul and Kansas, they advanced to the Final Four in San Francisco to meet their 1959 nemesis, Pete Newell's California Bears, who were ranked tops in the UPI poll. Basketball history repeated itself, as Newell's highly structured team held Robertson to 18 points and again defeated Cincinnati, 77-69.

With Robertson thwarted, the mantle was seized by another Ohio team, third-ranked Ohio State, and another star, consensus All-American Jerry Lucas, a 6-foot-8 center with incredible fluidity. He could shoot, run the break, pass, and generally displayed the mobility of a guard. But he was no one-man team.

To go with Lucas, Ohio State Coach Fred Taylor had John Havlicek, Larry Siegfried and Mel Nowell, the core of one of the greatest shooting teams in college basketball

history. Among the substitutes was another flash of brilliance, Bobby Knight. The Buckeyes sliced apart their competition in the Mideast Regional: Western Kentucky, 98-79, and Georgia Tech, 86-69. The Final Four brought more of the same. NYU was humbled, 76-54, and the championship match with Cal was a 75-55 snoozer.

Obviously, Taylor's Buckeyes were well prepared for their opponents. The Ohio State coach had spent the summer studying defense with Pete Newell, with neither man considering the likelihood of their teams meeting in the NCAA finals.

To go with the defense, Ohio State had a potent, balanced offense. Lucas led five Buckeyes in double figures with 16 points and 10 rebounds.

Denied the championship, Robertson was left to deal with his frustration. But his college career had ended with his winning a third consecutive national scoring title. In three years of varsity eligibility, Robertson scored 2,973 points and added 1,338 rebounds.

TOURNAMENT NOTES: Lucas was selected tournament MVP. He, Robertson, Jerry West and California's Darrall Imhoff were selected concensus All-Americans.

Ohio State Coach Fred Taylor

1960

Ohio State	fg-fga	ft-fta	rb	pf	tp
Havlicek	4- 8	4- 5	6	2	12
Roberts	5- 6	0- 1	5	1	10
Lucas	7- 9	2- 2	10	2	16
Nowell	6- 7	3- 3	4	2	15
Siegfried	5- 6	3- 6	1	2	13
Gearhart	0- 1	0- 0	1	0	0
Cedargren	0- 0	1- 2	1	1	1
Furry	2- 4	0- 0	3	1	4
Hoyt	0- 1	0- 0	0	0	0
Barker	0- 0	0- 0	0	0	0
Knight	0- 1	0- 0	0	1	0
Nourse	2- 3	0- 0	3	1	4
Team			1		
Totals	31-46	13-19	35	13	75
California	**fg-fga**	**ft-fta**	**rb**	**pf**	**tp**
McClintock	4-15	2- 3	3	3	10
Gillis	4- 9	0- 0	1	1	8
Imhoff	3- 9	2- 2	5	2	8
Wendell	0- 6	4- 4	0	2	4
Shultz	2- 8	2- 2	4-	4	6
Mann	3- 5	1- 1	0	0	7
Doughty	4- 5	3- 3	6	1	11
Stafford	0- 1	1- 2	0	1	1
Morrison	0- 0	0- 0	1	1	0
Averbuck	0- 0	0- 1	1	0	0
Pearson	0- 1	0- 0	0	0	0
Alexander	0- 0	0- 0	0	0	0
Team			7		
Totals	20-59	15-18	28	15	55

Half time: Ohio State 37-19.

An Interview With John Havlicek

John Havlicek was an All-American at Ohio State. For 1960-62, the Buckeyes won 78, and lost six, and made three appearances in the NCAA finals. He was elected to the Hall of Fame in 1983.

Packer—John, you were a multi-talented, multi-sport athlete. How did you happen to go to Ohio State?

Havlicek—I was first recruited by Woody Hayes because I'd played football in Bridgeport, Ohio. I was probably recruited more for football than basketball. I visited Ohio State three times for football and once for basketball. Woody Hayes had talked at our high school sports banquet and tried to talk me into playing football. However, my mother wasn't very happy about me thinking about playing football, and I decided I liked basketball better. When Woody realized I wasn't going to play football, he told me he still wanted me to come to Ohio State. Fred Taylor had been involved in the recruiting process, also, because he was about ready to take over the basketball job from Floyd Stall, who was retiring. He had recruited a great class, including Jerry Lucas, Mel Nowell, and Gary Gearhart, players I had played against in high school all-star games. And I had a great feeling for State, being an Ohio person. Miami of Florida had a distinct flavor for me also, maybe because I had relatives down there. I also considered West Virginia, which was only 90 miles from home. "Hot Rod" Hundley had played there, and I could have played a couple years with Jerry West.

Packer—Mel Nowell and Jerry Lucas were also highly recruited. Had Jerry committed to Ohio State before you decided to go there?

Havlicek—Yes, he committed much earlier than I did. I was the last to commit. Of course, the other prominent fellow on our team was Bobby Knight. I met him in 1958 at a barn used for recruiting parties and that sort of thing. He had that line-drive jump shot that he took from about 35 feet, and I thought, "This guy can really shoot." He wasn't the quickest man on foot, but defensively he played hard. When you got fouled by Bobby, you knew you had been fouled.

Packer—When you went to college, nobody could play as a freshman, so you were a sophomore your first year on the varsity. That year, many people thought Ohio State would be good, but you weren't expected to end up number one in the nation. Do you remember your first game?

Havlicek—I got my first chance to play when one of the co-captains of our team took an elbow right above the eyebrow, and he had to get six stitches. I was inserted into the line-up and I had a pretty decent game, with 18 points or something like that.

Packer—Your team progressed quickly. When did your team begin to feel that it could go all the way?

Havlicek—When we played Indiana tough on their home floor, we knew we could play with just about anyone in the country. We also lost to Bill "The Helm" McGill out in Utah and to Kentucky. All those teams were highly ranked and we played them pretty competitively. As sophomores, we really didn't fear anything. We just went out and played as hard as we could.

Packer—That ball club had Joe Roberts and Larry Siegfried, two outstanding players who must have provided leadership and maturity for your team.

Havlicek—Larry had been the leading scorer for Ohio State the year before with a 20-point average, and Joe Roberts was a seasoned veteran who had played with Frank Howard. Howard, by the way, was a gifted basketball player, and his baseball ability is well known. He was a great rebounder. Siegfried had great confidence and, of course, Jerry never played like a sophomore. He always played beyond his years.

Packer—When was the first time you thought about the Final Four?

Havlicek—I can remember two Final Fours. The first was when I was in high school, and I listened on my car radio to the Kansas-North Carolina game in 1957 when Wilt Chamberlain faced Lennie Rosenbluth. The second was when I was a freshman at Ohio State in 1959. One of my high school coaches gave me a ticket, and we went to the tournament in Louisville. We stayed in a hotel room that only had one bed and a common bath used by everybody on the floor.

Packer—Not exactly uptown.

Havlicek—Not uptown. Everything was booked, so we just took what was left. I remember Imhoff and California beat West Virgina and Jerry West by one point. That was one of the most fantastic games I've ever seen.

Packer—You were just a freshman at the time?

Havlicek—Yes, a freshman who couldn't have imagined that his team would end up in the Final Four the next year and win it. Although I think the Final Four was televised in Columbus, it really wasn't a national event at that time. I think you really date yourself when you look at film of that game and see that it's not even in color. But the thing I remember best about the tournament is that I cut two fingers on my shooting hand two days before we went to California. The cuts required 10 stitches. But in the championship game, we shot a phenomenal percentage the first half. We were something like 18-for-21 or 19-for-22, and I missed two of the three shots I took, and I felt I was a real burden to the team.

Joe Roberts had a great game. I remember a long hook shot he hit from the top of the key. The hook shot is a shot I really don't understand, but it's an impossible shot to defend against, as Kareem Abdul-Jabbar has shown. You would think that the players who play against Kareem would realize the effectiveness of the shot and try to use it, but somehow they don't seem to want to use it. It seems to be the older players who take up the hook once their legs go a little bit. I started shooting a hook shot a little more when I was posting people up later in my career.

Packer—Let's talk about the tournament matchups. In the semifinals, who did you go up against?

Havlicek—We played NYU. Tom Sanders was on that team and two fellows named Ray Paprocky and Al Filardi. Filardi was known as a garbage man, a guy who gets a lot of cheap baskets inside. My assignment was to keep Filardi away from the boards so he couldn't come up with all the loose balls. We played a similar style, so I ended up doing a decent job on him. Tom Sanders was a person who looked like he came from outer space because he wore wire rim glasses with a big rubber piece between them and an eyeglass band that wrapped around his head. He also had those huge, long knee guards that were quite unusual at that time. And Satch just had such a distinctive style and flavor all his own. Later on, when we were both with the Celtics, we became roommates, and I used to kid him a lot about those things. But against NYU, he had a fairly decent game. He was 6'6" and had to play Jerry Lucas. There was no way he could defend against Jerry's hook shot. Siegfried and Mel Nowell played very well that particular game.

Packer—The final ball game was really over at halftime. That first half may have been the most awesome half a team ever had in a championship game.

Havlicek—Yes, it was really over very quickly, and it was very surprising to us to find that we were that far ahead of them. As sophomores, you always feel like someone is going to come back on you. Fred Taylor had been a student of Pete Newell's, and I think the tables were sort of reversed that night because Fred utilized a lot of things he had learned from Pete. The great thing about Pete is that he really loves for people to learn more about the game, and he was one of the masters. He wasn't afraid to give pointers to other people, and I think we benefited from it greatly.

Packer—Now to jump ahead to Pete Newell. He and Bobby Knight are real tight. Bobby was a sub on your ball club. Do you think Bobby has become Pete's equal in terms of his basketball knowledge?

Havlicek—Bobby is throwback in a lot of ways because he requires a lot of discipline. He admires the great coaches like Hank Iba, Clair Bee, Red Auerbach, Fred Taylor, and Pete. These are the people he believes taught him the basics of how basketball should be played. I think he's taken a little bit from each of these people and added a few things of his own.

Packer—As you said, you were not a starter on the team at the beginning of the season. You become a starter, and the team ends up at the Final Four, the first of three straight Final Four appearances for Ohio State. What happened your junior year?

Havlicek—My junior year, we went 30-and-O until the final game. We didn't have anyone standing in our way. I think we had a couple of games that were pretty close. The final game of the tournament that year was against Cincinnati in Kansas City, The semifinal game, or consolation game as they used to call it, was between St. Joseph's and Utah. As we were about to take the floor, someone tied it up and the game went into overtime. We went back to the locker room. There ended up being four overtimes, and each time we had to retreat from the edge of the floor to the locker room. Well, our game with Cincinnati went into overtime, too, and I can remember a fellow by the name of Bonham hitting a couple of 20- or 25-footers, the types of shots you normally want people to take in that situation. He drained us, and that was the end of us. I did not have a particularly good scoring game. My role at that time was not as a shooter; most of that was taken care of by Lucas, and Nowell, and Larry Siegfried. A fellow named Bob Wiesenhahn played very well against me. Cincinnati's Paul Hogue was hitting that 15- and 20-footer, which was something he generally didn't do, and by the time we adjusted, the game was in overtime, and they ended up winning by about five points.

Packer—It had to be quite a letdown, not only because you were undefeated, but because you had been ranked number one all season. And then you were beaten by a team down the road that was kind of like a stepchild.

Havlicek—They were a very good team. Tom Thacker played forward at 6'1" or 6'2," and Wiesenhahn and Hogue were in the middle. Their guards were Bouldin and Tony Yates, two very good guards. They were good defensively and handled our press easily.

Packer—So you had to be committed for that senior year. Again you made it back to the Final Four. That Final Four was the first for Johnny Wooden. Back in '62, did the name Wooden mean anything to you?

Havlicek—It didn't mean as much certainly as it does now, but I could see that his teams were developing in a way that would make them contenders, particularly in the PAC Ten, or PAC Eight, as it was back then. Wooden was from Indiana, and he had a great basketball heritage. We had beaten them earlier in the year in Los Angeles in

The Ohio State Buckeyes celebrate their 1960 championship.

the Holiday Festival, so we felt we could play them quite well. They had a player, Cunningham, who just lit me up in the Holiday Tournament in California. I never played a guy so well who still was so effective. I was in his face on every shot, and everything he threw up went in. I think he scored 19 or 21 points, and he shot a high percentage, something like seven-for-nine or eight-for-ten. We felt that we could beat them, but we ended up against Cincinnati, again. They had basically a different team than the year before, with George Wilson and Ron Bonham the forwards. Yates was still one of the guards and Thacker had moved to the back court. Of course, they had Paul Hogue.

Packer—I want to jump back to the semifinal game. You beat Wake Forest, my ball club, and Lucas went down with a knee problem.

Havlicek—I was rooming with Jerry at that time, and I really didn't know how effective he was going to be. It was one of those things where you couldn't tell what was going to happen until he got on the floor. In those days, you played back-to-back games in the tournament, Friday and Saturday. When we went out on the floor I knew right away he wasn't going to be as effective as usual. I know that I could have taken over more offensively, and it kind of bugs me that I didn't. The night before, in the game against you when Jerry got hurt, I played well and got 20 points or so.

Packer—Against Cincinnati, you were four-for-six with eight points.

Havlicek—If I had shot 20 times, maybe it would have been a different ball game. But I played my role. I remember that the Cincinnati coach did not want me involved defensively while they were running their patterns. So my assignment, Ron Bonham, and I more or less held hands at half court while the other guys played four-on-four.

Packer—Until Kareem and Walton, I don't think there had been a center who had played in back-to-back championship games, except for Paul Hogue. Yet, Bonham never really advanced as a pro player.

Havlicek—He played sensationally in both championship games and was drafted by the New York Knicks. Going from Cincinnati to New York was quite a jump, and he had a great deal of media attention. He ran into a lot of personal problems and never really developed.

Packer—What did the Final Four mean to you?

Havlicek—The Final Four was what everyone was striving for. And I think it was a lot tougher to get to the Final Four back in those days because you had to win your conference championship or go through some other elimination process, so there were only 28 teams who had a chance to get there. It meant a great deal for us to get there, but it also was very disappointing to lose the last two years after we had won the first one.

Bearcats!

The NCAA tournament settled more than the national championship in 1961 and '62. It resolved the bragging rights issue in Ohio, as Cincinnati and Ohio State battled in the finals both years.

Fred Taylor's talented sophomores from 1960—Havlicek, Lucas, and Nowell—returned as juniors and defending national champions. Senior Larry Siegfried was another important element in the chemistry. The basketball world was their oyster, or so it seemed throughout much of the regular season, as they dominated both the UPI and AP polls.

Their neighbors in Cincinnati lingered in the shadows, but not too much in the shadows, finishing at the number two spot in both polls. Bearcat Coach George Smith had moved up to the athletic director's post, and Ed Jucker, his assistant, had taken over. Oscar Robertson had graduated, but his presence had attracted a number of other talents to the program—Paul Hogue, Tom Thacker, Tony Yates, Bob Wiesenhahn and Carl Bouldin. Yet, early in the season, they all seemed to struggle with the notion of filling Robertson's legendary shoes. Instead of Robertson's elegant greyhound game, their forte was inside power with 6-foot-9 Hogue and 6-foot-7 Wiesenhahn. Accordingly, Jucker shifted strategy from a running offense and zone defense to a control offense and pressure man-to-man. The experiment produced a 17-point loss to St. Louis and a 19-point defeat by Bradley. Fortunately, the identity crisis resolved itself in time, and the '61 Bearcats went on to accomplish the only thing Robertson hadn't: a national championship.

In its wisdom, the 1961 tournament selection committee sent Ohio State to the Mideast Regional and Cincinnati to the Midwest. The Buckeyes struggled to a 56-55 victory over Louisville in the second round, advancing only after Havlicek hit a jumper with six seconds left and Louisville missed a crucial free throw. Then Ohio State finished Kentucky, 87-74, in the regional finals.

The Bearcats had an easy second-round game, deleting Texas Tech, 78-55. But the regional final against Kansas State was another matter. With 10 minutes left in the game, Cincinnati trailed by seven. Yet somehow, its deliberate offense generated a flurry of baskets and outdistanced Kansas State down the stretch, 69-64.

The 1961 Final Four in Kansas City offered few semifinal thrills. Ohio State pounded St. Joseph's, 95-69, and Cincinnati blitzed Utah, 82-67. From there, however, the proceedings acquired a wild tension. In consolation, Utah and St. Joseph's battled through a four-overtime thriller before the Utes succumbed, 127-120, the highest scoring post-season game ever played. The event would later be nullified and wiped from the record books when Jack Egan and other St. Joseph's players were implicated in the 1961 point-shaving scandal.

The overtime fever carried over into the finals, where the Buckeyes and Bearcats scrapped the entire game. With a minute left, Cincinnati held a 61-59 lead, but State's Bobby Knight drove for a layup, his only two points, to tie the game. Both teams had a chance to win as the seconds drained off in regulation, but Lucas missed connections on an alley-oop pass. The onlookers found themselves treated to another overtime.

Left—Cincinnati's Paul Hogue (22) pressures Ohio State's Jerry Lucas in the 1961 national championship game. Above—UCLA's Walt Hazzard (right) guards Cincinnati's Tom Thacker in the 1962 semifinals.

1961

Cincinnati	fg-fga	ft-fta	rb	pf	tp
Wiesenhahn	8-15	1- 1	9	3	17
Thacker	7-21	1- 4	7	0	15
Hogue	3- 8	3- 6	7	3	9
Yates	4- 8	5- 5	2	3	13
Bouldin	7-12	2- 3	4	4	16
Sizer	0- 0	0- 0	1	0	0
Heidotting	0- 0	0- 0	0	0	0
Team			6		
Totals	29-64	12-19	36	13	70

Ohio State	fg-fga	ft-fta	rb	pf	tp
Havlicek	1- 5	2- 2	4	2	4
Hoyt	3- 5	1- 1	1	3	7
Lucas	10-17	7- 7	12	4	27
Nowell	3- 9	3- 3	3	1	9
Siegfried	6-10	2- 3	3	2	14
Knight	1- 3	0- 0	1	1	2
Gearhart	1- 1	0- 0	0	1	2
Team			8		
Totals	25-50	15-16	32	14	65

Half time: Ohio State 39-38. Regulation Score: 61-61. Officials: Fox and Filiberti.

1962

Ohio State	fg-fga	ft-fta	rb	pf	tp
Havlicek	5-14	1- 2	9	1	11
McDonald	0- 1	3- 3	1	2	3
Lucas	5-17	1- 2	16	3	11
Reasbeck	4- 6	0- 0	0	4	8
Nowell	4-16	1- 1	6	2	9
Doughty	0- 1	0- 0	2	2	0
Gearhart	1- 4	0- 0	4	3	2
Bradds	5- 7	5- 6	4	2	15
Totals	24-66	11-14	42	19	59

Cincinnati	fg-fga	ft-fta	rb	pf	tp
Bonham	3-12	4- 4	6	3	10
Wilson	1- 6	4- 4	11	2	6
Hogue	11-18	0- 2	19	2	22
Thacker	6-14	9-11	6	2	21
Yates	4- 8	4- 7	1	1	12
Sizer	0- 0	0- 0	0	0	0
Totals	25-58	21-28	43	10	71

Half time: Cincinnati 37-29. Attendance: 18,469.

There, Cincinnati gained the slightest edge, 66-64, on two Tony Yates free throws. Siegfried made one of two foul shots for the Buckeyes, meaning that when the Bearcats went into a stall seconds later, State was forced to foul. Yates again converted two points, and after a little last-second scrambling, Cincinnati had its first championship, 70-65. Jerry Lucas had 27 points and 12 rebounds to earn the MVP award.

Strangely, circumstances would repeat themselves the next year, with a few changes in the script. Added to the Final Four's cast of characters was the Wake Forest team I played on with Len Chappell, the AP All-American. We had won the East Regional, but the Buckeyes were our undoing in the semifinals. Ohio State was again the top-ranked team in both polls, with only Siegfried and Rickie Hoyt gone from the '61 team.

College basketball had again been rocked by point-shaving scandals, as players and teams across the country were caught up in the investigation. But the atmosphere seemed to have little effect on the Buckeyes' march to the top. They nailed Western Kentucky, 93-73, in the second round of the Mideast, then pushed past third-ranked Kentucky, 74-64.

Cincinnati, on the other hand, had two early-season losses, then struggled past Bradley and Drake to win the Missouri Valley Conference and a bid to the NCAAs. Wiesenhahn and Bouldin had finished their eligibility and were replaced by Ron Bonham and George Wilson. But the basic Bearcat format hadn't changed, and once in the tournament, Cincinnati found it was ready for the competition. In the Midwest, Creighton fell first, 66-46, and Colorado second, 73-46.

But the Final Four in Louisville was different. Ohio State hammered our Wake Forest team, 84-68, but Lucas was seriously injured with eight minutes left in the game. In the other semifinal, Cincinnati's easy run ended. John Wooden's first Final Four team, the 1962 UCLA Bruins, with Walt Hazzard, John Green and Gary Cunningham, pushed the Bearcats to the brink of elimination. Cincinnati ran out to an early lead, but UCLA came back, setting up a second half of changing leads. Finally, Tom Thacker scored with 10 seconds left to give the Bearcats a shot at their second title. Hogue had the best game of his college career, scoring 36 points and pulling down 19 rebounds.

With Lucas injured, that accomplishment was easier than expected. The final was anticlimactic as Cincinnati won, 71-59. Later, Ohio State Coach Fred Taylor acknowledged that even with Lucas the outcome might not have been different.

TOURNAMENT NOTES: Paul Hogue, with 22 points and 19 rebounds in the final, was named MVP.

Cincinnati's Paul Hogue defends the basket in the closing seconds of regulation in the 1961 NCAA championship game. Cincy's Carl Bouldin (34) grabbed the loose ball moments later. In the backcourt are Ohio State's Mel Nowell (3) and Larry Siegfried (21).

Ramblers On A Roll

Cincinnati center Paul Hogue finished his eligibility with the 1962 season, but the Bearcats still returned to the Final Four in '63 and almost claimed a third straight championship. The only thing that stopped them was a little five-man team from Loyola of Chicago.

Ultimately, the NCAA championship would come down to a confrontation between the country's highest scoring team, Loyola, averaging 91.8 points per game, and its stingiest defensive team, Cincinnati, giving up just 52.9 points per game. But before that occurred, two interesting subplots developed.

First, the reverberations of the point-shaving scandal had taken their toll. Caught in the nightmare of headlines were players from NYU, North Carolina, NC State, St. John's, Columbia, St. Joseph's, and Connecticut. In the aftermath, Frank McGuire left North Carolina and was replaced by his assistant, Dean Smith. And the famed preseason southern tournament, the Dixie Classic, ceased to exist. In New York, the scandal had brought an end to all NCAA post-season games at Madison Square Garden. St. Joseph's Coach Jack Ramsay was disillusioned by revelations of his players accepting bribes and decided to become an NBA coach.

The revelations had led to an outcry against recruiting irregularities and academic deficiencies, sending college basketball into a period of re-examination. But by the start of the 1962-63 season, the uproar had already begun to settle. By the time the 1963 NCAA tournament rolled around, the controversy had shifted. Mississippi State, with its all-white basketball team, had turned in another outstanding year, the third time in five seasons that the team won the SEC race. Each year, however, the team had not been allowed to enter the NCAA tournament where it might meet an opponent with black players. Finally, in 1963, Coach Babe McCarthy and his players voted to go despite pressure from Mississippi's segregationist governor, Ross Barnett. The school's president and Board of Regents approved the team's decision, but when Barnett learned of the coach's plans, he sought and received a restraining order. McCarthy, however, was able to get his team across the state line into Tennessee just ahead of a sheriff serving the order.

Mississippi State met Loyola, which started four black players, in the semifinals of the Mideast Regional in Evanston, Illinois. Loyola's Ramblers had embarrassed Tennessee Tech in the first round, 111-42. But the expected tension in their game against Mississippi State never materialized. Instead, the atmosphere was eerily polite, as Loyola won, 61-51. The regional finals pitted the Catholic school from Chicago against the University of Illinois, the Big Ten power. Ranked third nationally, the Ramblers converted what remained of their doubters by finishing off the Illini, 79-64.

The nation was learning that Loyola Coach George Ireland had a high-scoring but finely-disciplined team that featured All-American guard Jerry Harkness. In the frontcourt, Ireland worked 6-foot-7 Leslie Hunter and 6-foot-6 Vic Rouse, giving the Ramblers a blend of speed and power.

In the national semifinals at Louisville's Freedom Hall, Loyola faced another southern team in second-ranked Duke, coached by Vic Bubas. The Blue Devils, with their own All-American, Art Heyman, and Jeff Mullins, had won the ACC and worked their way through the East Regional with victories over NYU and St. Joseph's. But their ride ended at the Final Four, despite 29 points and 12 rebounds by Heyman. Loyola ran past Duke, 94-75.

Cincinnati had emerged from the Midwest to find an even easier time in the semis, blowing right by Oregon State, 80-46. Heisman Trophy winner Terry Baker started for Oregon State but went 0-for-9 from the floor.

Behind Ron Bonham, who had been named All-American, Cincinnati took a strong lead in the championship game and appeared headed for an unprecedented third straight championship. At the midpoint of the second half, the Bearcats led 45-30. But then a stretch of fouling chilled their momentum. Loyola closed the gap with its potent offense, and Cincinnati responded with missed shots and turnovers. Finally, the game came down to a 53-52 Cincinnati lead with seconds left and Bearcat Larry Shingleton at the line for one-and-one. He made the first but missed the second, giving Harkness just enough time to rebound, drive the length of the floor and score to send the game into overtime.

Once there, the teams traded baskets until the last second when Rouse rebounded a miss and banked it back in to give the Ramblers the title, 60-58.

TOURNAMENT NOTES: Despite the heroics, the Ramblers hit only 23 of their 84 shots from the floor. Duke's Art Heyman was voted the tournament MVP.

Above—Loyola Coach George Ireland with players John Egan and Floyd Bosley. Left—Cincinnati's Larry Shingleton drives against Loyola's Ron Miller (Left) and Vic Rouse (Right) in the 1963 championship game.

1963					
Loyola, Ill.	fg-fga	ft-fta	rb	pf	tp
Harkness	5-18	4- 8	6	4	14
Rouse	6-22	3- 4	12	4	15
Hunter	6-22	4- 4	11	3	16
Egan	3- 8	3- 5	3	3	9
Miller	3-14	0- 0	2	3	6
Team			11		
Totals	23-84	14-21	45	17	60
Cincinnati	fg-fga	ft-fta	rb	pf	tp
Bonham	8-16	6- 6	4	3	22
Thacker	5-12	3- 4	15	4	13
Wilson	4- 8	2- 3	13	4	10
Yates	4- 6	1- 4	8	4	9
Shingleton	1- 3	2- 3	4	0	4
Heidotting	0- 0	0- 0	1	2	0
Team			7		
Totals	22-45	14-20	52	17	58

Half time: Cincinnati 29-21. Regulation Score: 54-54.

Bruins Begin

Looking from the hindsight of history, modern basketball fans have been known to view John Wooden's UCLA dynasty as something put together with luck and ease during college basketball's "formative" years. In reality, there was nothing easy about Wooden's effort to build a program at UCLA. And no matter how often an observer attempts to downplay it, what Wooden and his teams achieved—10 national championships in 12 years—is an incredible level of triumph for any endeavor, whether it be basketball or mathematics.

As a young man, Wooden had achieved notoriety as a three-time All American for Piggy Lambert at Purdue and later as a successful Indiana high school coach.

After two years at Indiana State, Wooden came to UCLA in 1949 and immediately turned a loser into a winner. But then his instant success quickly became mired in a struggle as his teams fought for more than a dozen years to rise above regional competition. For much of that period, UCLA had a tiny gym. And although he won, Wooden's ability as a coach was held in question in the West, where Phil Woolpert at San Francisco and Pete Newell at California were winning with disciplined, patient offenses. Wooden, being true to his Indiana heritage, put his faith in a controlled fast-break offense. Beyond that, he showed a countenance of pious discipline that didn't endear him to his fellow coaches.

Yet Wooden persisted in working the pieces into place. He added Jerry Norman as an assistant coach, which improved recruiting. He increased his player rotation to where he was working a first unit of seven or eight men. And he studied various forms of the full-court press, which he had used off and on during his years at UCLA.

The big breakthrough came in the signing of Walt Hazzard, a Philadelphia schoolboy star. His 1962 team had featured Hazzard, 6-foot-5 powerhouse center Fred Slaughter, forwards Gary Cunningham and Pete Blackman, and guard John Green. They went to the Final Four and took champion Cincinnati to the wire before losing by a basket in the semifinals.

The 1963 season brought Gail Goodrich, Keith Erickson, Fred Goss and Jack Hirsch into a unit with Hazzard and Slaughter. By the '64 season, Wooden had added sixth man Kenny Washington and the 2-2-1 zone press and turned his squad loose to run off into basketball history. The team was a thing of beauty in its spare precision. There was no starter taller than 6-5. The Bruins generated their offense like lightning off the press.

Hirsch and Goodrich were on the front line, pressuring the inbounds pass. Slaughter and Hazzard were the second line, the center with his speed and jumping ability there for the steal, and Hazzard the scorer to convert the turnover into automatic offense. The safety valve was Erickson. The unit stripped and dismantled taller, slower opponents like a band of LA car thieves working over a parked car.

The first national notice came that December of '63, when the Bruins took apart second-ranked Michigan with Cazzie Russell. They whisked their way, despite a few close calls, through an undefeated 26-game regular season and entered the West Regional in Kansas City ranked number one in both polls. There, however, their momentum sputtered as they struggled past Seattle, 95-90, and San Francisco, 76-72. For the second time in three seasons, Wooden was taking a team to the Final Four.

In the first game, Kansas State had a zone defense and 29 points from Willie Murrell, but the Bruins came from behind on Erickson's 28 points to win, 90-84. In the other bracket, Duke had returned as the East champion and faced Russell and Michigan from the Mideast. The Blue Devils prevailed, 91-80, setting up a match of UCLA's speed against Duke's height. Coach Vic Bubas mixed balanced scorer Jeff Mullins with a pair of 6-foot-10 frontcourt players, Jay Buckley and Hack Tison. Duke's height helped them to an early lead, but Wooden called a timeout, switched to a zone and sent Doug McIntosh and Washington into the game. The rest is history. The Bruins raced off to 16 points, and eventually, a big chunk of basketball history. Duke could never catch up and finally expired, 98-83.

Goodrich had scored 27 points, and Washington 26 in the final, but Hazzard, the quarterback running the offense, was named the tournament MVP.

The Philadelphia phenom, Slaughter, and Hirsch had completed their eligibility and would not be back for '65. Just how sorely they would be missed was apparent in the season opener as Illinois deflated UCLA, 110-83. However, the '65 unit - Goodrich at playmaker, McIntosh at center, Goss at the other guard, sophomores Edgar Lacey and Mike Lynn at forwards, and Washington as sixth man - quickly found its stride. The Bruins lost another game, later in the season, this time at Iowa. But beyond that, their only rub was a mild squeeze with San Francisco in the West Regional finals. Earlier, UCLA had numbed

UCLA's Walt Hazzard beats two Kansas State defenders in the 1964 national semifinals.

Duke Coach Vic Bubas

Brigham Young, 100-76. They outlasted the Dons, 101-93, and found themselves facing Wichita State at the Final Four in Portland, Oregon. With Goodrich scoring 28 and Lacey 24, they breezed, 108-89.

Cazzie Russell and Michigan had eliminated Bill Bradley and Princeton in the other semifinal, 93-76, despite Bradley's 29 points. The press mentioned a showdown in the finals, but Goodrich scored 42 points and turned the affair into another day at the beach and another championship, 91-80.

Earlier in the evening, Bradley had mesmerized the audience, his opponents and his teammates by scoring 58 points in the consolation game against Wichita State.

TOURNAMENT NOTES: Some observers were confused when Bradley was selected MVP over Goodrich. Yet the Princeton senior had captured the fans' fancy by carrying his underdog team to the Final Four.

1964

UCLA	fg-fga	ft-fta	rb	pf	tp
Goodrich	9-18	9- 9	3	1	27
Slaughter	0- 1	0- 0	1	0	0
Hazzard	4-10	3- 5	3	5	11
Hirsch	5- 9	3- 5	6	3	13
Erickson	2- 7	4- 4	5	5	8
McIntosh	4- 9	0- 0	11	2	8
Washington	11-16	4- 4	12	4	26
Darrow	0- 1	3- 4	1	2	3
Stewart	0- 1	0- 0	0	1	0
Huggins	0- 1	0- 1	1	2	0
Hoffman	1- 2	0- 0	0	0	2
Levin	0- 1	0- 0	0	0	0
Totals	36-76	26-32	43	25	98

Duke	fg-fga	ft-fta	rb	pf	tp
Ferguson	2- 6	0- 1	1	3	4
Buckley	5- 8	8-12	9	4	18
Tison	3- 8	1- 1	1	2	7
Harrison	1- 1	0- 0	1	2	2
Mullins	9-21	4- 4	4	5	22
Marin	8-16	0- 1	10	3	16
Vacendak	2- 7	3- 3	6	4	7
Herbster	1- 4	0- 2	0	0	2
Kitching	1- 1	0- 0	1	0	2
Mann	0- 0	3- 4	2	1	3
Harscher	0- 0	0- 0	0	0	0
Cox	0- 0	0- 0	0	0	0
Totals	32-72	19-28	35	24	83

Half time: UCLA 50-38. Officials: Mihalik and Glennon. Attendance: 10,864.

1965

UCLA	fg-fga	ft-fta	rb	pf	tp
Erickson	1- 1	1- 2	1	1	3
Lacey	5- 7	1- 2	7	3	11
McIntosh	1- 2	1- 2	0	2	3
Goodrich	12-22	18-20	4	4	42
Goss	4-12	0- 0	3	1	8
Washington	7- 9	3- 4	5	2	17
Lynn	2- 3	1- 2	6	1	5
Lyons	0- 0	0- 0	0	1	0
Galbraith	0- 0	0- 0	0	0	0
Hoffman	1- 1	0- 0	1	0	2
Levin	0- 1	0- 0	1	0	0
Chambers	0- 0	0- 1	0	0	0
Team			6		
Totals	33-58	25-33	34	15	91

Michigan	fg-fga	ft-fta	rb	pf	tp
Darden	8-10	1- 1	4	5	17
Pomey	2- 5	0- 0	2	2	4
Buntin	6-14	2- 4	6	5	14
Russell	10-16	8-10	5	2	28
Tregoning	2- 7	1- 1	5	5	5
Myers	0- 4	0- 0	3	2	0
Brown	0- 0	0- 0	0	0	0
Ludwig	1- 2	0- 0	0	0	2
Thompson	0- 0	0- 0	0	0	0
Bankey	0- 0	0- 0	0	0	0
Clawson	3- 4	0- 0	0	2	6
Dill	1- 2	2- 2	1	1	4
Team			7		
Totals	33-64	14-18	33	24	80

Half time: UCLA 47-34. Officials: Mihalik and Honzo. Attendance: 13,204.

An Interview With Walt Hazzard

Walt Hazzard was one of the key figures in John Wooden's first national championship team at UCLA, the 1964 Bruins. He was named the outstanding player of the 1964 NCAA tournament. He played on the 1964 U.S. Olympic team and later enjoyed a 10-year professional career. Today, h e is UCLA's head coach. His teammate from 1964, Jack Hirsch, is his assistant.

Lazenby—The 1964 Bruins were one of the greatest teams in basketball. What made you unique?

Hazzard—I think of our chemistry, of people accepting their roles. We went 30-0, and we had no starter larger that 6'5".

The chemistry of that ball club was incredible. First, the architect was Coach Wooden, the philosopher of basketball. He found five players who liked his style, who were extremely competitive and were winners, and accepted their roles with pride.

My role was the leader, the spirit of the team. I had come from a great basketball tradition in high school in Philadelphia, where I had been a scorer. At UCLA, I became the playmaker and offensive quarterback. I accepted that role. I knew I could have been the leading scorer, but Gail Goodrich was a great scorer. If he missed five in a row, that was no big deal to him. He would just hit the next five. He was a hungry guy who liked to score points. The other players on the team realized that in the fast-break situations, if he was the guy in the middle, he was gonna take the shot.

Jack Hirsch, a 6'3" forward, was our top defender, always assigned to the other team's top scorer. He had the instincts, the tenacity. He knew how to shut a guy down. In junior college he had averaged 38 points a game, but at UCLA he was the defender.

Fred Slaughter, our 6'5" center, weighed about 250 pounds. He was ideal for the high-post offense John Wooden ran. Even with that size, he was the high school 100-yard dash champion in Kansas. He played up front on our press, but when the ball crossed half court, he'd still beat everybody back.

That's what was so brilliant about Coach Wooden. He took the strengths of his individual players and adjusted his system to maximize those abilities.

Keith Erickson, at 6'5", was our fifth man on the 2-2-1 press. He was a great player, and athlete with great reactions, a great rebounder with excellent timing. Above all, he was a fierce competitior.

To that, Wooden added his two players off the bench, Kenny Washington and Doug McIntosh. Coach Wooden just fit all these pieces together to make a great team.

Two-time All-American and UCLA Coach Walt Hazzard with Coach John Wooden (UCLA—retired).

The Miners Take A Major

Lew Alcindor matriculated as a student at UCLA in the fall of 1965, and a few months later the talented freshman team engaged the varsity in a pre-season scrimmage. At the time, the Bruins were ranked number one in the country. With no disrespect intended, the freshmen defeated their elders, 75-60, a score that was reported nationwide.

Sportswriters kept the game in mind that March when the NCAA playoffs began. Figuring Alcindor and his mates would dominate college basketball for the next three years, the press dubbed the 1966 event the "Last Chance Tournament," suggesting that it would be the last chance for some other college team to win the championship for quite some time.

The press, history shows, was only a bit short-sighted in its prophesying. Instead of retaining the title for three years, John Wooden's teams kept it for seven straight seasons.

So the 1966 tournament was a last chance of sorts. In picking a team to seize the opportunity in 1966, the national polls figured the likes of Kentucky or Duke or Kansas or Michigan or Cincinnati. Anybody but the little team that could, the Texas Western Miners.

The United States was in the throes of racial strife in 1965-66, as ghettoes flared up in protest. As circumstance would have it, the 1966 NCAA championship in Cole Field House at the University of Maryland offered a mirror of the nation's racial polarization.

There, Adolph Rupp's all-white Kentucky team was pitted against Don Haskins' Miners, a club whose eight primary players were black. It was the stuff sociologists' dreams were made of.

Texas Western (now Texas-El Paso) had a storybook season from start to finish. The only blemish was a late-season loss to Seattle.

Led by 6-foot-8, 240-pound Dave Lattin, the Miners entered the Midwest Regional with a 23-1 record and a third-place ranking in the national polls. But Haskins held out most of his starters in their first-round game against Oklahoma City because of curfew violations. After Western fell behind by 15 points, he inserted them and watched them work comeback magic, salvaging an 89-74 victory.

From there, the Miners survived a 78-76 overtime match against Cincinnati as Lattin scored 29. The next night against fourth-ranked Kansas, the menu was again overtime, this time a double helping. Kansas' Jo Jo White made a 32-foot shot at the close of the first overtime, but the referee disallowed it, pointing to where White had stepped on the sideline.

The second overtime was just as tight until Western's Willie Cager won it, 81-80, with a last-second shot.

The Miners were joined at the Final Four by second-ranked Duke, top-ranked Kentucky and surprise entry Utah, with Jerry Chambers. Most sportswriters gave the Duke-Kentucky semifinal clash the top billing. The Blue Devils with Bob Verga and Jack Marin were the third Vic Bubas team to make the Final Four in as many years.

Rupp, on the other hand, had brought Kentucky back after an absence of seven years. With no starter taller than 6-5, the Wildcats were dubbed "Rupp's Runts." Their lineup included Larry Conley and Pat Riley. The Baron had reluctantly moved them to a 1-3-1 zone defense, although he wouldn't admit that's what it was.

They escaped Duke in the semifinals, 83-79, setting up the meeting with Haskins' defense-minded Miners, who had beaten Utah, 85-78. Keyed by the press nickname for the tournament, Rupp sensed this would be his last chance at a fifth title, and he wanted it badly. "It was just a tremendous, cohesive team," Rupp said of his Runts years afterward. "Losing to Haskins that year was possibly the biggest disappointment of my life, because that was my finest coaching effort."

With their pressing defense, the Miners dominated from the start and won easily, 72-65. Haskins had drunk from the championship cup just before the long drought settled in. The next decade would belong to Wooden.

TOURNAMENT NOTES: Utah's Jerry Chambers was named tournament MVP although his team lost both Final Four games. He had scored 143 points in four tournament games, a record.

1966

Kentucky	fg-fga	ft-fta	rb	pf	tp
Dampier	7-18	5- 5	9	4	19
Kron	3- 6	0- 0	7	2	6
Conley	4- 9	2- 2	8	5	10
Riley	8-22	3- 4	4	4	19
Jaracz	3- 8	1- 2	5	5	7
Berger	2- 3	0- 0	0	0	4
Gamble	0- 0	0- 0	0	1	0
LeMaster	0- 1	0- 0	0	1	0
Tallent	0- 3	0- 0	0	1	0
Totals	27-70	11-13	33	23	65
Texas Western	fg-fga	ft-fta	rb	pf	tp
Hill	7-17	6- 9	3	3	20
Artis	5-13	5- 5	8	1	15
Shed	1- 1	1- 1	3	1	3
Lattin	5-10	6- 6	9	4	16
Cager	1- 3	6- 7	6	3	8
Flournoy	1- 1	0- 0	0	0	2
Worsley	2- 4	4- 6	4	0	8
Totals	22-49	28-34	35	12	72

Half time: Texas Western 34-31. Officials: Honzo and Jenkins. Attendance: 14,253.

Above—Adolph Rupp had his last Final Four team in 1965.
Right—Utah's Jerry Chambers shoots against Texas Western in the semifinals. Western's Nevil Shed (33) looks on.

LewCLA

John Wooden was never known for his recruiting prowess. In that respect, Jerry Norman was the perfect assistant for the UCLA coach. Norman could handle the face-to-face work, the selling of the program to recruits, which Wooden was reluctant to do.

In the mid 1960s, the basketball world witnessed the most significant recruiting struggle in the history of the game. At the same time, it was the most subtle recruitment, because Jack Donahue, Lew Alcindor's coach at Power Memorial High School in New York, dictated that it would be low-key. Recruiters weren't allowed to so much as speak to the 7-foot-1 Alcindor.

Those circumstances aided Wooden and Norman. In their unassuming way, they brought every resource to luring Alcindor to UCLA. One after another, the school's black luminaries - Jackie Robinson, Willie Naulls and Ralph Bunche - made their pitch to Alcindor. The bright, sensitive young center listened to their reasoning and accepted it.

From the perspective of two decades, it is obvious that the young All-American made just the right decision, good for himself, good for Wooden, good for the game. Arguably, Alcindor could have gone to other schools and won three NCAA championships. But more than any other coach, Wooden was the man to appreciate Alcindor's bountiful talent and to mold a system to reach its potential.

Alcindor spent much of his freshman year working with Jay Carty, a 6-foot-8 graduate student from Oregon State, in developing his presence around the basket. Also on the freshman team were Lucius Allen, a gazelle of a shooting guard from Kansas; Lynn Shackelford, a forward with a deadeye from the corner; and Kenny Heitz, a 6-foot-3 guard/forward who realized his potential on defense. Their freshman team went undefeated, many of their games being little more than a monster feasting on helpless prey.

Their sophomore season, 1966-67, quickly acquired the same atmosphere. The four sophomores were paired with junior guard Mike Warren to create a unit that made a mockery of competition. Alcindor ran through a variety of dunks and bankshots in his first varsity game, against Southern Cal, and set a school record with 56 points, as the Bruins won, 105-90. Wooden had set Alcindor in a low-post offense, making him a terror offensively and defensively. His rebounds and strong outlet passes keyed a quick break . When the zones became a little too tight

around Alcindor, Shackelford loosened things with shots deep from the corner. The only rub in their path to a perfect season was the stall tactics adopted by some opponents. Southern Cal was the most successful, about midway through the season. The Trojans took the game to overtime, but the Bruins escaped there, 40-35.

For the most part, however, UCLA's progress was unimpeded. They entered the NCAA tournament after slicing through 26 opponents and continued the pace, paring Wyoming, 109-60, Pacific, 80-64, Houston and Elvin Hayes, 73-58, and Dayton 79-64, to match the 1964 team's 30-0 record and hand Wooden his third championship in four years.

Alcindor was the obvious choice as tournament MVP. He had averaged 29 points over the season by making 66.7 percent of his field-goal attempts, an NCAA record. Allen, Warren and Shackelford had all averaged in double figures.

For 1968, the NCAA outlawed dunking, an apparent attempt to neutralize Alcindor, yet it only made him more

Lew Alcindor (Kareen Abdul Jabbar). Opposite—UCLA's Lew Alcindor dominates the boards against Houston in the 1968 semifinals.

1967

UCLA	fg-fga	ft-fta	rb	pf	tp
Heitz	2- 7	0- 0	6	2	4
Schackelford	5-10	0- 2	3	1	10
Alcindor	8-12	4-11	18	0	20
Allen	7-15	5- 8	9	2	19
Warren	8-16	1- 1	7	1	17
Nielsen	0- 1	0- 1	1	3	0
Sweek	1- 1	0- 0	0	1	2
Saffer	2- 5	0- 0	0	1	4
Saner	1- 1	0- 0	2	2	2
Chrisman	0- 0	1- 2	1	2	1
Sutherland	0- 0	0- 0	0	0	0
Lynn	0- 1	0- 0	0	0	0
Team			7		
Totals	34-69	11-25	54	15	79

Dayton	fg-fga	ft-fta	rb	pf	tp
May	9-23	3- 4	17	4	21
Sadlier	2- 5	1- 2	7	5	5
Obrovac	0- 2	0- 0	2	1	0
Klaus	4- 7	0- 0	0	1	8
Hooper	2- 7	2- 4	5	2	6
Torain	3-14	0- 0	4	3	6
Waterman	4-11	2- 3	1	3	10
Sharpenter	2- 5	4- 5	5	1	8
Samanich	0- 2	0- 0	2	0	0
Beckman	0- 0	0- 0	0	0	0
Inderrieden	0- 0	0- 0	0	0	0
Wannemacher	0- 0	0- 0	0	0	0
Team			8		
Totals	26-76	12-18	51	20	64

Half time: UCLA 38-20.

Above—Alcindor led UCLA over Dayton in the 1968 finals.

1968

UCLA	fg-fga	ft-fta	rb	pf	tp
L. Shackelford	3- 5	0- 1	2	0	6
M. Lynn	1- 7	5- 7	6	3	7
L. Alcindor	15-21	4- 4	16	3	34
M. Warren	3- 7	1- 1	3	2	7
L. Allen	3- 7	5- 7	5	0	11
J. Nielsen	1- 1	0- 0	1	1	2
K. Heitz	3- 6	1- 1	2	3	7
G. Sutherland	1- 2	0- 0	2	1	2
B. Sweek	0- 1	0- 0	0	1	0
N. Saner	1- 3	0- 0	2	2	2
Team			9		
Totals	31-60	16-21	48	16	78

North Carolina	fg-fga	ft-fta	rb	pf	tp
L. Miller	5-13	4- 6	6	3	14
B. Bunting	1- 3	1- 2	2	5	3
R. Clark	4-12	1- 3	8	3	9
C. Scott	6-17	0- 1	3	3	12
D. Grubar	2- 5	1- 2	0	2	5
E. Fogler	1- 4	2- 2	0	0	4
J. Brown	2- 5	2- 2	5	1	6
G. Tuttle	0- 0	0- 0	0	0	0
J. Frye	1- 2	0- 1	1	0	2
G. Whitehead	0- 0	0- 0	0	0	0
J. Delany	0- 1	0- 0	0	0	0
R. Fletcher	0- 1	0- 0	0	0	0
Team			10		
Totals	22-63	11-19	35	17	55

Half time: UCLA 32-22. Officials: Honzo and Fouty. Attendance: 14,438.

1969

UCLA	fg-fga	ft-fta	rb	pf	tp
L. Shackelford	3- 8	5- 8	9	3	11
C. Rowe	4-10	4- 4	12	2	12
L. Alcindor	15-20	7- 9	20	2	37
K. Heitz	0- 3	0- 1	3	4	0
J. Vallely	4- 9	7-10	4	3	15
B. Sweek	3- 3	0- 1	1	3	6
S. Wicks	0- 1	3- 6	4	1	3
T. Schofield	1- 2	0- 0	0	0	2
S. Patterson	1- 1	2- 2	2	0	4
B. Seibert	0- 0	0- 0	1	0	0
G. Farmer	0- 0	0- 0	0	1	0
J. Ecker	1- 1	0- 0	0	0	2
Team			5		
Totals	32-58	28-41	61	19	92

Purdue	fg-fga	ft-fta	rb	pf	tp
H. Gilliam	2-14	3- 3	11	2	7
G. Faerber	1- 2	0- 0	3	5	2
J. Johnson	4- 9	3- 4	9	2	11
R. Mount	12-36	4- 5	1	3	28
B. Keller	4-17	3- 4	4	5	11
F. Kaufman	0- 0	2- 2	5	5	2
T. Bedford	3- 8	1- 3	8	3	7
L. Weatherford	1- 5	2- 2	1	3	4
T. Reasoner	0- 1	0- 1	1	2	0
R. Taylor	0- 0	0- 0	0	0	0
Team			5		
Totals	27-92	18-24	48	30	72

Half time: UCLA 50-41. Officials: DiTomasso and Brown. Attendance: 18,669.

The 1969 edition of the Bruins. Back row (L to R)—Lynn Shackelford, Curtis Rowe, Steve Patterson, Lew Alcindor, Sidney Wicks, John Ecker, Bill Seibert. Middle row—George Farmer, Bill Sweek, Ken Heitz, John Vallely, Terry Schofield. Front row—Ducky Drake, Denny Crum, John Wooden, Gary Cunningham, Manager Bob Marcucci.

powerful, because the slam was the only shot he found difficult to defend. With opponents forced to shoot from short range, he spent much of his time swatting their attempts to the hinterlands.

Wooden found himself with something of a talent traffic jam for the 1967-68 season, as Edgar Lacey and Mike Lynn, starters from the '66 team, returned after a year's absence. The team switched to a high post/low-post offense that required some adjustments, as Lynn and Lacey alternated at the high-post. In the opening game, Purdue and Rick Mount pushed the Bruins to 71 all before UCLA reserve Bill Sweek scored at the buzzer to preserve the win streak.

It would continue through 47 games, until UCLA met Houston and Hayes in the Astrodome before 52,693 fans (an NCAA record) and a national television audience. Alcindor had injured his eye the week before the game

but elected to play anyway. The result was a moment in the sun for Hayes. In what was billed as a legendary showdown, the big forward scored 39 points, including two free throws in the waning seconds, to give Houston a 71-69 victory.

In the aftermath, Lacey quit the team, and Wooden reverted to the low-post offense with Alcindor as the single center. Their defensive teeth were their 2-2-1 and 1-2-1-1 zone presses. With that set of tools, the Bruins hammered their competition on the way to a rematch with Houston in the national semifinals at the Final Four in the Los Angeles Sports Arena. The payback was more than a bit unpleasant for the Cougars. Alcindor led five scorers in double figures with 19 points and 18 rebounds, as UCLA advanced, 101-69. Hayes finished with 10 points.

North Carolina with Charlie Scott and Larry Miller

Above (L to R)—L. Allen, Mike Warren, Alcindor, John Wooden after the '68 championship. Opposite—Alcindor against Carolina in the 1968 finals

had ousted Ohio State in the other semifinal, but the Tar Heels didn't have the talent to stay with UCLA. Alcindor scored 34 points with 16 rebounds to claim his second MVP award, and Wooden picked up his fifth championship, 78-55.

The deck was reshuffled again for Alcindor's third varsity season, as Warren graduated on his way to Hill Street Blues fame and Lucius Allen left school. Sophomores Curtis Rowe and Sidney Wicks moved into the picture at forward, and Wooden acquired junior college transfer John Vallely for the backcourt, where he was teamed with Heitz.

The Bruins won their first 23 games, then hit a bump with two overtime wins over Cal and Southern Cal before losing their first game, the season finale, to the Trojans a night later. Their momentum resumed the first two games

of the NCAA tournament, 53-38 over a stalling New Mexico State and 90-52 over Santa Clara. But they played poorly against Drake in the national semifinals in Louisville. John Vallely scored 29 points while Drake played a strong man-to-man defense against Alcindor. The Bruins escaped 85-82 and met for the national championship with Rick Mount and Purdue, who had pounded North Carolina, 92-65, in the semis.

Alcindor was never more dominating than in his final college game, scoring 37 points on 15 of 20 from the floor with 20 rebounds as UCLA won its fifth championship, 92-72.

TOURNAMENT NOTES: Alcindor was named MVP for an unprecedented third time. In three years, he had led the Bruins to an 88-2 record.

Talent Plus

Perhaps even more than its first, UCLA's sixth championship surprised the world of college basketball in 1970. With the graduation of Alcindor (now Kareem Abdul-Jabbar), many observers had assumed the competition would revert to Before Alcindor climate. Instead, the Bruins' subset of talent found room to flourish. Their game wasn't the domination of the Alcindor years. They had to work for their wins. They got them all the same.

Guard John Vallely and forward Curtis Rowe were the returning starters, but Sidney Wicks was the emergent leader at forward. Wooden's new look was a strong front line, slashing inside power moves and aggressive rebounding. Wicks and Rowe were aligned with high-post center Steve Patterson, and all three registered ample numbers of points and rebounds. Wicks led the three by averaging nearly 19 points and 12 rebounds per game.

Moving into the guard slot opposite Vallely was sophomore Henry Bibby from North Carolina, who could drill jumpshots from downtown.

Despite the relatively low expectations of many observers, the tone of Wooden's 1970 team was decidedly cocky. Nonchalant was another term used frequently to describe their play. They blasted by many teams, but struggled with mediocre Minnesota and Princeton. Past the midpoint of the season, Oregon whipped 'em 78-65, then three games later Southern Cal nipped the Bruins in Pauley Pavilion, 87-86.

After a bit of intra-team confrontation and soul searching, they headed into the NCAA tournament's West Regional (where no other team was ranked in the top 10) as the number two team in the nation at 24-2. The nation's talent seemed to be jammed into the Mideast Regional, where top-ranked Kentucky with Dan Issel, ninth-ranked Notre Dame with Austin Carr, and Jacksonville with Artis Gilmore would have to battle with solid Iowa and Western Kentucky teams.

The traffic tie-up was resolved with a shootout. All three of the big teams - Kentucky, Notre Dame and Jacksonville - were high scoring. But Jacksonville was the least regarded, it being a low-profile program with what was considered a soft schedule. The Dolphins, however, were fairly convincing with a 106-100 upset of Kentucky that sent them to the Final Four, held again in College Park, Maryland.

The team to emerge in the East was St. Bonaventure with Bob Lanier. The big center was injured in the Bonnies' regional finals win over Villanova and was unable to play in Final Four. Despite the absence of their big man,

St. Bonaventure kept their national semifinal against Jacksonville reasonably close before losing 91-83.

Using mostly his five starters, Wooden negotiated his way through a regional, whipping Jerry Tarkanian's Long Beach State team, 88-65, and Utah State, 101-79. In the Midwest, New Mexico State whipped Drake, but proved to be little trouble for the Bruins in College Park, losing 93-77.

The championship game was an interesting match of inside power, with Gilmore and Jacksonville taking the early advantage. Wicks was playing the 7-foot-2 Dolphin, and after a defensive adjustment, UCLA took the lead just before the close of the first half. The second half was all Bruins, and although the final score was 80-69, the game wasn't that close. Wicks, with 17 points and 18 rebounds, was named MVP. "Every time somebody mentions three in a row, they say Lew did it," Rowe told reporters. "Now we just proved four other men from that team could play basketball."

For all its success, UCLA's basketball program was laced with a basic unhappiness generated by the circumstances. First, Wooden had drawn a broad collection of talented high school players to his program, and many of them were forced to settle into the obscurity of his second and third teams. Also, the period of the late 60s and early 70s brought a movement of unrest and protest to college campuses across America, particularly at UCLA. Athletes were challenged to be more than athletes, and some felt the need to make political statements. Although a firm disciplinarian, Wooden reluctantly acknowledged the players need for expression and adjusted to it.

Still, he was hurt deeply when departing substitute Bill Seibert used the team banquet to attack the coach, the program and what Seibert saw as a double standard - treatment for subs as opposed to that of the starters. Wooden and assistant coaches Gary Cunningham and Denny Crum, both former players who had joined the staff in '69, attempted to resolve the problem before the negative publicity damaged the program and its ability to recruit.

However, there was only so much they could do. Talented players are given to having their own minds, and one of the negative byproducts of assembling a first-rate program is dealing with discontent. All in all, the UCLA coaches showed a remarkable ability for handling the personalities.

The 1971 team was known for its seemingly uninspired play. That didn't seem to matter, however, as

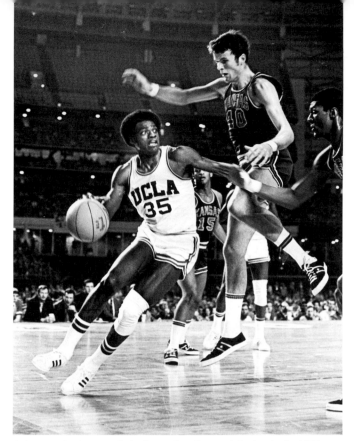

Sidney Wicks drives to the basket against Kansas defenders in the 1971 national semifinals.

the Bruins won on the sheer force of their talent. Wicks, Rowe and Patterson returned as seniors. Bibby, the junior, led the backcourt and shifted to playmaker. He was joined by senior Kenny Booker with another senior, Terry

Schofield, serving as sixth man. The inside power look remained the same.

There were a few close games, but only one loss, 89-82, to Notre Dame in South Bend at midseason, where Austin Carr scored 46 points. Wooden could find no way to stop him. Then the Bruins tiptoed through a string of narrow wins and come-from-behind victories over Southern Cal, Oregon, Oregon State, Washington and Washington State. Regardless, they entered the NCAA tournament at 25-1. After blasting Brigham Young in the first round, Tarkanian's Long Beach State team froze UCLA with a zone and took an 11-point lead. Larry Farmer and John Ecker came off the bench to lift the team, 57-55, to yet another Final Four, this time at the Astrodome in Houston.

In the national semis, Henry Bibby took charge in defeating Kansas, the Midwest winners who featured Dave Robisch, 68-60. Again, the Mideast Regional had been a traffic jam of talent with Western Kentucky, Jacksonville, Ohio State, Kentucky and undefeated second-ranked Marquette (26-0), all of them top 10 teams. Western Kentucky emerged, after Ohio State knocked off Al McGuire's dream team with Dean Meminger.

In the East, 6-foot-8 All-American Howard Porter and Villanova ended the dreams of undefeated Penn with a nightmare 90-47 defeat in the finals, setting up a battle in Houston between the Wildcats and Western Kentucky. The dome crowd of 31,428 saw a double-overtime death match. WKU's Jerry Dunn knotted the regulation at 74 by missing a one and one. Porter tied the first overtime at 85 with a baseline jumper, then continued the strain to deliver Villanova, 92-89.

In the championship game, Wooden used a zone press to slow down Villanova's running game. Then with Bibby and Schofield launching bombs over the Wildcat zone, the UCLA coach slowed the tempo. The second half dragged with the Bruins' stall, until Villanova worked a couple of steals and cut UCLA's lead to four. Patterson, however, was having the game of his career, finishing with 29 points. The Wildcats closed to within three with just over two minutes left but could get no closer, and the Bruins gave Wooden his fifth straight title, 68-62.

TOURNAMENT NOTES: Porter, with 25 points in the final, was named MVP. The Final Four teams each received $60,000 as their share of TV and game revenues.

1970

Jacksonville	fg-fga	ft-fta	rb	pf	tp
V. Wedeking	6-11	0- 0	2	2	12
M. Blevins	1- 2	1- 2	0	1	3
R. Morgan	5-11	0- 0	4	5	10
P. Burrows	6- 9	0- 0	6	1	12
A. Gilmore	9-29	1- 1	16	5	19
G. Nelson	3- 9	2- 2	5	1	8
C. Dublin	0- 5	2- 2	1	4	2
R. Baldwin	0- 0	0- 0	0	0	0
R. McIntyre	1- 3	0- 0	3	4	2
D. Hawkins	0- 1	1- 1	1	1	1
K. Selke	0- 0	0- 0	0	0	0
Team			2		
Totals	31-80	7- 8	40	24	69
UCLA	fg-fga	ft-fta	rb	pf	tp
C. Rowe	7-15	5- 5	8	4	19
S. Patterson	8-15	1- 4	11	1	7
S. Wicks	5- 9	7-10	18	3	17
J. Vallely	5-10	5- 7	7	2	15
H. Bibby	2-11	4- 4	4	1	8
K. Booker	0- 0	2- 3	0	0	2
B. Seibert	0- 1	0- 0	1	1	0
J. Ecker	1- 1	0- 0	0	0	2
R. Betchley	0- 0	0- 1	0	0	0
J. Chapman	0- 1	0- 0	1	0	0
A. Hill	0- 0	0- 1	0	0	0
T. Schofield	0- 0	0- 0	0	0	0
Team			3		
Totals	28-63	24-35	53	12	80

Half time: UCLA 41-36. Officials: Scott and Wirtz. Attendance: 14,380.

1971

Villanova	fg-fga	ft-fta	rb	pf	tp
C. Smith	4-11	1- 1	2	4	9
H. Porter	10-21	5- 6	8	1	25
H. Siemiontkowski	9-16	1- 2	6	3	19
T. Ingelsby	3- 9	1- 1	4	2	7
C. Ford	0- 4	2- 3	5	4	2
J. McDowell	0- 1	0- 0	2	0	0
J. Fox	0- 0	0- 0	0	0	0
Team			4		
Totals	26-62	10-13	31	14	62
UCLA	fg-fga	ft-fta	rb	pf	tp
C. Rowe	2- 3	4- 5	8	0	8
S. Wicks	3- 7	1- 1	9	2	7
S. Patterson	13-18	3- 5	8	1	29
H. Bibby	6-12	5- 5	2	1	17
K. Booker	0- 0	0- 0	0	0	0
T. Schofield	3- 9	0- 0	1	4	6
R. Betchley	0- 0	1- 2	1	1	1
Team			5		
Totals	27-49	14-18	34	9	68

Half time: UCLA 45-37. Officials: Bain and Brown. Attendance: 31,765.

Walton Gang

The next wave of talented sophomores crested in the UCLA program in 1972. They would play two full seasons and win two national championships before they tasted defeat. Never had a college basketball team, not even one of John Wooden's, enjoyed such success.

The key figure, of course, was the fiery red-headed center, Bill Walton, the 6-foot-11 son of a San Diego social worker. Off the court, he was a radical student in a radical age. On the court, he was the picture of precision, the ultimate passing center, schooled and polished in every phase of the game. It was fortunate that he was a team player, for Wooden and his assistants had assembled a team to go with him. The other starting sophomores were Keith Wilkes, the silky smooth forward, and Greg Lee. Junior Larry Farmer had moved into the lineup after being a key reserve the year before. Henry Bibby, the senior guard, was the only returning starter. Swen Nater,

another big, strong sophomore center, served as Walton's backup for three years, then was taken in the first round of the NBA draft.

This group set an NCAA record for obliterating opponents, with an average margin of victory of 30.3 points over 30 games. They scored more than 100 points in their first seven games, not against Divison II patsies mind you, but against Iowa, Iowa State, Notre Dame, Texas A&M, and Texas. The ninth game of the season, Oregon State came close at 78-72, but from there the Bruins zoomed off again, leaving 17 more teams strewn in their wake to enter the NCAA West Regional 26-0. At Provo, Utah, they zapped Weber State and Long Beach and headed back home for the Final Four at the Los Angeles Sports Arena.

Former Wooden assistant Denny Crum had left the program for Louisville. His Cards were the Bruins' meat

John Wooden presided over some talented but turbulent teams.

1972					
Florida State	fg-fga	ft-fta	rb	pf	tp
R. Garrett	1- 9	1- 1	5	1	3
R. King	12-20	3- 3	6	1	27
R. Royals	5- 7	5- 6	10	5	15
L. McCray	3- 6	2- 5	6	4	8
G. Samuel	3-10	0- 0	1	1	6
R. Harris	7-13	2- 3	6	1	16
O. Petty	0- 0	1- 1	0	1	1
O. Cole	0- 2	0- 0	2	1	0
Team			6		
Totals	31-67	14-19	42	15	76
UCLA	fg-fga	ft-fta	rb	pf	tp
K. Wilkes	11-16	1- 2	10	4	23
L. Farmer	2- 6	0- 0	6	2	4
B. Walton	9-17	6-11	20	4	24
G. Lee	0- 0	0- 0	2	0	0
H. Bibby	8-17	2- 3	3	2	18
T. Curtis	4-14	0- 1	4	1	8
L. Hollyfield	1- 6	0- 0	2	2	2
S. Nater	1- 2	0- 1	1	0	2
Team			2		
Totals	36-78	9-18	50	15	81

Half time: UCLA 50-39. Officials: Brown and Scott. Attendance: 15,063.

Walton made 21 of 22 field goal attempts against Memphis State in the 1973 finals.

1973

UCLA	fg-fga	ft-fta	rb	pf	tp
K. Wilkes	8-14	0- 0	7	2	16
L. Farmer	1- 4	0- 0	2	2	2
B. Walton	21-22	2- 5	13	4	44
G. Lee	1- 1	3- 3	3	2	5
L. Hollyfield	4- 7	0- 0	3	4	8
T. Curtis	1- 4	2- 2	3	1	4
D. Meyers	2- 7	0- 0	3	1	4
S. Nater	1- 1	0- 0	3	2	2
G. Franklin	1- 2	0- 1	1	0	2
V. Carson	0- 0	0- 0	0	0	0
B. Webb	0- 0	0- 0	0	0	0
Team			2		
Totals	40-62	7-11	40	18	87

Memphis State	fg-fga	ft-fta	rb	pf	tp
B. Buford	3- 7	1- 2	3	1	7
L. Kenon	8-16	4- 4	8	3	20
R. Robinson	3- 6	0- 1	7	4	6
B. Laurie	0- 1	0- 0	0	0	0
L. Finch	9-21	11-13	1	2	29
W. Westfall	0- 1	0- 0	0	5	0
B. Cook	1- 4	2- 2	0	1	4
D. McKinney	0- 0	0- 0	0	0	0
C. Jones	0- 0	0- 0	0	0	0
J. Tetzlaff	0- 0	0- 2	0	1	0
J. Liss	0- 1	0- 0	0	0	0
K. Andrews	0- 0	0- 0	0	0	0
Team			2		
Totals	24-57	18-24	21	17	66

Half time: 39-39. Officials: Howell and Shosid. Attendance: 19,301.

in the semifinals. As Crum would say later, his team played hard but stood no chance. Wooden paddled his former assistant, 96-77. Walton, whom Crum had recruited for the Bruins, scored 33.

In the other semifinal, Robert McAdoo and second-ranked Carolina faced Hugh Durham's Florida State team, a Cinderella. The Seminoles had upset Minnesota, then defeated Kentucky in what would prove to be the last game coached by Adolph Rupp. Durham had a gifted scorer in Ron King, and he put him to work early against the Tar Heels. Carolina shot poorly and struggled early, but then came back from a 23-point deficit. It wasn't enough, and the Seminoles earned the right to be the Bruins' next meal, 79-75. Except Durham's bunch proved not to be so easily digestible as the earlier entrees on Wooden's menu.

With King lofting deadeye jumpers, Florida State took an early lead until Walton began scoring. When he slipped into foul trouble the second half, State had the savvy to keep close. Walton returned sporadically and played gingerly but still collected 24 points and 20 rebounds to earn the MVP honor.

Wooden had added another link to his chain of 30-0 teams. To prove it was no fluke, the Walton gang went out and did it again the next season, 1972-73. Bibby, of course, had moved on to the NBA, and Larry Hollyfield moved into the lineup. That January 25, UCLA beat Loyola of Chicago for their 60th straight victory, tying San Francisco's record in 1955-56. Two nights later, the Bruins beat Notre Dame and would ring the number all the way up to 75 by the end of the season. A few teams came as close as six points, but not many.

The feast continued at the Final Four in St. Louis, where Bobby Knight's young Indiana team fell 70-59 in the semis. NC State, the other great undefeated team with David Thompson, was on NCAA restriction and wasn't allowed to play. In the other semi, Gene Bartow's Memphis State team with Larry Finch, Ronnie Robinson and Larry Kenon upset Providence 98-85. The Friars featured Ernie DiGregorio and Marvin Barnes, but they weren't enough.

The finals became a showcase of Walton's inside offensive prowess, as he made 21 of 22 field goal attempts for 44 points and 13 rebounds. His performance loosened a game that had been tied at 39 at half time. UCLA glided over the last 20 minutes to an 87-66 win for Wooden's seventh consecutive championship. If anything, UCLA seemed primed to make it eight straight the next year. Yet even in the days of Wooden, not everything was a foregone conclusion.

TOURNAMENT NOTES: Walton was named MVP for the second consecutive year. Finch of Memphis State had averaged 26.8 points over four tournament games.

Larry Farmer

Larry Farmer was a member of three national championship teams at UCLA, 1971-73. Farmer was the head coach at UCLA from 1981-84, compiling a 61-23 record in three seasons.

Packer—Larry, in the NCAA Final Four, your record turned out to be 6-0; three times in the tournament, three times national champions. When was the first time you heard of a thing called the Final Four?

Farmer—My first recollection of the Final Four was when I was a senior in high school, back in '69. I had followed professional basketball but I hadn't watched a lot of college basketball. The only reason I paid any attention to it was because I wanted to go to UCLA, and they had this kid whom everyone kept talking about named Lew Alcindor. I was just curious to see how good he was.

Packer—You got an opportunity to play as a sophomore, a year that was supposed to be a down one for UCLA. Kareem was gone and other teams felt it might be the year to catch Coach Wooden. But it didn't happen. Why?

Farmer—It was really exciting for me. I had played in a state high school championship game before, and to me that was the end of the world. All of a sudden, I'm playing for the national championship. I tried to be sophisticated because Sidney Wicks and those guys had all been through it before.

Packer—The next two seasons brought even greater success for the Bruins. You won two more national crowns, including the game with Memphis State in which Bill Walton had one of the greatest performances of all time. Tell me about that performance.

Farmer—It's interesting what happened. I played on the weak side of the offense and a lot of my offense was derived from Bill missing his shot and me tipping them from the weak side. Halfway through the second half of that game, it dawned on me that I hadn't gotten tip-ins and it hit me that the guy hadn't missed many shots. Every time he got the ball inside, he scored. During the game, I didn't realize that he had missed only one shot.

Packer—That was the first time we had seen the big man play the lob so effectively. Was that a strategy that was set or was it something between the players?

Farmer—It was strictly by accident. You're going to think I'm pulling your leg, but you can ask Coach Wooden. That play got started between Greg Lee and me as a weak side entry to the offense. The first couple of times we did it, Coach didn't say anything. But he had us

practice it once and said if the lob didn't work or if we started to turn the ball over to stop it. But it was a big factor in that ball game because it was one of the few times that a team tried to match up with us man to man, with Larry Kenon on Bill. The way our offense was spread out, he tried to deny Bill the ball by playing in front of him. Greg just started throwing the ball over the top, and the next thing you know Bill Walton and Greg Lee had developed the lob pass.

Packer—Then it wasn't devised before the game?

Farmer—No, it just developed that way. After I had finished playing at UCLA, Coach told me that he liked coaching players who had great basketball savvy, as did Greg Lee and Bill Walton, kids who were smart enough to read what the defense was giving them and adjust. When Memphis State decided to play an agressive man-to-man and try to deny Bill the ball by getting in front of him, Greg picked up on it right away. Bill was a smart enough player to move his man up the lane so we could throw it to him near the basket. I think he got called once for offensive goaltending, but that was it.

Packer—In your three year varsity career, you fellows were 89 and 1, an all-time record in NCAA play. What was your toughest Final Four game?

Farmer—The Florida State game my junior year stands out as the toughest. We were behind at the beginning of the second half. My junior year, our average winning margin was 30.3 points a game. Nobody had touched us. When we got into the tournament, we played Louisville in Denny Crum's first year there. That was a tough game. The Bruin Blitz, our press that generated momentum for us, betrayed us. They threw the ball up court, and we dared them to shoot out of the corner. They did and hit the shots. I don't remember what the final margin was, but it was one of the closest games we played.

Packer—During your three years, did you ever have a really difficult game getting through the Final Four?

Farmer—We had a very difficult game against Long Beach State my sophomore year. Tarkanian was there and they had Ed Ratleff. They got up by about 12 points. They were in a 1-3-1 zone, and we were just not doing a good job of attacking it. I played most of the second half, and I remember Coach Wooden called a time out. It was one of the few times that he did not use the timeout for instruction. He spent it yelling at us to go out and play hard and play from the neck up. We ended up turning the game around in the final two minutes of the ball game. I blocked

1972 UCLA team photo. Back row(L to R)—Tommy Curtis, Greg Lee, Larry Hollyfield, Jon Chapman, Keith Wilkes, Bill Walton, Swen Nater, Vince Carson, Larry Farmer, Gary Franklin, Andy Hill, Henry Bibby. Middle row—John Wooden, Ducky Drake, Gary Cunningham. Front row—Manager Les Friedman.

a shot, threw it to Sidney, who got fouled. He hit two free throws to put us ahead, and we went on to win. That was the only time in any of the games in the tournament that I thought we might not win.

Packer—Let's go into Coach Wooden a little bit. You had a very unusual experience in that you not only had a chance to observe him as a player during a very successful period, but you also had the opportunity to work with him as a coach. Why do you think he was so successful as a coach?

Farmer—I've talked about that many times. Coach Wooden is a genius, and I don't mean that in the sense of being an intellectual, though obviously, he's that, too. But he was the perfect motivator for the kids. Coach could figure out what it would take to get each kid on his team motivated to play and get the most out of him. I played with Dave Meyers. He was a very sensitive kid and Coach got him to play hard by patting him on the back and giving him the attention he needed. By the same token I was just the opposite. Had I been given a pat on the back I probably would have folded up shop, thinking I was God's gift to basketball. But Coach ignored me, and that kept me working hard. As I look back, I can see where he would do little things for everyone to maximize his ability. So, not only did he get great players, but he got the greatness out of them. He made us think as a team. You look back at some of the great players we had, players who could have averaged 30 points a game, who could

have been great individual players. They were always part of a team. My last year, Walton averaged 20 points a game, but before that he averaged 16 or 18 points. He taught us a system and made us play within that system. He treated us all the same when we were on the basketball court. He had us in great shape and we were fundamentally sound players. I guess the combination of all those things, and the fact that he was a great teacher, led to his incredible win streaks that I don't think will be matched in any sport.

Packer—Let's talk about some of those individuals. Bill Walton—how did he handle him during those days of campus unrest in the 60's?

Farmer—Coach knew that Bill was a very impressionable guy. If some guy talked to Bill one day and told him the sky was pink, Bill would believe that; and then if he talked to someone the next day who told him the sky was red, Bill would believe that, too. Coach wanted us to be individuals and experience college as students, not just as basketball players. In his system, he had rules off and on the court, but within that system he let us be ourselves. I don't think coach minded Bill expressing his views on war at all. I think he was mad at Bill when Bill got arrested for voicing his views, and I'm sure he told Bill that. I know they had disagreements about length of hair from time-to-time. Bill thought that because it was fashionable to wear hair on his shoulders he should be able to do that during the season. I know Coach told him one day that if it was more important for him to wear his hair long, he should wear it long. He believed in a person being able to take a stand. But he told him if he were going to wear his hair long, not to come out for the team. Needless to say, Bill cut his hair. But he did give us freedom to be our own person within his system.

Packer—How about Sidney Wicks—a completely different personality?

Farmer—Coach knew Sidney had a certain flamboyance about him, and Sidney had a little con in him. I think Coach would let Sidney con him a little bit just to keep him happy, but behind closed doors he had Sidney completely in control, just like the rest of us. I'm sure there were times when Sidney tested him more than we ever knew as players, but I'm sure Coach had his way. Sidney, despite the fact that he came across as a wild kind of crazy guy, was very respectful of Coach Wooden, and I never saw him smart-off to Coach or talk back to him. I saw them get into some heated discussions, and Coach would let Sidney speak his piece. But I never saw any disrespect.

Packer—You had great depth of talent there. How did Coach Wooden keep guys happy?

Farmer—The guys who weren't playing obviously weren't real thrilled about it. Coach made no bones about telling us right at the beginning of the game that he would play the best eight players until the game was won or lost; didn't take long to learn who those eight were. In a situation like UCLA, with the team winning every game, it's difficult to walk into a coach's office and say you think you ought to be playing more. In my case, the two guys who were ahead of me were consensus All-Americans. I would not have had a good argument asking to play more. Coach was very sensitive to the fact that there were guys who were not happy about their playing time, and he tried to make us aware that you had to pay your dues. When the opportunity came to play, he said we should have our heads screwed on right and not be disgruntled, and make the most of the opportunity. He was bluntly honest and if you went to one of those meetings where you wanted to find out why or when or what, you might walk out of there with your tail between your legs wishing you hadn't gone in.

Packer—He was the boss then?

Farmer—No question.

Packer—When you got to the Final Four, how much time did he spend talking about the opponent as opposed to what UCLA was going to do?

Farmer—The day before the game, Coach would spend time talking a little bit about what we would see. We might work on our defensive drills and isolate a particular thing, but mention of the team we were going to play would never come up. Mention of any individual player on that team would never come up. There were actually days, and this is true, when I was a junior and senior in college, when we would play that weekend and I wouldn't know during the week who we were going to play. Kids would walk up to me and ask, "Who are you playing this week?" And I'd say I didn't know, and they'd laugh. But we never focused on the opponent except for about five minutes the day before the ball game, and that was it.

Packer—Was it surprising to you the way coach Wooden exited college basketball?

Farmer—When I heard he'd announced his retirement after the semifinal game, the first thing I felt was sadness. I'd never been close to Coach when I was a player, and I didn't get close to him until after I graduated. I was sad that that whole era had come to an end. I wondered what Coach was going to do because basketball had been so much of his life. I thought if he is going to quit, I hope he wins his last ball game. I was in Europe and I listened to his last game on armed forces network when they played Kentucky. I cheered like crazy. I started crying. I was happy, but it was more for him than the fact that I was a part of that thing a few years back.

When I played at UCLA, we weren't emotional when we won championships. I cut down the net and put it around my neck because that was what we were supposed to do. Today, I watch kids and they jump up and down and stand on the rims and, hell, I wish I'd done that.

Packer—What's the major change in the Final Four, from the first one you appeared in to the way you see it today?

Farmer—Oh, the press coverage. I wished they'd covered that stuff then like they do now. I'd be a stock broker now or something with all the attention these kids get. It's a much bigger event with all the coverage. I think because the number of teams that participate has increased, there are a lot of people who follow the tournament all the way to the end. Now, I watch kids and they look with pride to just being a part of the Final Four. Looking back, I've grown to appreciate how special you've got to be to get to the Final Four.

Packer—Did Coach Wooden talk about winning the Final Four?

Farmer—He never mentioned the Final Four. The first coach I worked with who used that terminology was Coach Gene Bartow. It was sort of strange because I hadn't heard that term used before.

Coach always played them one at a time, and the Final Four was no more special, at least not in terms of the way Coach portrayed it to us, than any other game we played in. Obviously, there was more tension and there was a lot of color and atmosphere. But when we practiced and had our team meetings or our pre-game meal, it was exactly like any other game. The night before we played the national championship, we would run the same drills that we ran when we began practice on October 15.

Larry Farmer usually worked from the weak side to collect rebounds, but with Walton making 21 of 22 shots against Memphis State, there weren't many rebounds in the 1973 finals.

The State Break

It was perhaps the greatest season in all of college basketball. The on-court struggles were legendary, elevated almost to the level of myth. The Walton team flexed its muscle early, then stumbled. NC State shook loose the shackles of NCAA restriction and engaged in a fierce ACC struggle with Maryland, from which the Wolfpack emerged to claim the national championship.

Such a turn of events seemed highly unlikely to UCLA fans heading into the 1973-74 season. The team of super sophomores had become super juniors and seemed poised at the edge of divinity for their senior season. Solid, stable Larry Farmer had graduated. Keith Wilkes, Bill Walton and Greg Lee were joined by fellow senior Tommy Curtis at guard. Junior Dave Meyers added a strong element of hustle to the lineup.

Wooden took all comers in challenges to the crown and agreed to play both Maryland and NC State early in the season. The Bruins warmed up by blasting Arkansas, 101-79, in the season opener then entertained Maryland and Pauley Pavilion for what was the Terps' first game.

Having come to Maryland for the 1970 season, Coach Lefty Driesell had claimed much to his later regret that he was building the "UCLA of the East." His Terps had won the NIT in 1972, but lost to Providence in the 1973 East Regional finals. Arguably, his 1974 edition was his greatest team with center Len Elmore, forward Tom McMillan and guard John Lucas, all of whom would earn All-American honors during their college careers.

They almost pulled UCLA from the throne in Pauley Pavilion. Going into the closing minutes, the Bruins led 65-57, but the Terps rushed back to 65-64. John Lucas had a shot to win it in the dying seconds, but Meyers blocked it and the win streak lived a little longer.

After a win over Southern Methodist, Wooden's bunch played NC State in St. Louis, a game sought by State Coach Norm Sloan. Coming off probation and a riding a 29-game win streak, Sloan was eager to test his team's mettle. He, too, had a grand collection of players. The heart of the team was 6-foot-4 David Thompson with a 42-inch vertical leap. He was aided by 5-foot-6 playmaker Monte Towe and 7-foot-4 center Tom Burleson.

Walton picked up four fouls early on and watched from the bench as his team struggled to 54 all. But the Wolfpack's dreams were dashed late in the second half when Walton's return boosted UCLA to a convincing 84-66 win.

The Bruins seemed in position to roll to yet another title. But in retrospect, one might say they were caught up

NC State's Monte Towe. Opposite —NC State's David Thompson soars to the boards against UCLA's Keith Wilkes (52) in the 1974 national semifinals. Thompson holds Bill Walton at bay to his left.

in the times. The mood in the country was nasty, with Watergate and Vietnam creating constant debate. The fiery Walton's emotions were a lightning rod for those controversies. UCLA took on the air of the counterculture and reflected the disillusionment felt by students across the country. Perhaps those distractions cracked their concentration. Perhaps the players buckled under the pressure of their win streak. Whatever the cause, the Walton team ran through 13 games that season, pushing their win streak to an incredible 88 games before heading to South Bend to play undefeated Notre Dame, coached by Digger Phelps. With three minutes left in the game, things seemed business as usual. UCLA led, 70-59. That's when Adrian Dantley and crew magically blitzed through 12 points and won, 71-70. The streak had died of a sudden, unexpected heart attack.

Having felt their mortality, Walton's version of the Bruins felt it again four games later in a 61-57 loss to Oregon State, then again the next game to mediocre Oregon, 56-51. Losing their top ranking in the polls, they resumed their pace after that, pausing only at the close of the regular season with a close win over Stanford. Then

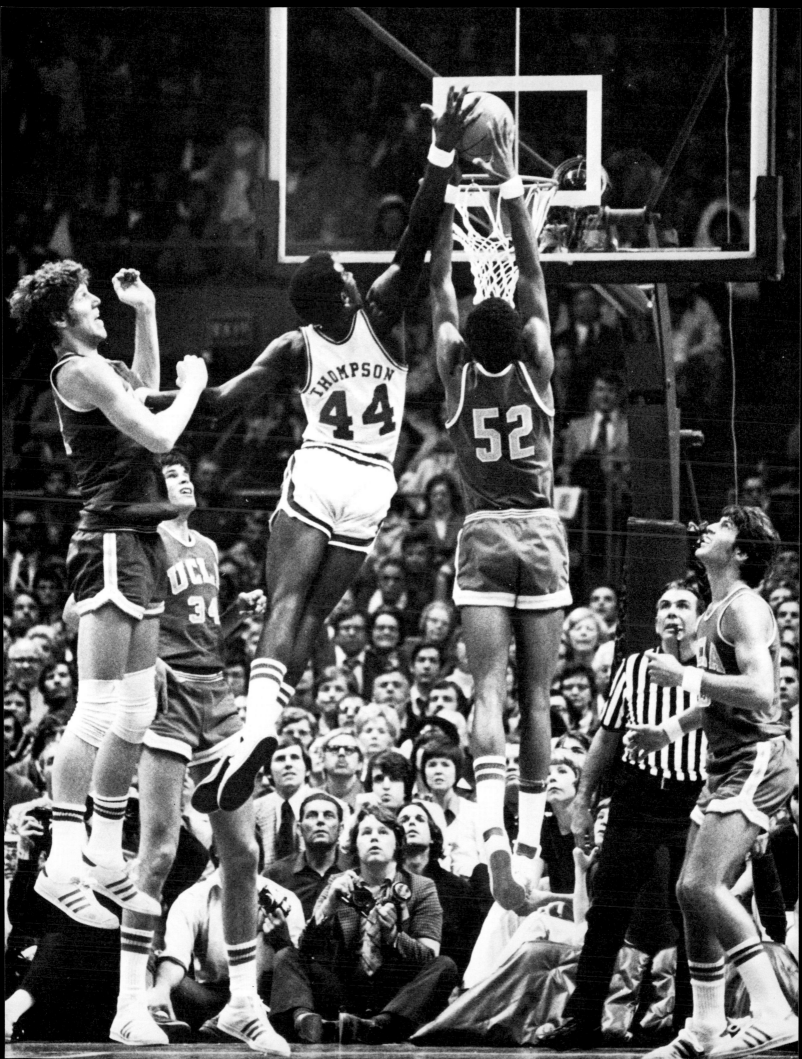

Above—The Wolfpack celebrates a championship. Bottom left—Thompson, Towe and Burleson on the bench.

1974

Marquette	fg-fga	ft-fta	rb	pf	tp
M. Ellis	6-16	0- 0	11	5	12
E. Tatum	2- 7	0- 0	3	4	4
M. Lucas	7-13	7- 9	13	4	21
L. Walton	4-10	0- 0	2	2	8
M. Washington	3-13	5- 8	4	3	11
D. Delsman	0- 0	0- 0	0	2	0
E. Daniels	1- 3	1- 2	0	3	3
R. Campbell	2- 3	0- 0	1	3	4
J. Homan	0- 4	1- 2	6	2	1
B. Brennan	0- 0	0- 0	0	1	0
Team			3		
Totals	25-69	14-21	43	29	64
North Carolina St.	fg-fga	ft-fta	rb	pf	tp
T. Stoddard	3- 4	2- 2	7	5	8
D. Thompson	7-12	7- 8	7	3	21
T. Burleson	6- 9	2- 6	11	4	14
M. Rivers	4- 9	6- 9	2	2	14
M. Towe	5-10	6- 7	3	1	16
P. Spence	1- 2	1- 2	3	2	3
M. Moeller	0- 0	0- 0	0	0	0
Team			1		
Totals	26-46	24-34	34	17	76

Half time: North Carolina State 39-30.
Officials: Howell and Brown. Attendance: 15,742.

The 1974 title put NC State Coach Norm Sloan in the spotlight.

State's Tommy Burleson battles Marquette's Bo Ellis

came a three-overtime screamer against Dayton in the first round of the West Regional, which they won finally, 111-100. In the finals they whipped San Francisco soundly and headed to the Final Four in Greensboro, North Carolina.

There they encountered NC State again. The Wolfpack was ranked number one in both polls after surviving an overtime scare of its own in the ACC tournament finals. In overtime, they had escaped Maryland, 103-100, a game billed as the greatest in the league's history. In the East Regional on their home floor, Reynolds Coliseum, State had turned away fourth-ranked Providence and eighth-ranked Pitt, but Thompson had been knocked cold in a brutal fall against the Panthers in the final. He lay in a motionless heap that left the home crowd aghast, but returned from the hospital toward the end of the game, a development that brought relieved cheers from Pack supporters.

The semifinal pairing of UCLA and State was immediately pronounced the true championship. In the other bracket, Al McGuire's Marquette team with Maurice Lucas had come out of the Mideast Regional, where Michigan had upset Notre Dame. From a weak Midwest Regional, Kansas had survived Oral Roberts in overtime. Their Final Four meeting was settled by Marquette rather easily, 64-51.

The championship, er, the other semifinal, was nothing less than a masterpiece. Wilkes found foul trouble early. Walton was grand with 29 points and 18 rebounds. So was Thompson, with 28 and 10. Both coaches played conservatively, using only seven men. At the half, the score was 35 all. At the end of regulation, 65 all. The first overtime ended in a knot at 67. Then UCLA shoved off with a 7-point lead in the second overtime, and it seemed settled. Somehow, the Pack found the fuel for one final, miraculous acceleration and blew past the Bruins at the wire, 80-77, a victory they're still celebrating down in Raleigh.

Wooden was graceful in defeat and said the final would be worth watching. Walton on the other hand had second thoughts about playing in the consolation game but decided to go ahead after consultation with his father. The Bruins downed Kansas, 78-61.

The final against Marquette was tight in the first half, but State pulled away after McGuire was slapped with two technicals. The lead stretched to 19 in the second half before State settled down and won it, 76-64.

TOURNAMENT NOTES: Thompson scored 21 points in the final and was named MVP. The Pack finished the year at 30-1.

An Interview With Bill Walton

Bill Walton led UCLA to national titles in 1972 and 1973. He was twice named the outstanding player in the tournament.

Packer—Bill, when one thinks of the greatest individual performances in the Final Four, everybody points to your game against Memphis State. You shot 21-of-22 from the field. How do you remember that game?

Walton—We knew we had to play great basketball to beat Memphis State, so we were really rolling as a unit right from the beginning. We had won seven straight games before that game, and we had a tremendous amount of confidence. Memphis State had a powerful front line, but they were not particularly tall, so we tried to go to the hoop with the ball. I was feeling great and we were really moving the ball around.

People talk a lot about my scoring, but it was really our team offense that had to click perfectly for me to get 21 baskets in that game. Our starting guards, Greg Lee and Larry Hollyfield, had 22 assists between them. Most of those were to me. We had the kind of offense that really thrived on passing that ball. Most of my shots were very short, so I had a very fortunate day. Normally, we had a fast-break team that relied on pressure defense to get our offense going. We would score bunches of points on the fast break after our defense forced turnovers. Then after we scored we would get into our press. This game was different; we weren't fast breaking that much because they were able to control the flow, and they weren't going to let our defense take them out of their game. So we had to rely on set offense. Everybody was moving and passing at a faster pace then Memphis State, and once I got hot shooting, the guys found me for easy baskets underneath. Although I was hot, I missed three of five free throws. I still get teased by all my teammates for going 21-of-22 from the floor and only two-of-five from the line.

When I got in foul trouble, they went to a 3-2 zone with everybody in front of me and nobody between me and the basket. Greg Lee was running the point for our team, and I told him, "What do you say you throw it up high, and I'll go over the top for a layup?" If our fast break and pressure defense had been on fire, as they often were, I really wouldn't have gotten much involved in the set offense.

Packer—The lob pass was very effective. I talked to Greg Lee and Larry Farmer, and both of them said the lob pass did not originate as a set play for you, but was the result of a bad pass from Lee to Farmer.

Walton—Definitely. It was a mistake. We had very few set plays; basically we had positions on the court. I played

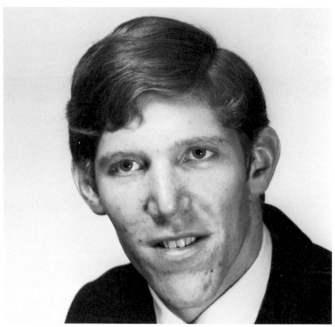

UCLA's Bill Walton.

low post, Larry played the left box, Henry Bibby played the left wing. Basically, it was a 1-3-1 offense, with Bibby and Farmer as the wing players and Wilkes and myself at the double low post. Wilkes would break to the middle to make it a 1-3-1. Lee was right in the middle of the court, and he would set up the plays. Coach Wooden, Henry Bibby, Keith Wilkes, and I always demanded that Lee bring the ball to our side, and Larry Farmer just got shafted in terms of the number of opportunities he had to score. So we ran our offense to the left side of the court. It wasn't complicated; just get the ball to people in good spots and let them do what was best with the ball. There wasn't a lot of screening, but there was a lot of cutting and passing, not many trick plays. As we overloaded the left side, the defense would react to that and come to the left side. One day, Greg Lee was standing at the point and was trying to feed the ball inside. Farmer was at the right wing all alone, and he just ran to the basket, and Greg threw it up and Farmer grabbed it and put it in. They did that a couple more times, and I said, "Wait a second, that looks like something I can do." I went and talked to Greg and told him to look for me on that play because they were trying to deny me the ball and I could just go back door. Greg would toss the ball high, I would catch it and put it in.

Packer—The game against Memphis State was one of

1971 team photo. Back row (L to R)—Larry Hollyfield, Larry Farmer, John Ecker, Curtis Rowe, Steve Patterson, Sidney Wicks, Jon Chapman, Kenny Booker, Rich Betchley, Terry Schofield. Middle row—Manager George Morgan, Denny Crum, John Wooden, Gary Cunningham, Ducky Drake. Front row—Andy Hill, Henry Bibby.

the magic moments in your collegiate career. One of the most disappointing moments came a year later against NC State. You had the game all wrapped up in overtime, but let it slip away. How about that day?

Walton—Those are the days you never forget. You forget the great days like the Memphis State game and winning championships, but the ones you can never get out of your mind are the ones you lose when you should have won. You can't take anything away from NC State. They beat us and they won the championship. But I feel we beat ourselves in that game. We had it won. We did not play nearly as well in that game as we had played most of the season. The last two months of the season, our team started playing poorly. After our 88 game win streak was broken, we lost four of our last 10 games. We lost four games to teams we should have beaten. We should have won 105 in a row. NC State had a lot of talent, and in David Thompson they had a game-breaker, a guy who could make the big play at the end of a game. We had a seven-point lead in the overtime, but we made turnovers. We were not a good team when it was a slow-down game. They went to a slow-down four corners, and that really took it out of us. I missed a lot of shots around the basket down the stretch when I should have put the game away for us. Thompson had a big, big game, and we didn't have a big enough game out of any of our players. We were incredibly disappointed. You just don't have the opportunity to win championships that often, and when you do and lose, it changes your life.

Packer—Was UCLA the place you knew you wanted to play?

Walton—Without a doubt, UCLA was the only place to go. I wanted to go there even before they contacted me. I went to a John Wooden basketball camp for a day as a kid

in San Diego. He and Bill Sharman came down to San Diego and gave a one-day clinic.

Packer—You were how old at the time?

Walton—I was young, 10 or 12. I came from a family that wasn't able to afford to send their kids to camp, and really there weren't that many camps when I was a kid. I wouldn't have been in a financial situation to go anyway. But I got to go to this one-day camp. I don't think it was very expensive. My mom and dad had gotten me the book *Facts in Modern Basketball*. I watched UCLA in the early '60's when they were playing for the national championship with Hazzard and Goodrich. I loved the way they played. I loved the fast-break style and the pressure defense. UCLA was the first school to recruit me. I got my first letter from Denny Crum, the assistant coach, when I was a sophomore in high school.

Packer—Did you ever have the feeling that you would be compared to Kareem?

Walton—No. I wanted to go to UCLA, not only because of Coach Wooden, but because Pauley Pavillion was the nicest basketball building in the country. Equally important were the guys I would be playing with. I knew Greg Lee and I knew he was a great player. I knew Keith Wilkes and I knew he was a great player. I figured that to be most effective, I needed to play with that caliber of player. I also loved the enthusiasm and intensity of the fans. It's funny, but most of the players who played here talk about the wonderful days at UCLA and the sense of family and how they come back to events like this and how wonderful it is. I second those emotions. I'm very lucky because I'm on the Boston Celtics and their ball club is exactly like that in terms of the tradition, the long-term comradery of the players, and the management. It's just a wonderful situation for me.

The '75 Surprise

It seemed North Carolina State had broken the 11-year spell that John Wooden and UCLA had cast over college basketball. For the 1974-75 season, the attention shifted to the many revived programs sprouting up across the land. The NCAA tournament was expanded to 32 teams, and for the first time in years, there was an sense of hope in the air. For the first time in years, Wooden didn't have an Alcindor or Walton waiting in the wings.

Yet the Wizard of Westwood took one final opportunity to prove a point to the basketball world. As a number of ambitious coaches were sizing up each other, wondering who would be the next to seize the championship mantle, Wooden whisked an odd collection of players into the Final Four, captured his tenth title and retired. Seldom in any occupation has a man dominated with such precision then stepped aside with such panache.

Bobby Knight might argue that fate had set up the circumstances. He declared his 1975 Indiana team the greatest he has ever known after watching his Hoosiers, led by Scott May, Kent Benson and Quinn Buckner, win their first 28 games. But with four games remaining in the season, May broke his arm. He played with a cast but wasn't nearly as effective. Regardless, Indiana drove to the Mideast Regional finals, where Joe B. Hall's Kentucky team, a team they had beaten earlier in the year, 98-74, ended Knight's hopes of a first national championship, 92-90.

Over the course of the season, Wooden's team had slipped a step out of the spotlight. Dave Meyers was the only returning starter. He was teamed with the next set of

Richard Washington drives inside against Kentucky's power game in the 1975 finals.

1975

UCLA	fg-fga	ft-fta	rb	pf	tp
D. Meyers	9-18	6- 7	11	4	24
M. Johnson	3- 9	0- 1	7	2	6
R. Washington	12-23	4- 5	12	4	28
P. Trgovich	7-16	2- 4	5	4	16
A. McCarter	3- 6	2- 3	2	1	8
R. Drollinger	4- 6	2- 5	13	4	10
Team			5		
Totals	38-78	16-25	55	19	92

Kentucky	fg-fga	ft-fta	rb	pf	tp
K. Grevey	13-30	8-10	5	4	34
B. Guyette	7-11	2- 2	7	3	16
R. Robey	1- 3	0- 0	9	5	2
J.D. Conner	4-12	1- 2	5	1	9
M. Flynn	3- 9	4- 5	3	4	10
J. Givens	3-10	2- 3	6	3	8
L. Johnson	0- 3	0- 0	3	3	0
M. Phillips	1- 7	2- 3	6	4	4
D. Hall	1- 1	0- 0	1	0	2
J. Lee	0- 0	0- 0		1	0
Team			4		
Totals	33-86	19-25	49	28	85

Half time: UCLA 43-40. Officials: Nichols and Workman. Attendance: 15,151.

sophomores, Marques Johnson and Richard Washington, to create a solid frontcourt. Junior Andre McCarter was the playmaker, and Pete Trgovich moved into the other guard slot.

They won their first 12 games, then were upset by Stanford and dropped another three games later to Notre Dame. After a demoralizing 22-point defeat to Washington late in the season, they picked up enough to win the PAC 8. But in the West Regional in Pullman, Washington, the Bruins immediately ran into trouble. In overtime, they finally ousted Michigan, 103-91. And they couldn't subdue Jud Heathcote's Montana team in the next round, only managing to win late, 67-64. Eighth-ranked Arizona State with Lionel Hollins figured to be more trouble in the finals, but Wooden found it to be the closest thing they'd seen to a breather, an 89-75 ticket to yet another Final Four, this time in that least assuming of basketball towns, San Diego.

Denny Crum, Wooden's former player and assistant, was just as ambitious as any of the young coaches in the game. He was making his second trip to the Final Four in the four years since he had left Wooden's program. The Cards featured Wesley Cox and Junior Bridgeman and came to the party from the Midwest Regionals, where they had defeated Maryland, 96-82. Louisville vs. UCLA, Crum vs. Wooden. Not a bad story line, the media decided.

Hall's Kentucky Wildcats, victors over Indiana in the Mideast, faced East champion Syracuse in the other bracket. But the game was a foul fest, with 61 whistles, and the Wildcats prevailed, 95-79. It was the Bruins' game that history smiled on. Even Denny Crum will say today that it was a great one. His Cards led by four with 48 seconds left. In the sequence frozen in time, Meyers tried twice to score, and Bill Bunton blocked both shots. Washington retrieved the second rejection and shot, and Bunton blocked it, too, but was called for the foul. Washington made both free throws, then UCLA tied the game moments later when Marques Johnson picked off a pass and scored. In overtime, Louisville led by one with seconds left when Johnson dished to Washington at the baseline. His shot killed the Cards, 75-74.

At the press conference after the game, Wooden announced his retirement at the close of the season. Joe B. Hall and everyone else knew his players weren't about to let the Wizard go out anything but a winner. The Kentucky lineup was studded with 6-foot-5 All-American Kevin Grevey, plus 6-foot-10 freshman bookends Rick Robey and Mike Phillips, and Jack "Goose" Givens. The Wildcats kept it close until just under seven minutes to go

Washington pulls up for a jumper in the 1975 finals.

in the game, with UCLA leading 76-75, when Meyers was called for a charging foul, then a technical. Wooden rushed onto the court in anger and had to be restrained. Kentucky, however, missed the shots and moments later turned over the possession. The Bruins rushed out to the win, 92-85, and Wooden took number 10 home to the trophy case.

TOURNAMENT NOTES: With 26 points against Louisville in the semis and 28 against Kentucky in the finals, Washington was named MVP.

Wooden was a three-time All-American in the 30s.

An Interview With John Wooden

John R. Wooden won 667 games and lost 161 in 29 years of college coaching. He has been elected to the Hall of Fame as both a player and a coach.

Packer—Coach, a lot of people wonder if, during the years before you took a team to your first national championship in 1962, you had a club capable of going to the Final Four?

Wooden—Well, I definitely think so Billy. Prior to winning our first championship, which was my 15th year, we had three or four teams that could have won. My second year at UCLA, in 1950, we came very close in the regionals at Kansas City, when Bradley beat us in a very close game. Bradley then lost to CCNY, and we had beaten CCNY by 10 points in Madison Square Garden. And I believe it was '56 or '57, when I had Willie Naulls, that we had a fine team. But we weren't quite as good as the University of San Francisco, and they knocked us off in the regionals. But I think we were good enough to have won that year.

Packer—Everyone says it's much more difficut now to get to a Final Four, much less win it. What do you think?

Wooden—I don't think it is. In my day, for example, you had to win your conference to get in. So we only played conference champions, and I think there were more quality teams then than there are today. In a recent Final Four, three of the teams had lost eight, nine or 10 games each during the year. My 10 national championship teams lost a total of 10 games. When three teams get to the Final Four that have lost eight or nine games during the year, I can't believe that it is more difficult to get to the Final Four today.

Packer—When was the first time that the NCAA championship meant anything to you personally?

Wooden—The first NCAA tournament was in '39. I didn't get interested in the tournament until after World War II when I got the coaching position at Indiana State. Of course, I played high school ball in Indiana, and I would say that, in my day, winning the Indiana high school tournament was as meaningful as winning the NCAA. I was involved in both. I'm an Indiana high school state champion and an NCAA champion. The state of Indiana was crazy about basketball.

Packer—At UCLA, you put together a winning string that most people say will never be matched again. I'd like to talk about two particular eras, the Jabbar years and the Walton years. The teams seemed so different, yet the results were the same. How would you compare them?

Wooden—Let's take the two individuals who were the outstanding individuals on the two teams. Kareem, of course, was the best performer of them all, and I think he is quite possibly the most valuable college player who ever played. Most valuable. That doesn't necessarily mean the same thing as saying he is the best player. But I believe he caused opponents more problems at each end of the court than any other center I know of. Bill probably was a better basketball player than Kareem. He passed a little better, not that Kareem was a bad passer, and I would say that Bill could probably shoot a little better. But he still wasn't that tremendous threat in there. Bill could rebound and initiate the fast break with the outlet pass better than anybody I have ever coached. Overall, I would say our set offense might have been better with Walton because we had people to fill all the roles. But our overall game was probably a little bit stronger in the Jabbar era just because I think he is tremendously valuable.

Kareem's first years I had Mike Warren and Lucius Allen, and when you got it out to them, they were gone. Our guards during the Walton era were not quite the equal of Warren and Allen, so even though we got the ball out better on our fast break, the fast break as a whole wasn't any better. Both Kareem and Bill were fine students, and they were both devoted to basketball when they came on the floor. Off the floor, they were two entirely different individuals. Kareem was somewhat of a recluse. You didn't know much about him off the floor. Bill was a rebel. Of course, during Bill's playing days, it was probably a little more rebellious time. He was fighting to end the Vietnam war and had various other causes. In between practice, I was always concerned about him.

Packer—You have one guy from San Diego who admitted he wanted to play for you since he attended one of your basketball clinics when he was 10 or 11 years old. And you have Kareem, a fellow who probably never met you until he came out here. Did you recruit these fellows the same way?

Wooden—Bill had an older brother, Bruce, who was on our football team. He was two years ahead of Bill, but Bill had come to football games with his parents. I had met Bill earlier. He was one of the few players outside the greater Los Angeles area that I went to watch play in high school and one of the few players I ever visited in his home. I thought from the very beginning he was going to come to UCLA.

Jabbar was most unusual. His high school coach called me after his junior year and said, "Coach, you're speaking in Valley Forge, Pennsylvania, in April. I'd like to come and talk to you about my player, Alcindor. You'll be pleased about what I have to say." He went on to tell me that Jabbar was going to visit five schools his senior year and that UCLA was one of his picks. Of course, that pleased me very much. When I talked to Jabbar's coach in Valley Forge, I asked him a favor. I asked him to let UCLA be the last of Jabbar's five visits, if possible. He said that nobody else had asked for that: he thought it would be all right. At the conclusion of his 48-hour visit, he said, "I'm coming to UCLA." Then, to show you what kind of individual he is, sometime later he called me and asked me if I would come and visit his folks. He said his parents would like to meet the coach for whom he was going to play. I talked to our athletic director and he said, "They're Catholic, so why don't you take along Jerry Norman [my assistant] because he's Catholic and they might want to ask you some questions." So Jerry and I took the trip, and we met Kareem's parents at one o'clock in the morning because his father was working the noon-to-midnight shift. I think what probably swayed Kareem more then anything was that we had just won our first national championship and had gone undefeated that year. The next year, his senior year, we won again. Now we really had his attention. Then, when he came out to UCLA, he saw that he would be playing in the new building, Pauley Pavilion. We would never have gotten him if we'd still been playing in that old gym with only two baskets, where I swept the floor every day before practice, and if we were still playing our home games at Santa Monica City College or Venice High School. To give you a better idea of his character, Kareem called me sometime after he had committed to UCLA and told me that his high school coach had taken the job at Holy Cross and had asked him to visit. He explained, "I said I was only going to visit five schools, but I feel I owe my coach a visit. I'm not going to Holy Cross, and he knows I'm not going to Holy Cross." I told him, "I agree with you one hundred percent, and I think you certainly owe him the visit." So, as far as recruiting was concerned, I hardly recruited Bill or Kareem at all. They more or less just came to UCLA on their own.

Packer—We hear a lot of coaches talk about the pressure of getting to the Final Four. Guys like Bobby Knight, who has won three championships, and Denny Crum, who has won two, say the pressure eases after that first one. Did you feel pressure to win the national championship in order to be accepted as a coach, and, after you won your first title, did the pressure decrease?

Wooden—Billy, I think the only pressure that really matters is the pressure you put on yourself. If you're affected by outside pressures, that's going to hamper your performance no matter what you're doing. I don't think I've permitted outside pressures to affect me ad-

versely. I wanted to do well, and I put pressure on myself. I wanted to win a national championship very much, and I think it's quite possible that, prior to winning one in 1964, I might have wanted it so much I hurt my players in one or two instances. I may have overworked them thinking that I had to really work hard, and that may have caused us not to play as well as we could. I never wanted to win one as badly as I wanted to win that first one. I never thought of winning it in terms of being accepted as a coach. But maybe I felt that without realizing it. After the first win, I never wanted one as badly, and, you know, they seemed to flow. Someone asked me, "How come it took you 15 years to win your first one at UCLA?" I said, "I'm a slow learner, but when I learn something, I get it down pretty good."

Packer—Today, coaches talk about getting their teams ready for the March run. Did you have a process where you tried to have your team to peak at tournament time?

Wooden—In my day, you had to win the conference to get into the NCAA tournament. It's a little different today. You can be fourth or fifth in your conference and still get to the tournament. When I was coaching, the ACC was the only major conference that was having a tournament that you had to win to get to the NCAAs. I felt that hurt their chances in the NCAA very much. When I would go back to Campbell College every summer and the reporters would ask me about this, I said I hoped they would keep it up as long as I was coaching because I think that lessened their chances of winning the NCAA tournament. Now, just about everyone is having a tournament. But to be quite honest with you, I don't like it. I like conference champions who are determined by playing each opponent home-and-home. I think that determines the best team in that conference. One year we were undefeated and won the championship, and USC lost only two games all year, both of them to us, and we didn't exactly run away from them in those two games. I think they were the second best team in the country and they didn't even get into the tournament. And I don't think they should have gone to the tournament. If I'd been in their position, I don't think I would have wanted to be in the tournament. At the beginning of the season, from the fifteenth of October to the first of December, I was trying to get our team in shape and trying to analyze personnel and find combinations that could work. By January, when conference play began, I wanted to know who the top seven players were and what combinations I was going to use. If we won the conference championship early enough, I slowed the team down to keep them fresh for the NCAA. Had I coached in the ACC, I wouldn't have coached the same. I would be playing for that ACC tournament. There would be some things against certain opponents in a regular season game that I wouldn't do I might have been saving something for the ACC tournament.

Wooden on the bench with assistant coach Gary Cunningham.

Packer —We've had some emotional championships lately. In watching your teams play all those times, they seemed to maintain a consistent level of performance without the need for inspirational speeches or anything. Was that by design?

Wooden—I don't believe in artificial motivational things; maybe with some individual now and then. For example, I might try to get Hazzard mad at me because, when he'd get mad at me, he'd show me. And there were times when I wanted to get Sidney Wicks mad at me because he'd show me. But if I tried to get Gail Goodrich mad at me, he'd go into a shell. You have to learn the personalities of the players. But generally speaking, I don't agree with the emotional approach. I think for every peak, there is a valley. If you were standing in the hallway of our dressing room when we came out for warmups, you never had to worry about being run over. I wanted our team to walk out slowly and warm up and not expend a lot of energy. I wanted to save that energy for the game. I didn't want a lot of cheering and yelling in the dressing room. I wanted peace and quiet so we could consider things and analyze things. I think there's the tendency by many coaches to get players overly motivated. Once in a while it works, but I think for every time it works, there may be a couple of times it affected them adversely.

Packer—Your first club that won the national championship was not considered to be a great team until you won the title. What was the makeup of that club?

Wooden—A lot of people don't realize that that team was very good the year before, and I had all five starters back. I had instituted the 2-2-1 zone press, and we won the conference championship. We were knocked off in the regionals by Arizona State. They had a tremendously hot-shooting team; they just hit everything they shot, and we got behind early and couldn't catch up. Our five starters on that team had different personalities. Keith Erickson was a great athlete. I've coached better basketball players, but never a better athlete. And to play that number five position in the press, he was just tremendous. I've never seen anyone come close to being his equal. And other players filled their roles in the zone press. In the one and four positions in the press, I prefer left-handers. And just by chance, I had left-handers in Gail Goodrich and Jack Hirsch. In the four position, I like a ball-handler, and I put Hazzard there. In the number two position, I had Fred Slaughter, not tall, but big and quick-of-foot. I had two quality substitutes, Kenny Washington and Doug McIntosh. I didn't think they were that good at the beginning of the year, but they came along very well and enabled us to have the type of rotation we needed. The players complemented each other extremely well, and they got to the point where being behind didn't mean anything to them. They knew they were going to get one of those spurts through our press, and they expected it. They expected a spurt in each half and, for the most part, we got them.

Packer—With the press, I think opponents start looking for it and get psyched out. Don't you think teams started looking around the corner anticipating the press?

Wooden—I think that's definitely true and I think that happened in the championship game at Duke. They led us 19-to-7, but it only took us two or three minutes to catch up, and we had a 12-point lead at the half. But the lead wasn't the thing, it was the look they had on their faces. They looked whipped.

Packer—Going back over your record in the championship matches, I see that in the Final Four you fellows were never behind at halftime.

Wooden—In every one of the championship games against 10 different opponents incidentally, we had the game won before the last minute. Now one or two ended up with a five- or six-point spread. Florida State came close, but we had the game won and were in no danger of losing. After we'd won two or three championships, I think opponents subconsciously might have been wondering if they could catch us.

Packer—Let's go through some individual games and tell me some memories you have of it. In '64, you beat Duke 98-83. Washington got 26 points.

Wooden—Washington came in; did a tremendous job. Most everyone felt Duke would win the game. In the hotel Saturday afternoon before the game that night, a group of coaches were talking and some of them said, "Johnny, Duke's a remarkable team. Remarkable and big. You've got a nice team, but it's amazing you've won 29." There was a Czech coach there who had spent some time during the year at different schools around the country, and somebody asked him, "What do you think about the game?" In cryptic English, he said "UCLA win." "And how can you say that, Duke's a big team?" they asked. He said, "Yeah, UCLA is team," and he held up his hand to represent our team. That's about as nice a compliment as a coach can get. And that year, we really played as a team.

Packer—In '65, you played Michigan, Cazzie Russell's great team, a team with a lot of power. You beat them 91 - 80 with Gail Goodrich getting 42 points.

Wooden—We were too quick for Michigan, even with Erickson hurt with a pulled groin muscle, Kenny Washington came in, and, for the second national championship in a row, got 26 or 27 points and just played a beautiful game. And Goodrich had taken over as the leader, the way Hazzard had done the year before.

Packer—Bill Bradley got 58 in the consolation game that year. People talk about that a lot but you said games

on the line might be a little tougher. That 42 might have been bigger then the 58.

Wooden—Bradley got his 50-some points in the consolation game against Wichita State. If you check the records, I think you will find that Goodrich got 42 in that championship final and played only half the game. I'm not saying that Goodrich is a better basketball player than Bill Bradley. I have nothing but great respect for Bill Bradley because I thought he was one of the all-time greats. But I did feel that, in that particular tournament, Goodrich was the most valuable player.

Packer—You were out of the Final Four in 1966, but in 1967, you were back and beat Dayton by 15 points. Kareem starts his run of championships.

Wooden—Kareem was amazing. As a freshman the year before, he was largely instrumental in beating our varsity. I think he amazed a lot of people in his early career, and I think a lot of them got so interested in watching him that they forgot to play on occasion. But he, like Walton, was a very unselfish player, and he made every player on our team much better at each end of the court.

Packer—In 1968, you beat North Carolina in the finals, 78-55, in what had to be one of the most crushing defeats for Dean Smith. But that year, the game I remember is the semifinals when you beat Houston 101 to 69. Elvin Hayes got just 10 points. I think that game was one of the greatest games any college team ever played.

Wooden—Of course, Houston was a great basketball team. They had a lot of talent, and Hayes was a great individual player. Early in the second half, we led them by 44 points, and we could have won by a lot more than we did. Our starting five all scored something like 14 to 18 points. Our players still felt from the loss to them in the Astrodome earlier in the year, which was a great spectacle. I don't think it was a great basketball game, but it was a great spectacle in which Elvin Hayes had one of the greatest individual performances I've ever seen. But, generally speaking, individual performances don't win basketball games. We felt that we were a better basketball team, and we sincerely hoped we would play them again, and when we did, we were ready.

Packer—You said earlier that you didn't get your team ready emotionally, but there had to be something a little special about that game with Houston.

Wooden—Unquestionably. We felt we were a better basketball team, and from the time they beat us they were the number one ranked team, as far as the polls were concerned. Polls are only man-made types of things and aren't all that meaningful, but, nevertheless, we knew about them. I felt my biggest problem would be to keep us from becoming too emotional, because the players really wanted that one. After that game, I thought we might have a tremendous letdown against North Carolina in the

UCLA's Gail Goodrich takes the hook shot amid a crowd of Stanford defenders.

championship game. Fortunately, we didn't.

Packer—The next year, Kareem was going for three straight championships. Against Purdue, your alma mater, he gets 37 in his final game as a UCLA player.

Wooden—Purdue had Rick Mount, a great player, and I had Kenny Heitz, a 6-3 guard play him. Kenny did a tremendous job of controlling Mount until we had the game well in hand. All our team wanted to see Kareem finish his college career with an outstanding game, and he did in every aspect.

Packer—Maybe the toughest game you ever had in the Final Four was in the semifinals that year against Drake

Wooden—They were very quick, and, as a coach, I always wanted quickness over size. I'd always take quickness over size. I think coaches want two things: you want players big, and you want them quick. But where some coaches would give up a little quickness for more size, I tried never to do that. Drake was about as quick as we were. Their center was not a great basketball player, but he was a great high jumper and he just played an outstanding game. They had good guards who gave us a lot of problems. It was a tight game right down to the wire.

Packer—OK, the whole nation breathes a sigh of relief; Kareem has left; it's all over for John Wooden; everybody has a shot at the national championship. But Sidney

Wicks leads you right back to the championship, and you beat Jacksonville 80-69.

Wooden—That is the team I call "The Team Without." And, of course, I mean without Alcindor. That was a team that gave me, among all the teams that I have coached, about as much personal satisfaction as any team. We had a lot of close games that year, but somehow they would pull them out at the end. Chuck Dressen, when he managed the Brooklyn Dodgers, used to tell his team, "Stay close for seven innings, and I'll think of something." And I used to say, if this team can stay close for 30 to 35 minutes, somehow we'll pull it out. Sidney had a great game against Artis Gilmore in the championship game.

Packer—The decision to put Sidney on Artis, was that a decision of the moment or the result of your scouting reports?

Wooden—I never scouted much Billy. We played man-to-man, but a good man-to-man must play zone principles. We were floating back and helping Sidney front Gilmore. But Sidney didn't want to play in front and he wasn't doing a very good job. Sidney said he could stop Gilmore by playing behind him. When we called timeout, I said, "Sidney, we'll go it your way and see what you can do." I had told him, essentially, "I don't think you can do it but you say you can." So Sidney got inspired. He played

UCLA'S Sidney Wicks

behind Gilmore and blocked a couple of Gilmore's shots, and got a couple of fast breaks on him, and before long, the game is going in our favor. Sidney did a magnificent job.

Packer—Sidney was always a bit of a renegade, and some coaches might have resented his attitude. But even in the heat of the battle, you maintained some flexibility about what you could do.

Wooden—I think you have to. I think you learn from your players and from your assistants, but you have to make the decisions. But you're not perfect and you're going to make mistakes. I think there are some who think they're perfect, and they're the ones I like to play against. I think you must be flexible. Sidney was a spirited individual, but I liked spirited players. I didn't want them temperamental, but I liked them very spirited. The next year, in the Villanova game, Sidney gave me one of the greatest thrills I've ever had. At the end of the ball game, we were shooting a free throw. There was just a second or so to go, and there was a timeout. Sidney came over and the whole team was huddled around me. When they turned to go back on the floor, Sidney came back and put out his hand and said, "Congratulations on another

championship, Coach." Then he returned to the sideline, and he leaned down and put out his hand and said, "Coach, you're really something." The tears came to my eyes because, just prior to that, I'd disciplined Sidney rather severely. No one likes to be disciplined, I know that. But he accepted it and then congratulated me . That was one of my most treasured moments of coaching.

Packer—You beat Villanova in '71. In '72, you have an entirely different cast again. The team is no longer "without" because here comes Bill Walton, although a lot lof people doubted that a sophomore could carry the team. Maryland had the highly touted Tom McMillan. But you made it back to the championship finals and you beat Florida State.

Wooden—Two years earlier, Tom McMillan was considered to be the greatest prospect in the country. I thought, "If he's better than this Walton boy, then he's really something." I'd never seen Tom, and I'd never been in contact with him. But I had seen Walton, and I knew his capabilities. He's another one who made all the players around him better. He was probably the greatest at getting the ball off the boards and initiating a fastbreak. I had another great player who was so smooth and silky that he never got due credit, in my opinion. That was Keith Wilkes. Players have a tendency to nickname teammates, and they gave Keith the name "Silk." Speaking of that, let me add something that has nothing to do with this. In the late '50s, I had two players, one called "Iron Hands" and the other called "Stone Fingers." And do you know what those two have become?

Packer—Not surgeons, please!

Wooden—They are dentists, and both have done exceptionally well. I tease them whenever I see them. They'd never work on my teeth!

Packer—We get to the game against Memphis State. Everybody I have talked to who are students of the game consider Walton's performance in that game to be the finest in Final Four history.

Wooden—All I can say is they apparently didn't see Goodrich against Michigan in '65. Walton had a great game scoring-wise. But he let Kenon score more against him than Kenon should have scored. Kenon got rebounds against him that he should have never gotten. Bill took 22 field goal attempts and made 21, but most of them were lay-ins from passes.

Packer—Well, Bill admits that himself. He says he didn't have a hard shot all night.

Wooden—Well, he's modest. Greg Lee had something like 11 or 12 assists, and Larry Hollyfield, who wasn't particularly known for his assists, had 9 or 10. But Bill did a great job, and it was a great game, and I don't want to take anything away from him, but I don't think that was his greatest game. I think I can name many games when he played all-around better for us.

Packer—The lob pass was so popular in that game and has obviously become a critical weapon on the college scene and in the pros. In talking with Larry Farmer, he said the first time that was put in your offense was not for Walton, but as a Lee to Farmer pass.

Wooden—Yes, he's right. We pulled Bill up halfway to the high post. Then we reversed Larry on the weak side, faked the pass to Bill, and threw it high to Larry for the dunk. Larry was a fine jumper and he had good hands.

Packer—Most people assumed that your ball club, with Walton in his senior year, would win the championship again. But NC State knocked you off in the semifinals. Most of your players feel they should have won that game.

Wooden—I don't know if it would be fair to North Carolina State to say we should have won . I'll certainly say we could have won, and I think in most times we could have won. But you know they weren't a bad team. They lost one game all year long. And do you know to whom they lost that game.

Packer—Yes, to UCLA early in the year.

Wooden—Yes, we won the wrong one. Even today, people remind me of that. But they were a fine basketball team and I don't believe I would be giving them due credit if I said we should have won, because there are many games where it may appear that the wrong team won. We made some critical mistakes when we had a seven-point lead in the overtime, which I don' t think we were normally prone to make. Normally, we weren't going to blow a seven-point lead. We missed a couple of easy shots and made a couple of turnovers and had two charging fouls when we were trying to protect the ball. Nobody was charging at all. So we made some critical mistakes and North Carolina State took advantage of them and won, and they deserved it.

Packer—Your last Final Four was the first one I had a chance to broadcast. I'll never forget the semifinal game when you went up against your old pupil for the second time. It was a semifinal game that you pulled out at the very end.

Wooden—I still say that our game against Louisville was one of the better-played games in NCAA basketball history. It was a game that I feel neither team should have won, because if one wins, the other has to lose. We knew each other's style of play so well, and we were both using the high-post offense and had quick players. I think they were a little quicker then we were, actually. It was a tremendous basketball game. Being very close to Denny, I didn't want to win, but I certainly didn't want to lose.

Packer—When the game ended, you shocked the sports community when you walked across the floor and announced that you would be coaching your last game that Monday. When did you make that decision?

Wooden—That moment. Not that it hadn't been contemplated, somewhat. My wife, Nellie, wanted me to retire. I had had a little heart problem a few years before, and she was concerned. But it wasn't that entirely. Something else happened earlier that had hurt me, to be honest Billy, and I've never talked about this before. I was hurt by something the chairman of the tournament committee said when the rule was passed that you had to let the press into your dressing room after games. I did not like the press in the dressing room. Dressing rooms for basketball are always small, and they only want to talk to a few people, and you've got a bunch of youngsters in there trying to shower and dress. I'd always let the press in on the last day of the season and all that. But if they felt that was necessary, I wouldn't complain about that. I didn't like it, still don't like it; but when they put it in I accepted it. But he didn't have to say, "This will take care of Johnny Wooden." That hurt me because, I say to this day, I don't think they've had a coach who was any more cooperative with them in all things. I attended all meetings at the Final Four for years. I saw many times when many coaches didn't show up, and I did everything that was asked, and then for him to come up and, because I disagreed with this one thing, make that statement, well; that hurt me and I didn't like it. The chairman of the committee wrote me a letter of apology and kind of indicated that he might have been misquoted, and maybe he was. I don't know but I

John Wooden talks to his players during a break.

was hurt by it. I went down to talk to Denny, and I felt wrung out. I felt completely wrung out, and I knew that there was going to be an enormous crowd in the press room and those lights were going to be in my face, and I got to the point where that kind of bothered me. I hoped I don't let them know, but I dreaded going in there. Instead of going straight to the press room, I went to the dressing room and told my players. I congratulated them on an outstanding game and said that this would be my last game. This shocked all of them of course. And then I went to the press room, and when the time came for press remarks, I made the statement that that would be my last

game. There were those who felt that I did it to hype up my team to play Kentucky. I never did it to hype up my team. I thought all along that we had a better chance against Kentucky than we had against Louisville because we were quicker then Kentucky. They were big and strong, but we were quick.

Packer—So you coach your last game, win another national championship, and finish an era that probably never is going to be duplicated by anybody. Everybody says that except one guy. You're the only one person who believes it could be done again.

Wooden—Billy, if anyone had said to you in 1962 that

in the next 10 or 12 years some team was going to win 10 national championships, what would you have said?

Packer—No way.

Wooden—You would have said, "You're crazy," wouldn't you?

Packer—That's right.

Wooden—Think you would be any crazier today to say it?

Packer—I think I would have been crazy then. I think I would be crazy now.

Wooden—I feel exactly the same way. I think it was a crazy thing to think anyone could do it. It happened, and I think it's no more crazy today. In some ways, I think it would be easier today because you can get into the tournament sometimes by finishing fourth or fifth in your conference. Also you have freshmen who can play, and you can get a roll started. I've always contended that it's more difficult to get to the Top Ten than it is to stay on top. As I said earlier, Alcindor wouldn't have come except that we'd won in '64 and '65. Our winning with him helped attract other players. One of my most disappointing recruiting loses was Paul Westphal. I have great respect and admiration for him as a person and as a player. I visited at his home on a Saturday, and his parents said he was coming to UCLA, but on Monday he signed to go with USC. He wanted to go somewhere and help knock UCLA off rather than go to UCLA and help us do what we'd been doing. It's with considerable pride that I say he wasn't able to do this. Through '85, the Big Ten had more teams than anyone else in the Final Four. They had 27. The Pack 10 was next with 25 times in the Final Four. The ACC was next with 20, the Big Eight was next with 19, and SEC was next with 13. But in the SEC, 10 of those 13 were by Kentucky. In the ACC, nine of those 20 were by North Carolina. The Big Eight was spread out a little more, with Kansas State 5, Oklahoma State 4, and Oklahoma 2. In the Big Ten, who would you say the leader is, Billy?

Packer—Well right away you say Indiana, but it isn't Indiana.

Wooden—Ohio State, with eight times and Indiana with 5. In the PAC 10, UCLA was in 14 times, two of those after I retired, once with Bartow, then with Larry Brown taking the championship. Cal was there three times and Oregon State was there twice. Stanford was there only one time, and won it.

Here's something that a North Carolina person brought up to me. A fellow came up to me and asked me how many times a team won the NCAA with undefeated seasons?

Packer—San Francisco did it. You did it on a number of occasions. North Carolina did it did it once. Indiana did it once. I'd say eight or fewer.

Wooden—You're right, plus Kentucky did it. We did it four times.

Henry Bibby, 1972 All-American guard for UCLA.

Bob's Brigade

Bobby Knight was frustrated by the '75 season and determined to win the title in '76.

If any coach could lay claim to dominating the post Wooden years of college basketball, perhaps Bobby Knight could. His Indiana teams won three titles between 1976 and 1987. But in reality, no coach can claim superiority. As the NCAA tournament expanded, opportunity increased with it. College ball became a snazzy little round robin of competition with a variety of programs pausing in their share of the limelight. Marquette. Kentucky. Michigan State. Louisville. Indiana. North Carolina. North Carolina State. Georgetown. Villanova. Louisville, again. Indiana, again.

Knight got the kaleidoscope spinning with a perfect season, 33-0, from his 1976 team. Following the Hoosiers' defeat in the '75 regionals, Knight dragged his disappointment home to Bloomington and set to work immediately. Although Steve Green graduated from the "greatest team ever," Knight had Tom Abernethy as a waiting replacement. Kent Benson and Scott May were the All Americans around which the strategy was built. Quinn Buckner was the playmaker, and 6-foot-7 guard Bobby

Wilkerson, a role-playing rebounder, rounded out the starters.

The Hoosiers blasted UCLA—now coached by Gene Bartow—by 20 points during the regular season, then polished off the Big Ten and the rest of the schedule with nothing more than a few minor scrapes. They entered the Mideast Regional as the nation's raging power. May scored 33 and Kent Benson 20 as they blew by St. John's, 90-70. They struggled a bit with Alabama, but May's 25 points and 16 rebounds helped them over the hump. In the regional finals, second-ranked Marquette was the challenge. The Warriors led by one at intermission, but Knight's players turned on the afterburners in the second half to win, 65-56.

After the regular-season pasting by Indiana, UCLA regained its footing on the talents of Marques Johnson and Richard Washington. The Bruins pushed through the West Regional, putting away San Diego State, Pepperdine and Arizona to make yet another Final Four.

To help celebrate the United State's 200th birthday, NCAA officials held the 1976 Final Four in Philadelphia's Spectrum. In acknowledgement of the heartland, Michigan gave the Big Ten its second team in the Finals. (Before the finals, Knight would call me from the broadcast booth over to his team huddle and ask, "Packer, where the hell is the ACC now?" I thought he had wanted to discuss some important strategy, but before a big game all he was interested in was a little regional one upmanship).

Led by Rickey Green, Steve Grote, Phil Hubbard and John Robinson and coached by Johnny Orr, the Wolverines had sweated past Wichita State, Notre Dame and

Knight and Indiana Athletic Director Bill Orwig.

Missouri in the Midwest. Their mate in the national semifinals was undefeated Rutgers, the winner in the East over Princeton, Connecticutt, and Virginia Military The Scarlet Knights featured Phil Sellers, Mike Dabney and Ed Jordan, but their well of wins dried up against Michigan. The Wolverines loped to a 46-29 lead at the half and walked in from there, 86-70.

UCLA had no better luck against Indiana in the other semi. The Hoosiers gained control immediately and squeezed the score the whole way before finishing the Bruins, 65-51. Benson led four Hoosiers in double figures with 16.

The Big Ten matchup in the final seemed like it would be a thriller in the first half, as Michigan took a 10-point lead. But Indiana opened the second stanza with a burst of power. May scored 25, Benson 25, and the Hoosiers rolled to Knight's second title, 86-68.

TOURNAMENT NOTES: Benson was named MVP and was joined on the all-tournament team by May and Abernethy. Green from Michigan and Johnson from UCLA rounded it out.

Left—Indiana's Kent Benson was the MVP for 1976

1976					
Michigan	fg-fga	ft-fta	rb	pf	tp
W. Britt	5- 6	1- 1	3	5	11
J. Robinson	4- 8	0- 1	6	2	8
P. Hubbard	4- 8	2- 2	11	5	10
R. Green	7-16	4- 5	6	3	18
S. Grote	4- 9	4- 6	1	4	12
T. Bergen	0- 1	0- 0	0	1	0
T. Staton	2- 5	3- 4	2	3	7
D. Baxter	0- 2	0- 0	0	2	0
J. Thompson	0- 0	0- 0	0	0	0
A. Hardy	1- 2	0- 0	2	0	2
Team			1		
Totals	27-57	14-19	32	25	68
Indiana	fg-fga	ft-fta	rb	pf	tp
T. Abernethy	4- 8	3- 3	4	2	11
S. May	10-17	6- 6	8	4	26
K. Benson	11-20	3- 5	9	3	25
B. Wilkerson	0- 1	0- 0	0	1	0
Q. Buckner	5-10	6- 9	8	4	16
W. Radford	0- 1	0- 0	1	0	0
J. Crews	0- 1	2- 2	1	1	2
J. Wisman	0- 1	2- 3	1	4	2
R. Valavicius	1- 1	0- 0	0	0	2
M. Haymore	1- 1	0- 0	1	0	2
B. Bender	0- 0	0- 0	0	0	0
Team			3		
Totals	32-61	22-28	36	19	86

Half time: Michigan 35-29. Officials: Wortman and Brown. Attendance: 17,540.

(Al)—lelujah

College basketball and network television found the ingredients for a potent chemistry with the 1977 NCAA tournament. The reaction was a starburst. At its center was the key, albeit volatile, element: Marquette Coach Al McGuire.

McGuire wasn't the whole story in '77. It was also the year the dunk returned to college ball after a nine-year absence. And Dean Smith and North Carolina made the four corners offense famous, or infamous.

By now, almost everyone knows the book on my pal, Al. Schooled in the streets of Queens, New York. The younger, less talented brother of Dick McGuire. Played at St. John's, then a stint in the pros. Got his first head coaching at Belmont Abbey, a small college in North Carolina. Emerges there as a feisty, eccentric competitor. Gets the job at Marquette and focuses the full force of his competitiveness on building an independent power.

McGuire inherited a 20-game loser and turned it into a 20-game winner. He had a knack for attracting city-tough players to Wisconsin, although he was never a great recruiter. He took all that inner-city energy and harnessed it into the picture of precision basketball, teethed with a spirit-breaking defense.

By 1977, he had won the NIT and been to eight NCAA tournaments, rising to the finals in 1974 before losing to NC State. But, as he often reminds me, Al felt basketball; he didn't live it and breath it. He was never a hoops junkie. So early in the '77 season, while his team was struggling and appeared headed nowhere, he grew weary of the grind and announced his retirement, effective at the close of the campaign.

Pardon the cliche, but what happened from there was pure storybook. Al's Warriors came alive, hit a winning streak, and rode it into basketball history. When it was over, Al was an overnight sensation, a media star created by the moment, and Marquette was the NCAA champion.

Heading into the tournament, Johnny Orr's Michigan Wolverines appeared to be the chosen ones. They were top-ranked and had been to the finals the previous year. With forward John Robinson, center Phil Hubbard, and guards Rickey Green and Steve Grote, Orr had a team of pure power. Yet they sensed their power a little too much, grew a tad overconfident, and were upset in the Mideast Regionals by Cornbread Maxwell and UNC-Charlotte.

North Carolina also had a grand team with Walter Davis, Phil Ford, Mike O'Koren, Tommy LaGarde and Rich Yonakor, but injuries to Ford and LaGarde left the Heels limping into the Final Four at Atlanta's Omni. To overcome their injuries, they had come to rely on the four corners, the stall game. It would carry them to the finals, but not to the title.

The competition in Atlanta produced perhaps the most entertaining Final Four ever. The champion of the West Regional was Nevada-Las Vegas with Reggie Theus. Matched against Carolina in the semis, the Runnin' Rebels opened a 10-point lead, then watched Yonakor and O'Koren snatch it back with a burst of offense. Holding a slim lead, Smith called for the four corners with more than 15 minutes left in the game. The Heels held on, made their free throws, and somehow won, 84-83.

In the other semi, McGuire's team with guard Butch Lee, center Bernard Toone and Jerome Whitehead, squeezed through a tight, low-scoring match with UNCC. At the buzzer, Whitehead scored in close, and the officials had to think it over. Finally, they ruled the shot good and Marquette the winner, 51-49.

Smith had coached well to overcome his team's injuries, but in the final, luck left him. It appeared to be a runaway at the half, as Marquette led, 39-27. But the Tar Heels worked their way back and nosed into the lead, 45-43, with just under 14 minutes left. Smith called for the four corners, and McGuire was waiting. His players sagged to protect against the backdoor play, regained the lead, and gladly stepped to the free-throw line when Carolina was forced to foul.

McGuire then showed he had a mean little delay game of his own, as Marquette won, 67-59. Al, of course, wept on the bench before the TV audience. His zany antics had captured America's imagination, and suddenly network executives were thinking this NCAA tournament might be a bigger event than they had first thought.

TOURNAMENT NOTES: Butch Lee, with 19 points, was named the tournament MVP. My pal Al, of course, graduated to an analyst spot at NBC.

Marquette's Butch Lee splits the North Carolina defense as he heads to the basket in the 1977 championship game. He scored 19 points. Inset (L - R)—Marquette Coach Al McGuire, Asst. Coach "Hank" Raymonds and Asst. Rick Majerus begin to sense they have won the 1977 national championship.

1977

North Carolina	fg-fga	ft-fta	rb	pf	tp
W. Davis	6-13	8-10	8	4	20
M. O'Koren	6-10	2- 4	11	5	14
R. Yonakor	3- 5	0- 0	4	0	6
P. Ford	3-10	0- 0	2	3	6
J. Kuester	2- 6	1- 2	0	5	5
S. Krafcisin	1- 1	0- 0	0	0	2
T. Zaliagiris	2- 3	0- 0	0	3	4
D. Bradley	1- 1	0- 0	0	2	2
B. Buckley	0- 1	0- 0	0	1	0
J. Wolf	0- 1	0- 0	1	0	0
D. Colescott	0- 0	0- 0	0	0	0
W. Coley	0- 0	0- 0	0	0	0
G. Doughton	0- 0	0- 0	0	0	0
J. Virgil	0- 0	0- 0	0	1	0
Team			2		
Totals	24-51	11-16	28	24	59

Marquette	fg-fga	ft-fta	rb	pf	tp
B. Ellis	5- 9	4- 5	9	4	14
B. Neary	0- 2	0- 0	0	1	0
J. Whitehead	2- 8	4- 4	11	2	8
B. Lee	6-14	7- 7	3	1	19
J. Boylan	5- 7	4- 4	4	3	14
G. Rosenberger	1- 1	4- 4	1	1	6
B. Toone	3- 6	0- 1	0	1	6
Team			1		
Totals	22-47	23-25	29	13	67

Half time: Marquette 39-27. Officials: Galvan and Copeland. Attendance: 16,086.

Wildcats Once Again

The NCAA tournament came into its 40th birthday with a healthy mix of competition. There were newcomers in Indiana State, led by junior Larry Bird, and Michigan State, led by freshman Earvin Johnson. But the development of their fortunes was a year away.

The 1978 Final Four would be the domain of the Kentucky Wildcats and Coach Joe B. Hall, who had been a substitute on Adolph Rupp's 1949 championship team. Hall had served as Rupp's assistant in later years, then took on the unenviable task of succeeding the legend.

Hall's record as a coach was superior by any standards except those of Kentucky fanatics. He had taken his team to the NCAA championship game in '75, losing to Wooden's last UCLA squad. He had won the NIT the next year, then lost in the regional finals in '77.

Finally, the planets were aligned in Hall's favor in '78. His lineup featured the inside power of Rick Robey and Mike Phillips, the scoring finesse of All-American forward Jack "Goose" Givens and the guard play of sophomore Kyle Macy, a transfer from Purdue.

They entered the Mideast Regional ranked number one in the country with a 25-2 record. Third-ranked Marquette also was there, but the Warriors were upset in the first round by Miami of Ohio. With that, the Wildcats' real test came in the regional finals against Michigan State. In a snail's game, Kentucky squeezed by, 52-49, leaving some to argue that the NCAA championship had been settled in the regionals.

In the East, a young Duke team with Mike Gminski, Gene Banks and Jim Spanarkel struggled past Rhode Island and Penn before blasting Villanova to gain the Final Four in St. Louis.

Notre Dame rode through the Midwest in a scoring whirlwind blown up by Kelly Tripucka and Duck Williams. Their victims, by large margins, were Houston, Utah and DePaul.

In the West, it was Eddie Sutton's Arkansas bunch, with Sidney Moncrief and Ron Brewer, that prevailed over Weber State, UCLA and Fullerton State.

Gminski made 13 of 17 from the floor to score 29 points in pushing Duke past Notre Dame in one semifinal. Duke guard John Harrell made two free throws in the closing seconds to preserve the win, 90-86.

In the other semifinal, Kentucky fell back on its defense to defeat the small, determined Razorbacks. Forced to abandon their man-to-man because of foul trouble, the Razorbacks switched back to their pressure in the second half and pulled close before losing, 64-59. Givens led

Kentucky's Jack "Goose" Givens puts up a soft one-hander in the 1978 championship battle against Duke. Opposite—Duke's Gene Banks fires off a shot against a Kentucky defender.

Kentucky with 23 points and 9 rebounds. High-jumping senior sub James Lee had 13 points.

In the championship, Givens and Kentucky shredded the Duke zone. The All-American forward hit 18 of 27 from the floor, including a string of line-drive jumpers, for 41 points. The Blue Devils rushed on strong in the last two minutes when Hall pulled his starters with an 11-point lead. He put them back in, and Kentucky held on for its fifth national title, 94-88.

TOURNAMENT NOTES: Givens was named MVP and joined Robey, Gminski, Spanarkel, and Brewer on the All-Tournament team.

1978

Duke	fg-fga	ft-fta	rb	pf	tp
E. Banks	6-12	10-12	8	2	22
K. Dennard	5- 7	0- 0	8	5	10
M. Gminski	6-16	8- 8	12	3	20
J. Harrell	2- 2	0- 0	0	3	4
J. Spanarkel	8-16	5- 6	2	4	21
J. Suddath	1- 3	2- 3	2	1	4
B. Bender	1- 2	5- 5	1	3	7
S. Goetsch	0- 1	0- 0	1	1	0
Team			1		
Totals	29-59	30-34	35	22	88

Kentucky	fg-fga	ft-fta	rb	pf	tp
J. Givens	18-27	5- 8	8	4	41
R. Robey	8-11	4- 6	11	2	20
M. Phillips	1- 4	2- 2	2	5	4
K. Macy	3- 3	3- 4	0	1	9
T. Claytor	3- 5	2- 4	0	2	8
J. Lee	4- 8	0- 0	4	4	8
J. Shidler	1- 5	0- 1	1	3	2
C. Aleksinas	0- 0	0- 0	0	1	0
L. Williams	1- 3	0- 0	4	2	2
F. Cowan	0- 2	0- 0	2	1	0
T. Stephens	0- 0	0- 0	0	0	0
S. Courts	0- 0	0- 0	0	0	0
C. Gettelfinger	0- 0	0- 0	0	0	0
D. Casey	0- 0	0- 0	0	1	0
Team			0		
Totals	39-68	16-25	32	26	94

Half time: Kentucky 45-38. Officials: Bain and Clymer. Attendance: 18,721.

An Interview With Joe B. Hall

Coach Joe Hall led Kentucky to the NCAA championship in 1978. In the late 1940s, he played at Kentucky for coach Adolph Rupp.

Packer—Joe, I don't think during the time I've covered the Final Four that there's ever been a championship game in which a player had a more perfect game than Jack Givens. People talk about Bill Walton's game, but that day against Duke University, Jack played about as fine a game as you can play.

Hall—He certainly did. He had a hot hand and scored the last 16 points before the half ended. In the second half, one of his shots from the corner banked in from the side of the backboard. That showed the kind of streak he was on. But the Duke zone opened up the middle for Jack and allowed him to flash into the middle. We practically discarded the rest of our zone offense and had Jack flash from the weak side to the middle of the zone. The Duke zone was set up primarily to stop our big inside players, Rick Robey and Mike Phillips. We also had good outside shooters in Kyle Macy and Truman Claytor. Duke liked to stimulate action in order to produce turnovers and ignite their fastbreak. Their guards came out a little higher than normal to put pressure on Macy and Claytor. The big men, Gminski in particular, stayed back under the basket to protect against Robey and Phillips. That opened up the middle and allowed Jack to receive the pass in the middle and either get off a quick shot or pump fake and go up for his shot.

Packer—Joe, I can remember when that year started, it was one of those years when everybody said it's everybody against Kentucky. You were a prohibitive favorite to win, and you were able to do that. It's very difficult to start off the season in October with everybody shooting for you and come out at the end with the championship. How did you handle those great expectations?

Hall—I've often said that the '76-'77 year probably produced the national championship for us. We had a very good ball club that year, but it was a junior-dominated club. The only change in the team was the addition of Kyle Macy at one guard spot in '78. The '77 team really worked well all season long. They lost in the East finals to North Carolina, but we came out of that season with a renewed dedication. Each of our practices is rated by the coaching staff, and the '78 team only had about four practices that we felt were par, and all the rest had been excellent. It was the dedication of those young men that led to the championship. It was such a disappointment in

Kentucky Coach Joe B. Hall ponders game strategy.

'77 not to get to the Final Four that they rededicated themselves and worked hard the next year.

Packer—In the eyes of most people, the only way the '77 team could succeed was by winning the national championship. Anything less would have been seen as a failure. Did you feel the same or was that just something that members of the press or fans felt?

Hall—When you're picked number one, there's only one way to go. Sure we felt that pressure that we were supposed to win the championship. But I think that the real pressure came from within. The seniors on that club had been freshmen on the '75 team that was the first Kentucky team to get to the Final Four since 1966. In '75, we had a group of seniors and we had a group of freshmen. At that Final Four in San Diego, we just had a great time. Our players went to everything that was available—Marineland, the San Diego Zoo, all of the social events, an Easter egg hunt, an outdoor church service on

Easter morning. We enjoyed everything that was associated with the Final Four. We lost in that Final Four, however. When we came back in '78, the freshmen on that team were seniors, Robey, Phillips, Givens, and Lee. They set the tempo for the rest of the players, and they were there not to have a good time. They were there to win the national championship, not to be distracted, not to defeat themselves. When we played the semifinal game against Arkansas, I believe Duke had already defeated Notre Dame in the other semifinal game. After their win, the Duke players put Bill Foster in the shower and had a victory celebration in their locker room. After our victory over Arkansas, everything was quiet. The players went about their business, taking their uniforms off, getting their showers; the press kind of mingled in the locker room quietly. We had a squad meeting before we left the dressing room for the hotel, and I told the players you really worked hard, you're serious-minded, you won the game, we're going to the finals, so let's relax tonight, get away from the hotel and the crowd, go out someplace where we won't be distracted, have dinner, go to a movie, and get basketball off our minds. And I really thought that that was what they should do. Rick Robey spoke up, and he said, "Coach, did you tape the Duke-Notre Dame game?" I said we had, and he said, "Well, we would like to stay in our rooms and watch the tape of that game." Here was a group of young men who set a goal for themselves, had felt the pressure all year, but who were determined to win the national championship. I could not have orchestrated it any better than those kids did themselves. To the press, they were cold and calculating, but they were like any other group of young men. They had tremendous times. Now, at our yearly reunions of that championship team, they tell stories and joke and cut up about things that happened through the years. They did not celebrate until the race was won.

Packer—Along the way to the championship, it seems every team has had a game in which they really had to battle and show their merits early in the tournament. I think of your game against Michigan State, a strong club that marched through the tournament to the title the very next year. It was close, 52-49, and you win because Kyle Macy hit 10 of 11 from the foul line.

Hall—That was the toughest game we had along the way. Michigan State had Magic Johnson, Jay Vincent, and Greg Kelser. Jud Heathcote had a super 2-3 zone defense that was very difficult to penetrate. Their two men out front were very fast, and we went in at half time behind. We were having trouble getting the ball inside to our big people and also having trouble getting the outside shot that we normally got if the team defended well inside. We came out at halftime and decided to use Robey as a screen on the high post. But our feelings were that we had to get Macy the shot because we still were not effective inside. The screen worked, Macy got several baskets coming off

the pick, Michigan State begn to foul him, and he stepped to the foul line and hit the crucial free throws. That was probably a turning point in that game, our screening against their zone. After the game was over, I predicted that Michigan State would win the national championship the next year, which they did.

Packer—In 1975 in the semifinals, you beat Syracuse and UCLA beat Louisville. When John Wooden announced his retirement after that game, how did that extra emotional issue affect your team?

Hall—Well, I felt helpless. I was too young to resign at Kentucky! I knew the psychological impact Wooden's announcement would have. There was no question in my mind that 90 percent of the people in that arena would want to see John Wooden go out a winner. Plus we were playing in San Diego with a predominantly California crowd; the whole atmosphere was California. And here was the most successful coach in the nation playing his last game in an NCAA final, which he had already won nine times. And there was no question in my mind that that was going to be a big obstacle to overcome.

Packer—There probably has never been a half that was more frustrating to a coach or team than what happened in '83 when you played Georgetown in the Final Four in Seattle. I think if you had played Georgetown in a 20-game series, you would've ended up 10 and 10. They got a scoring run going and your team just couldn't get it together.

Hall—In the first half, we had shot a good 50 percent and went to the locker room with a seven-point lead. But I didn't feel too comfortable with the lead at the start of the second half, because Georgetown had begun to press with intensity and I could see the momentum starting to swing. I think John Thompson's team came out that second half with the attitude, "Look, we're behind, we have nothing to lose, we're going to really put our bodies on them, and see what the officials will allow us to do." And I think that's good coaching. They came out in a much tighter full court press and physically put the pressure on our players, and I think that swung the game. We had good shooters, boys like Jim Master, Dickie Beal, and certainly Bowie, Turpin and Kenny Walker, although Kenny was probably not up to par because of a back injury. But I had confidence that after each missed shot the next one was going to fall and that our scoring drought could not continue. But it did. But with just a few minutes to go, we were still very much in the game, and a basket could have put us within one or two points of Georgetown. But we missed layups, we missed tip-ins, we missed 15-foot bank shots from the side, and the ball just would not fall.

Packer—Joe, when you were a high school kid in Kentucky, how did the Baron, Adolph Rupp, and the Kentucky basketball fervor affect you?

Hall—Up in Bennett, Kentucky, about all that I had

ever known growing up was Kentucky basketball and Coach Adolph Rupp. And I guess that as a high school player, to have Coach Rupp in the stands was about as big a thrill as you could have. Every kid who loved basketball in the state of Kentucky followed the University of Kentucky. I was no different. I was a fan long before I was a player at Kentucky. I kept my scrapbook on Kentucky basketball from the time I could remember anything about the game. And I'm sure that many other aspiring players did, also. Coach Rupp had been at the University of Kentucky since 1931, so when I arrived on the scene, he'd been there 17 years. When I was a high school player, he attended one of my games. I didn't find that out until the game was over, but that was a great thrill to me as a young man.

Packer—Can you remember the first time you ever had a chance to talk to him?

Hall—I guess it was when I tried out. For the most part, Coach Lancaster and the team manager ran the tryouts, and Coach Rupp sat up high in the stands. I just remember that I was on the campus one weekend with high school all-staters from all over the nation, and we were on the floor when Coach Rupp and Coach Lancaster were coming out of their office, and Coach says, "Harry, lez go upstayers sinz yew can see so much damn better." And I guess that was the first thing I ever heard him say. After about 70 of us scrimmaged the whole Saturday morning, the manager came down and called my name, and asked me to come back the next weekend. I came back, and there was a new group of players and we went at it again. That's the way recruiting was done back then. I was a freshman the '47-'48 season, and Kentucky had the "Fabulous Five." Four of them returned my sophomore year, and we called our twelve-man squad the "Fabulous Five and the Sorry Seven." I was so far down at the end of the bench that I didn't get into the games very often.

Packer—The '48 and '49 teams certainly have to go down in collegiate history as among the best teams that ever played. Alex Groza and Ralph Beard, tell me a little about those two players.

Hall—Groza was the big man, certainly one of the finest in the country. He was only 6'7", but he was a scoring machine. He understood the game, and he wasn't intimidated. Yet he wasn't interested in roughing up his opponent; he was interested in winning and contributing to the team's success. He got along well with the players and was very likable. That team had tremendous maturity, because they had a lot of Army veterans, including Groza. Cliff Barker was 28-years-old and had been in a German prisoner-of-war camp for 18 months, and if that doesn't lend maturity to a ball club, then I don't know what would.

Packer-In the final game in '49, Kentucky played Oklahoma A&M and beat Coach Iba's team, 46-36. Groza got 25 and Beard only got 3.

Hall—I've often said that Ralph Beard could step on the floor today and be an outstanding basketball player without changing skills at all. He was such a competitor, a defensive ball-hawk and outstanding scorer, just a tremendous athlete. Beard had ups and downs because he had games that the opposition really concentrated on stopping him. Many teams felt that if they could stop Ralph Beard, they could stop Kentucky.

Packer—What was his forte?

Hall—He had the greatest quickness of anyone I've ever seen on the basketball floor. One time he was guarding me in practice, and we were on the fastbreak and I had the ball, dribbling as fast as I could go. I wasn't any speed merchant, but I was leading the way down the floor, and Beard was on my side and he tripped and fell. He rolled over on the floor and back up on his feet and never lost a step and took me away from the basket on the break.

Packer—I'm going to ask you about various teams and you can interject about Coach Rupp and so forth. In 1951, Kentucky beat Kansas State in the Final Four, with Spivey. Obviously another guy ahead of his time in terms of his ability to play. He had a great tournament there. Do you remember much about him?

Hall—I remember a lot about Spivey. He was a freshman my sophomore year. I remember when he first came in to try out at Kentucky in the spring of his senior year in high school. He was 7 feet tall and weighed something under 170 pounds. One of the first things they did was get some weight on him. The year that Spivey was recruited, Coach Rupp took the team on tour in Europe, but Coach Lancaster was back at the University working with Spivey, and he was watching his diet more than he was watching his playing. Coach Lancaster would send reports to Coach Rupp overseas about Spivey's weight. When Lancaster reported that Spivey had broken the 200-pound mark, Coach Rupp wired back, "I know he can eat, but can he play?" He played very well as a freshman, although he needed a lot of work in hand and eye coordination and developing his shot. But he developed a hook shot, became a good rebounder and shot blocker, and was one of the first really big men ever to play in Kentucky.

Packer—Ramsey and Hagan, two names synonymous with the great players in the history of the game. How about their abilities?

Hall—Hagan and Ramsey were different type players. Hagan, at 6-4, was a center and played pretty much with his back to the basket. Ramsey, also at 6-4, was a guard. Ramsey was a courageous, slashing type guard who would drive with the ball to the basket and either get the shot or kick off. He was a full court man and always in the action. Hagan was strong, an unbelievably effective player for his size, and I saw him dominate his opponent with physical strength and courage. He was a complete player. He was a great jumper, he could shoot facing the basket, he could use the hook shot, he positioned himself well, he had great hands, great touch, and tremendous passing ability. He was a six-time All-Pro in the NBA at 6-4, even going up against the likes of Oscar Robertson. Another player on that squad who was very effective was Lou Tsiropoulos, who was really a recruit for football at Kentucky. He became an outstanding basketball player, a catalyst and the enforcer.

Packer—Joe, Kentucky wins in '48, wins in '49, wins in '51 and became a dominant factor in the collegiate game. How was Kentucky able to be so dominant?

Hall—I guess there was a commitment to basketball early in its involvement that led Kentucky to develop this rich tradition. The administrators at the university, back before Coach Rupp, recognized basketball as kind of a salvation for Kentucky. The small rural communities on the high school level did not play football in the state of Kentucky. Many of the schools were so inaccessible back up in the hollows that they just couldn't get that many kids together to have a football team. Basketball became a way of life in the Kentucky mountains and in eastern Kentucky. That influence and public acceptance of basketball ecouraged the administration at the University to support basketball in the very early stages of the game.

Packer—Could it have been done without a coach like Rupp? I mean, was it waiting to happen or did he make it happen?

Hall- I think it was waiting to happen. I certainly don't want to take any credit away from him, but the coach who preceded Coach Rupp had had great success in Kentucky.

Packer—The team tryouts that you talked about, did the great players have to try out, too?

Hall —I can remember some great players who came in and tried out and didn't make it, guys like Frank Selvy, who went on to Furman and became a top scorer. The tryouts were interesting back in those days. It was dog-eat-dog. The players came in by bus, by train, or their families drove down. It was also the time when veterans were flooding the colleges, so you had a backlog of about four years of athletes who had been in the service. So those were great years, not only in Kentucky, but at a lot of schools. Sports in general took a big step forward with the influx of all those veterans.

Packer—Rupp went a few years without winning a national championship, but then he won in '58 with a team that you wouldn't consider dominant. What about that team?

Hall—That team was called "The Fiddlin' Five." Coach Rupp said that to play in Carnegie Hall, you had to have violinists, and he had fiddlers. But that team proved him wrong, and probably it was the maturity, the leadership they had and the sincerity of such players as Odie Smith and Adrian Smith, and the outstanding play of Johnny Cox and Vernon Hatton. There was a good chemistry on that ball club, and they won with team effort, good defense, and smart play.

Packer - Did you ever talk to Coach Rupp about how he had decided to defend aginst Elgin Baylor?

Hall - Coach Rupp had learned that Baylor was prone to foul on the drive. They set it up so that whoever Baylor was guarding would drive on him and try to get him to pick up some early fouls, which they did.

Packer - It seems that, in many Final Fours, the best two teams in the tournament meet in the semifinals. In 1966, Kentucky met Duke in the semis. What memories do you have of that game?

Hall - We had defeated Michigan with Cazzie Russell in the finals of the regional tournament. When we got back to Lexington, the whole squad came down with the flu. We nursed them throughout the week and most of them got back on their feet before we left for College Park. But Conley and Kron were still weak. Duke also had a player down, Bobby Verga. The playoffs became a contest beatween the ill and the weak. In the Duke game, the players gave their all and fought through their illness. But coming back to play the next night, the players could not get their strength back.

The four NCAA tournaments that I've been involved with have all been unusual. That '66 one, the players were sick; in '75, there was the Wooden resignation; in '78, of course, we won; then in '84, we had the half when we shot nine percent. I have been involved in some pretty unusual circumstances in Final Four play, and I know that you can go into it with a great team and have injury or illness or psychological problems that can throw you off balance and cost you a championship. That's why I treasure so much the '78 championship and respect so much the attitude of the players.

Packer - What is that moment like when that buzzer goes off and you finally say, "I've taken a team to the top?"

Hall - Well, there is relief. In basketball, anything less than the championship is a disappointment because that's what your goal is. Once you win it, it's an almost dangerously satisfying thing. It can almost bring about complacency, not only among your staff and the present players, but your fans and everyone. So you have to forget it and gear up for another year.

Bird Man, Magic Man

Indiana State's Larry Bird goes to the jumper against Michigan State's Jay Vincent. Magic Johnson watches.

The 1978-79 college basketball season unraveled like a script. The primary plot linked the emergence of Larry Bird and Earvin "Magic" Johnson.

Bird was basketball's debatable phenomenon that season as Indiana State's Sycamores ripped through the regular schedule undefeated. Some thought he was a great, great player headed for the Hall of Fame. Others thought his fame sprang from the Sycamores' second-rate schedule.

As with all great debates, only the first round would be settled in college basketball, and that not coming until the NCAA finals that March in Salt Lake City, Utah.

The Yang to Bird's Yin, Magic Johnson, was riding with his Michigan State teammates through an up- and-down season in the Big Ten. When it was over, they would have six losses and a share of the league crown, which was enough to get them into the NCAA tournament.

The field had been expanded to 40 teams to accommodate the burgeoning number of competitive college programs. Critics claimed the new format would be awkward. But it created opportunity for more teams.

One of the first to seize it was the University of Pennsylvania. Somehow the Quakers survived the East Regional. Their opponents in the semifinals were the chosen ones, Magic and the Spartans, who had blown away

Lamar, LSU and Notre Dame in the Mideast Regional.

In the Midwest, Indiana State and Bird had made quick work of Virginia Tech and Oklahoma before nipping Arkansas and Sidney Moncrief in the regional finals.

In the West, Ray Meyer's DePaul Blue Demons came out on top, vanquishing Southern Cal, Marquette and second-ranked UCLA.

The strange collection of teams in Utah produced some fairly good basketball, if you leave out Michigan State's 101-67 bombardment of Penn in the semis. The other game matched Indiana State against Mark Aguirre and DePaul, which proved to be a classic.

Meyer chose to go the whole distance with his five starters. Indiana State Coach Bill Hodges offered more rest to Bird, guard Carl Nicks, and their mates. Bird, however, was beyond rest as he registered one of the all-time stellar performances in Final Four history: He made 16 of 19 field goal attempts for 35 points and 16 rebounds.

Even so, DePaul guard Gary Garland scored and gave the Blue Demons a 73-71 lead with about five minutes to play.

Meyer called for the freeze moments later when DePaul got the ball back.

With less than a minute left, Indiana State's Bob Heaton scored off a Nicks' assist to give the Sycamores a 75-74 lead. Aguirre then missed an 18-footer, and State added a free throw to win, 76-74.

With a 33-game unbeaten streak and the top ranking in their back pockets, the Sycamores faced one last obstacle. Building on five impressive tournament victories, Michigan State had jelled around the multiple talents of Magic. But there was more. Coach Jud Heathcote had positioned Greg Kelser, Ron Charles, Mike Brkovich and Terry Donnelly around Johnson. Jay Vincent was injured and came off the bench.

In the finals, Heathcote solved the Bird riddle with a match-up zone. The Indiana State star was snared every way he turned. Hassled into missing 14 of 21 shots, he scored only 19. And while Michigan State found foul trouble early, the Sycamores made only 10 of 22 free throws.

The Spartans led by a dozen in the first half, and in the second, when Indiana State threatened, Donnelly doused 'em with five long-range jump shots.

TOURNAMENT NOTES: Johnson, with 24 points and 7 rebounds in the final, was named MVP. A sophomore, Johnson would claim hardship status after the season and enter the NBA draft.

Left—Larry Bird talks with Bryant Gumbel and me, from NBC.
Above—Magic Johnson goes for the jam over an Indiana State defender.
Below—Michigan State's Magic Johnson drives to the basket past Indiana State's Leroy Staley.

1979

Michigan State	fg-fga	ft-fta	rb	pf	tp
M. Brkovich	1- 2	3- 7	4	1	5
G. Kelser	7-13	5- 6	8	4	19
R. Charles	3- 3	1- 2	7	5	7
T. Donnelly	5- 5	5- 6	4	2	15
E. Johnson	8-15	8-10	7	3	24
J. Vincent	2- 5	1- 2	2	4	5
R. Gonzalez	0- 0	0- 0	0	0	0
M. Longaker	0- 0	0- 0	0	0	0
Team			2		
Totals	26-43	23-33	34	19	75
Indiana State	fg-fga	ft-fta	rb	pf	tp
B. Miley	0- 0	0- 1	3	1	0
A. Gilbert	2- 3	0- 4	4	4	4
L. Bird	7-21	5- 8	13	3	19
C. Nicks	7-14	3- 6	2	5	17
S. Reed	4- 9	0- 0	0	4	8
B. Heaton	4-14	2- 2	6	2	10
L. Staley	2- 2	0- 1	3	2	4
R. Nemcek	1- 1	0- 0	0	3	2
Team			3		
Totals	27-64	10-22	34	24	64

Half time: Michigan State 37-28. Officials: Nichols, Muncy and Wirtz. Attendance: 15,410.

An Interview With Jud Heathcote

Jud Heathcote coached Michigan State to the national title in 1979. He has also coached Montana to the NCAA tournament.

Packer—Before we get into the Final Four of '79, I want to go back to 1975. We didn't know at the time, but it was Coach Wooden's swan song. Your Montana team played UCLA in Portland in a game, for all intents and purposes, you should have won. Go back to that ball game.

Heathcote—We went in with the idea that we were overmatched, but we were going to give it everything we had. We had kind of an unusual team in that we had a catalyst in Eric Hays, who was a great great competitor. And we had two or three good basketball players in Ken McKenzie, our center, and Larry Smedley, our forward. We were kind of a blue-collar team, a hard-nosed team, and we weren't going to go out there and just show and figure it was over. I think we caught UCLA by surprise in terms of our defense and offense, and we were well prepared. I think they were looking past that to Las Vegas or Arizona State. With 30 seconds to go we're one down with the ball, and Eric Hays goes up. He drops it off inside to Larry Smedley, who thought he was going to shoot, and the ball goes out of bounds. Eric Hays scored 32 that night on both David Meyers and Marques Johnson, two All-American forwards. We had to foul then and they made both foul shots and the game was over, 67-64. Another interesting sidelight, Charles Fouty and Bob Workman, who is now the Big Ten commissioner, refereed that game and we had an unusual situation where Fouty called an elbowing foul on David Meyers. In the process of giving the call, he hit Eric Hayes in the chin and knocked him cold, and he was out for a minute or two.

Packer—Hays ended up shooting 13-of-16 with 32 points and got seven rebounds. Coach Wooden says to this day it was one of the finest individual performances any of his teams went up against.

Heathcote—Kurt Gowdy interviewed Eric after the game and said he just gave a great interview. Eric's articulate and smart. He was a second-team All-American. Kurt asked him how he could play so hard for so long. He mentioned that he played for his brother, then went on to tell how his brother had lost his leg because of cancer and was now, as a junior, the leading scorer on his high school team playing on a wooden leg. It captivated the listening audience. Eric said, "I made up my mind early that if my brother could shoot with a wooden leg, then I owed it to myself and to my brother to play as hard as I could because I have two good legs." Kurt Gowdy still mentions that story to me.

Packer—As a coach, what was it like to play Wooden?

Heathcote—No mystery for me because, up to then, I was 0-14 against John Wooden. I was an assistant coach with Marv Harshman at Washington State for seven years and we played UCLA down to the wire a couple times. I still remember when we were nine up with six minutes to go and Lucius Allen tipped one in just before the buzzer, and they won the game. I remember the time we played them in Lew Alcindor's first road game. They had played 10 pre-season games, all at home, and suddenly they're on the road in Washington. That's when we came up with the tennis rackets in preparation. Taped them to one of our players, Wayne Ellis. It was my idea but Marv Harshman got the credit for it. We still laugh about that. Assistants come up with ideas; head coaches take the credit. I think my Montana players believed that we had a chance. Maybe not a great chance, but a chance. John Wooden was just a great, great coach. I had the opportunity, because he liked Marv Harshman, to just sit in the background. I felt like I should be taking notes or recording their conversations because John would seek Marv out even more than Marv would seek John out. I kind of felt that John was a lonely coach; that he didn't have a lot of coaching friends. He had a lot of people who admired or respected him, but as far as friends, I think he looked at Marv Harshman as one of his coaching friends. So when they got together they would always visit.

Packer—You go on to Michigan State. In 1978 you have a really good basketball club and then you go on against Kentucky, a team that eventually wins the national championship. But in that game, your club is prepared and plays well enough to beat Kentucky.

Heathcote—Well we had a lead at half time. We came in and said, let's gamble at the tip-off play. We scored on the tip-off in the second half. I think we're up by seven or nine points, then Earvin Johnson, our "Magic Man," picked up his fourth foul with 10 minutes to go. We knew we couldn't win the game with him sitting on the bench, so he kept playing and played very conservatively, very cautiously. They put a 1-3-1 kind of zone trap on us. Everyone says we lost that game defensively because Rick Robey would come up and set the screens for Macy against Terry Donnelly. They would call the fouls on us and Macy would go to the foul line and he just killed us. We lost the game, in our minds, on the offensive end. We did not generate the offense against that 1-3-1 zone. My assistant and I have talked about that game and thought maybe if we'd done a little better coaching job, we would have won a national championship that year. We were in the final eight, and when I looked at Arkansas and Notre Dame in the Final Four, neither of those clubs was as good as we were. Not only that, the fact that Kentucky waltzed to the championship maybe indicated that we had played the championship in the final of the regionals. We won the Big Ten title very easily, winning our first eight games kind of sneaking up on everybody. No one gave us any credit. We were picked to be about fifth in the league. We played Providence, Dave Gavitt's club, first and just ran them right off the floor. And he said,"Watch out for Michigan State, they may go all the way." We did not play particularly well against Western Kentucky, but managed to get 90 points or something like that. We were looking past them to the Kentucky game. Kentucky had been rated number one all year and it was the big game for us.

Packer—Of course, that sets the stage for the next year. And everybody around the country knew there was no sneaking up on Michigan State. Magic had made his mark on the national scene. But you didn't blow everybody away at the start of that Big Ten year. When did the momentum change?

Heathcote—Well, I think you have to look at the whole season, Billy, and look at what went on. We took a trip to Brazil and Earvin did not want to go. He had been playing all summer, and he had just got back from Russia. He had played on some junior national team, and yet he knew he had to go if the team was going. We went down and played eight games. We won seven, and we won the Governors Cup in San Paulo after we lost to the same Brazilian national team in Rio de Janeiro. So it was a great trip for us, and an emotional trip, but in all honesty, our kids came back tired of basketball. We struggled in December to get any enthusiasm for basketball. Suddenly, I thought we came to life in the Far West Classic, and we just demolished a pretty good Washington State team. I think it was 92 to 58, and the kids said, "Hey coach, that one was for you and we're going home now." So, we had lost to North Carolina, we had beaten Fullerton State by 3. We'd played the first college basketball game in the Silver Dome against Cincinnati. We were behind at the half and barely pulled that off. Then we defeated Oregon State in the semifinals in the Far West Classic by about six points. Then we defeated Indiana in the finals, 70 - 57. Now we're rated number one in the country. We kept that rating for a week. Then we played Illinois on the road when they were rated number three in the country. They beat us with a last second shot. We went to Purdue; they beat us with a last second shot. And it looks like we were snake-bit or unlucky. But then if you look at the stats, we were out-rebounded two-to-one both places. We're just not playing well. We're not playing good defense. Then we went down and lost to Michigan with a foul shot by

Michigan State Coach Jud Heathcote can't believe the call.

Keith Smith after time had run out. Then we lost to Northwestern by 18 and by that time we're four and four. So we started talking that maybe it's our team, maybe we're not going anyplace, maybe this is the year that nothing goes. We had a team meeting. Everything in the world has come out of that team meeting. The players told the coaches off; Earvin took over the meeting; Gregory Kelser took over the meeting; the coaches did this; the coaches weren't at the meeting. . . . So much has been made over that meeting.

Packer—Was there ever a meeting?

Heathcote—Oh yeah, there was. We went in and said, "Let's talk about what the season has been; let's talk about where we are going." And we sat down and one of my all-time favorite players, Mike Longaker, a sub who ended up number one in his class at Harvard Medical School, had a lot to say. He was the only guy that Earvin would listen to. The consensus was, "Hey, we haven't worked hard enough; we haven't played hard enough; we're a lot better than we're playing, and the season isn't over." We proceeded to win 10 straight games. We go on the road needing two wins to get the NCAA bid. We beat Minnesota, Purdue loses and Iowa loses, and suddenly we're in.

Packer—So you win 15 of your last 16?

Heathcote—Yeah, so we get into the Final Four. It's amazing because we played the five games in the NCAA playoff. Our guys said, "We're where we should, so let's take advantage of it."

Packer—I want to interrupt for a minute. With Earvin, what 's the difference between the guy we know now and and the guy you first saw as a high school player?

Heathcote—Earvin has changed in the last two or three years as the grind of the pro game has turned it into a kind of a business rather than fun. The first three or four years Earvin was in the NBA, it was just like he was at Michigan State, like it was in high school, fun. The day he'd get home, he'd be in our gym. Now, a hundred games or whatever it is, takes its toll. Now he's just frazzled when the season's over. But he still comes and plays in the summer. He still probably prepares harder and better for the pro camp than the rookies do. Earvin is a dedicated player. I kid him every summer. I say, "Earvin, maybe this is the summer you should learn to shoot a jump shot." He says, "Maybe I should, but I don't quite need it yet." We kind of laugh about it as he zeroes in with that long, one-handed shot. But when I say Earvin has changed, I mean he's matured. Basketball is still fun, he still plays it with flair and enthusiasm. He hates to lose. He injured his ankle against Ohio State; then we had to play Northwestern and Kansas. He was averaging 17 or 18 points a game. With about two-and-a-half minutes left in the Northwestern game, they cut our lead to about six. So, I told Earvin it was time to go in, and he says, "Yeah Coach, time to get in there." He went in and controlled the ball for the last two- and-a-half minutes and scored two points. He couldn't have cared less that going into the game was going to lower his scoring average a couple of points a game. He cared next to nothing about scoring.

Earvin was a unique player in that he would practice hard. He and Gregory Kelser were our hardest working players in practice. Jay Vincent and Ron Charles were, I don't want to say lackadaisical, but there were times when they just didn't want to practice. I finally got to the point where, instead of the assistant coaches or myself, I'd say, "Earvin, get Jay and Bobo to practice harder today." He was the coach out there on the floor.

I still remember the first game that Earvin played. We were playing Central Michigan. I think he had seven points and about eight turnovers, and everyone said, "Heathcote's crazy. He's got Earvin handling the ball in the break, he's got him playing guard out there on offense, he' s got him running the break, he's got him doing so many different things. Nobody can do all those things." It's just that Earvin was nervous playing that first game and he didn't play like he played in practice because he was very uncomfortable in all those areas. When he went to the pros and right away they had him playing forward, I said sooner or later they'll realize that Earvin can play anywhere on defense and he has to have the ball on offense.

I'm asked a lot what was the greatest thing Earvin did. Many say passing the ball, his great court sense, the fact that he could rebound. I say the greatest things Earvin did were intangible. He always made the guys he played with better. In summer pick-up games, Earvin would take three or four non-players, and he'd make those guys look so much better and they would win, not because he was making the baskets all by himself, but because he just made other players play better. Larry Bird has that and so does Isiah Thomas, to some extent.

Packer—You mentioned Larry Bird. During that year, Indiana State was really a non-entity. I had seen Bird play with Magic in the World University games, but I really didn't appreciate his total skill level. You talk about making other players better. When you broke down that Indiana State club for the championship, what was your opinion of Larry Bird?

Heathcote—Larry Bird had put on a tremendous performance in the semifinals against DePaul, and that was the first I'd seen him in person. We'd seen him in film clips and on TV once. You know it's amazing when you get into the Final Four, there are lots of freelance writers looking for any angle, anything that's bizarre, different, or controversial. The way the format was set up, you had to pick two players to interview and then you'd have individual interviews. So, I took Gregory Kelser and Earvin to the interview room, and I told them, "Hey, when we go in, someone will try to get you to say something negative about Larry Bird so they can make an issue about it. Say what a great player he is and this and that." When they came back they said, "Coach, you can't imagine the questions they asked us to try to trap us; how Larry Bird is overrated and things like that." The guys handled it beautifully, but the writers were trying to trap them, which I resent.

After the game, we go to the interview room. Our feeling after winning the national championship was not extreme elation like you would think, but relief. It was like the Kentucky team the year before. They were just expected to do so. I figured our guys would go out and celebrate, but you know what our guys did? They all went home and went to bed. They said, "Coach, we're worn out. We'll celebrate when we get back home." In the game, Byrd had gone 7-for-21, and in our dressing room there's a guy trying to get the kids to say something negative about Larry Bird like, "Boy, Larry Bird really choked in that game, didn't he?" The players said Larry Bird played very hard and very well. And the writer continued, "Well, he took some pretty bad shots, didn't he?" Finally, I said, "Hey where are you from?" He told me and I said, "Well, if you say one more bad word about Larry Bird, I'm going to throw you out of the goddamn locker room. Let me tell you something. You're telling me how slow Larry Bird is, you' re telling me what his shot selection is. I'm going to tell you something Larry Bird has that no one realizes. Same thing as Earvin Johnson. They're the greatest play-

Earvin "Magic" Johnson looks for the inside play against Indiana State.

ers in the game of basketball. Larry Bird, in spite of his slow feet, is going to be a great professional basketball player because he has great hands and court vision. Put that in your goddamn paper." Well, not one word in the paper. I could have been famous for my prediction.

Anyhow, getting back to the Final Four. The Notre Dame game was the key game. Notre Dame had had a lot of publicity, and our guys kind of resented that because they felt the Irish got more publicity than they deserved.

Packer—Let's go back to that championship game. The 1-3-1 match up that you played gave you a little edge

with a lot of people. Was Magic a key to that defense because of his wing span, his anticipation, his ability to rebound and take the ball up the court, all by himself?

Heathcote—I've had two great players who have been able to play as forwards and still be totally involved in the breaks because they could take the ball off the offensive boards and immediately be in the break zone. They were Michael Ray Richardson at Montana and Magic Johnson. Magic was a great director of the defense. We joke, "Hey, you rest on offense, not on defense."

Crum's Delight

The University of Louisville met, at the 1980 Final Four in Indianapolis, with a collection of second-rung teams - UCLA with nine losses and a fourth-place finish in the PAC-10, Purdue with eight losses, and Iowa with nine.

The 40-team format meant that schools no longer had to be dominant during the regular season; they just had to be good enough to get in the tournament. From there, anything could happen.

In the 1980 regionals, anything did happen. After finishing in a fourth-place tie in the Big 10, Iowa and guard Ronnie Lester entered the East Regional and transformed into assassins, killing off Virginia Commonwealth, N C State, Syracuse and finally Georgetown to advance.

John Thompson's Hoyas, led by Sleepy Floyd, fell 81-80 in the regional final when Iowa center Steve Waite scored a three-point play in the dying seconds.

Larry Brown had succeeded Gary Cunningham as coach at UCLA and managed only 17 wins during the season with a young lineup - Rod Foster, Kiki Vandeweghe, James Wilkes, Mike Holton and Mike "Slew" Sanders. But the Bruins aged in the West Regionals with a first-round win over Old Dominion. Then they took on top-ranked DePaul, Ray Meyer's 26-1 dream team with Mark Aguirre and freshman Terry Cummings. With balanced scoring, UCLA broke open a close game and earned the upset, 77-71.

Next, they stretched past a strong Ohio State team featuring Kelvin Ransey, Clark Kellog and Herb Williams, 72-68. After that, reaching the Final Four became a matter of eliminating Clemson, which they did, 85-74.

Denny Crum's 1980 edition was carried by senior guard Darrell Griffith, a consensus All-American, a 6-foot-4 dunking spectacle. Freshman Rodney McCray was teamed in the frontcourt with center Wiley Brown. Jerry Eaves was the unsung backcourt mate for Griffith.

The Cards almost died against Kansas State in the Midwest Regional. But super-sub Tony Branch drilled a jumper from downtown in the final seconds of overtime to keep them alive, 71-69.

That scare was followed by another overtime, this time against Texas A&M, but Louisville again survived, 66-55. From there, LSU played poorly in the regional final and provided easy meat for the Cards, 86-66.

The fourth Final Four entry, Purdue, was coached by Lee Rose, who had taken UNC-Charlotte to the dance in '77. Rose's ticket in '80 was 7-foot-1 All-American Joe Barry Carroll. The Boilermakers' victims in the Mideast were LaSalle, St. John's, Indiana and Duke.

Louisville's Rodney McCray pulls down the rebound against Louisiana State.

The Big Ten had two teams in the Final Four, but the conference party ended in the semifinals.

Crum was taking his third team to the Final Four, after falling to his alma mater, UCLA, in 1973 and '75. In 1980, he was determined to shake the championship monkey from his back, even if it meant cajoling and badgering his team from the sidelines when it drooped into stale play.

Iowa's hopes were deflated in the first half, as Louisville jumped to a lead and Lester aggravated a knee injury from earlier in the tournament. On top of that, Griffith was at his best, hitting 14 of 21 from the floor to finish with 34 points. The Hawkeyes kept it close, but Crum's team moved into the finals confidently, 80-72.

Brown had worked out a way of holding down Carroll in the other semifinal. While the Purdue center struggled for 17 points and eight rebounds, Vandeweghe paced UCLA with 24 on 9 of 12 from the floor. In the end,

Brown's team gained the title flight, 67-62, with a patience that belied their youth.

And once in the title game, they almost worked the UCLA jinx on Crum's team again. They led by two at the half and by five with just under seven minutes left. Crum pushed his players awake and watched them blitz to the title over the last few minutes, 59-54. Griffith led the champions with 23 points, but it was Eaves with several key late baskets that spurred the turnaround. Denny Crum had given the basketball-hungry Louisville crowd its first championship.

TOURNAMENT NOTES: Darrell Griffith was named Outstanding Player. Making the All-Tournament team with him were teammate Rodney McCray, and Foster and Vandeweghe from UCLA, and Carroll from Purdue.

Left—Darrell Griffith soars for the finger roll. Below (L-R)—Former UCLA Coach John Wooden, Louisville's premier player Darrell Griffith and Louisville Coach Denny Crum at the presentation of the John R. Wooden Award to Griffith in 1980.

1980

UCLA	fg-fga	ft-fta	rb	pf	tp
J. Wilkes	1- 4	0- 0	6	3	2
K. Vandeweghe	4- 9	6- 6	7	3	14
M. Sanders	4-10	2- 4	6	4	10
R. Foster	6-15	4- 4	1	3	16
M. Holton	1- 3	2- 2	2	2	4
C. Pruitt	2- 8	2- 2	6	2	6
D. Daye	1- 3	0- 0	1	1	2
D. Allums	0- 0	0- 0	2	0	0
T. Anderson	0- 0	0- 0	0	0	0
Team			3		
Totals	19-52	16-18	34	18	54
Louisville	fg-fga	ft-fta	rb	pf	tp
W. Brown	4-12	0- 2	7	3	8
D. Smith	3- 9	3- 4	5	2	9
R. McCray	2- 4	3- 4	11	4	7
J. Eaves	4- 7	0- 2	3	3	8
D. Griffith	9-16	5- 8	2	3	23
R. Burkman	0- 1	0- 0	1	4	0
P. Wright	2- 4	0- 0	4	1	4
T. Branch	0- 0	0- 0	0	0	0
Team			3		
Totals	24-53	11-20	36	20	59

Half time: UCLA 28-26. Officials: Weiler, Lembo and Nichols. Attendance: 16,637.

Knight Riders

The open tournament format brought an even greater flurry of upsets in 1981, creating a new pastime for TV broadcasters: Counting the carcasses. Arkansas over Louisville, James Madison over Georgetown, Kansas State over powerful Oregon State and Steve Johnson. And again DePaul, again top-ranked, again featuring Mark Aguirre, with a 27-1 record. This time St. Joseph's was the culprit, 49-48.

Yet even in the turmoil, basketball's tradition and power found a home. Bobby Knight's Indiana Hoosiers became the first team to win the title with as many as nine losses.

Although the Final Four games were settled with large margins of victory, the field hardly held any patsies. Virginia, with Ralph Sampson, Lee Raker and Jeff Lamp, had spent much of the year ranked number one and had defeated North Carolina twice. The Cavaliers advanced through the East with wins over Villanova, Tennessee and Brigham Young. Danny Ainge and Fred Roberts led BYU to the regional finals in Atlanta, but the 7-foot-4 Sampson, the consensus national player of the year, awakened there from his tournament slump as Virginia won handily, 74-60.

North Carolina found its footing in the West. The Heels had an incredible front line in James Worthy, Sam Perkins and Al Wood, all future first-round NBA draft picks. They beat Pittsburgh, Utah with Tom Chambers and Danny Vraines, and Kansas State to reach the Final Four.

Somehow, the Hoosiers had won the Big Ten championship despite their record. Then they exploded in the Mideast Regional with a burst of power, dumping Maryland, Alabama-Birmingham and St. Joe's. The Final Four setting was just right for Knight, Philadelphia's Spectrum, where he had won the title in 1976.

Out of the Midwest came Dale Brown's Louisiana State Tigers, powered by forward Rudy Macklin, guard Howard Carter and center Greg Cook. In their first tournament victory, 100-78, over Lamar, Macklin had 31 points and 16 rebounds. The Tigers then bumped Arkansas, 72-56, and claimed the regional title over Wichita State with Antoine Carr and Cliff Levingston, 96-85.

But Brown's Tigers lost their snarl in the national semis in Philly. The tamers were the Hoosiers - Isiah Thomas, Jim Thomas, Landon Turner and Ray Tolbert. LSU seemed in control in the first half, until Knight used his particular brand of motivation with his players at intermission. Indiana roared out in the second half, scored 40 points, and won going away, 67-49.

The other semifinal between the Atlantic Coast powers, Carolina and Virginia, was a tight game early. But the Heels had Sampson suffocated in a zone, and Al Wood fell into a scoring trance and had the game of his life, 14 of 19 from the floor for 39 points. His effort blew apart a game that had been tied at 37 early in the second half. Carolina had a surprisingly easy time of it, 78-65.

The atmosphere of the games was shattered that Monday by news that President Ronald Reagan had been shot and wounded. Officials from the NCAA, the two schools in the finals and NBC discussed postponing the game, but decided to proceed upon learning the President was out of danger.

It was Dean Smith's sixth trip to the Final Four and third shot at a national championship. The Heels held an early, tenuous edge over the Hoosiers, but Indiana eased to a one-point lead at the half. From there, the Hoosier advantage grew to the comfortable realm, as Isiah moved Indiana through the Carolina defense. From an 11-point edge, Knight's team coasted to the championship, 63-50.

TOURNAMENT NOTES: Isiah Thomas was named outstanding player. He was joined on the All-Tournament team by teammates Jim Thomas and Landon Turner, Wood from Carolina, and Lamp from Virginia. Virginia defeated LSU in the last consolation game played at the Final Four.

Opposite—Bobby Knight gave the Hoosiers another championship banner in 1981.
Above—Indiana:1981 National Champions. Front Row (L to R)—Manager Steve Skoronski, Eric Kirchner, Ray Tolbert, Glen Grunwald, Steve Risley, Phil Isenbarger. Middle Row—Asst. Coach Gerry Gimelstob, Asst. Coach Jene Davis, Chuck Franz, Randy Wittman, Isiah Thomas,Ted Kitchel, Asst. Coach Jim Crews, Trainer Bob Young. Back Row—Team Physician Dr. Brad Bomba, Coach Bob Knight, Landon Turner, Mike LaFave, Steve Bouchie, Tony Brown, Jim Thomas, Volunteer coach Steve Downing. Below—The Hoosiers huddled for victory in 1981.

1981

Indiana	fg-fga	ft-fta	rb	pf	tp
T. Kitchel	0- 1	0- 0	0	3	0
L. Turner	5- 8	2- 2	6	5	12
R. Tolbert	1- 4	3- 6	11	0	5
I. Thomas	8-17	7- 8	2	4	23
R. Wittman	7-13	2- 2	4	2	16
S. Risley	1- 1	3- 4	4	1	5
J. Thomas	1- 4	0- 0	4	2	2
Team			2		
Totals	23-48	17-22	33	17	63

North Carolina	fg-fga	ft-fta	rb	pf	tp
A. Wood	6-13	6- 9	6	4	18
J. Worthy	3-11	1- 2	6	5	7
S. Perkins	5- 8	1- 2	8	3	11
M. Pepper	2- 5	2- 2	1	1	6
J. Black	3- 4	0- 0	2	5	6
P. Budko	0- 1	0- 0	1	0	0
M. Doherty	1- 2	0- 1	4	4	2
J. Braddock	0- 2	0- 0	0	1	0
C. Brust	0- 0	0- 0	0	0	0
E. Kenny	0- 1	0- 0	1	0	0
Team			0		
Totals	20-47	10-16	29	23	50

Half time: Indiana 27-26. Officials: Turner, Lauderdale and Moser. Attendance: 18,276.

Heels and Hoyas

Six times Dean Smith had led his North Carolina Tar Heels to the well, and through six final fours they had come up dry. On his seventh trip, in 1982, Carolina finally made a splash. It was a piece of work, or some might say, a piece of luck.

Regardless, North Carolina's 63-62 victory over Georgetown in the NCAA finals is considered by many to be the most dramatic ever. Veteran broadcaster Curt Gowdy thinks it was the game, more than any other, to lift the Final Four to the entertainment level of the World Series and Super Bowl.

Held at the Superdome in New Orleans, the championship game broke attendance records with 61,612 spectators. Millions more caught it on television.

North Carolina entered the tournament number one and somehow managed to maintain that status despite a close call or two. The Heels had a legendary lineup. With Al Wood having gone to the NBA, James Worthy and Sam Perkins were joined by yet another superstar, freshman guard Michael Jordan. Jimmy Black at the point and Matt Doherty at forward were as fine a pair of role players as any coach could hope to have.

That, however, didn't seem to deter little James Madison from Virginia, a team that had upset Ohio Sate in the first round. The Tar Heels struggled to a 31-29 lead at the half, and things got no better in the second stanza. The only good Smith saw out of it was that his team escaped JMU, 52-50.

In the regional semifinals in Raleigh, North Carolina, Alabama served Carolina its next round of troubles before succumbing, 74-69. After a 10-point win over Villanova in the regional finals, the Heels were set to give Smith his much-wanted prize.

In the Midwest, the unranked Houston Cougars suddenly grew claws. With starters Michael Young, Rob Williams, Larry Micheaux, Lynden Rose and Clyde Drexler, Coach Guy Lewis pulled Akeem Olajuwon and Reid Gettys off the bench to form a potent rotation. By 1983, the Cougars would become known as Phi Slamma Jamma, the dunking fraternity. For 1982, however, they were just another hot Cinderella, burning Alcorn State, Tulsa, Missouri and Boston College on their way to New Orleans.

Louisville's path in the Mideast was cleared when Alabama-Birmingham upset Virginia. Denny Crum's 20th-ranked Cards polished off Middle Tennessee State, sixth-ranked Minnesota and UAB on the way to their second Final Four appearance in three years. Louisville had no dominant player, just the solid leadership of Jerry Eaves, Rodney McCray and Derek Smith.

The NCAA tournament selection committee had sent Georgetown to the West Regional, and the result was the greatest massacre since Custer. The Hoyas had added freshman center Patrick Ewing with All-American guard Eric "Sleepy" Floyd. The victims, in succession, were Wyoming, Fresno State and fourth-ranked Oregon State.

Sam Perkins took charge for Carolina in the semifinals with 25 points and 10 rebounds, while the Tar Heels held Rob Williams scoreless from the floor. North Carolina never trailed and advanced to the championship round, 68-63.

The Georgetown-Louisville matchup was a collision of defense-minded teams. The scoring was strained through a colander of full-court pressure. The Hoyas had the most pressure and the most points, 50-46, setting up a sportwriter's dream for the finals.

Dean Smith vs. John Thompson. Two friends and America's Olympic coaches from 1976 facing each other for the championship both wanted dearly.

Both men played it down. They weren't playing, they said, their teams were.

But the media seized the drama and squeezed. There were other plums. Carolina's Worthy and Georgetown's Floyd were both All-Americans, both from little Gastonia, North Carolina, both the stalwarts of their teams.

The pre-game tension and excitement were heavier than any Final Four I can recall. Ewing broke that somewhat in the early minutes by swatting away four Carolina shots. All four were ruled goaltending. The Heels scored their first eight points without putting the ball through the hoop.

From there, the game settled into the coaches' cat-and-mouse. The Hoyas grabbed a lead, then Carolina evened it at 18. Worthy came alive with 18 first-half points. The lead became a pendulum. Georgetown held it at the half, 32-31.

The swinging continued throughout the final 20 minutes. At the six-minute mark, Carolina eased ahead, 57-56, on a pair of Worthy free throws. The pace became agony after that. Somewhere under two minutes, Georgetown pulled to 61-60 when Ewing lofted a 14-foot shot. When Carolina missed on its next possession, the young Georgetown center rebounded. Floyd scored on a short jumper, and the Hoyas had the lead, 62-61, with just under a minute left.

Carolina worked for a good shot, and, with 15 seconds

The action heats up in New Orleans here, Georgetown's Patrick Ewing rejects a shot by North Carolina's James Worthy.

left, Doherty passed to Jordan for a 16-foot jumper from near the left sideline. The swish sent chills to Tar Heel Land.

Down 63-62 with adequate time, Georgetown attacked immediately with guard Fred Brown working the ball at the edge of the Carolina defense. He thought he saw Floyd out of the corner of his eye, but the shadowy form in white was Carolina's Worthy. He was surprised, then elated, to receive the ball and he headed downcourt, where he was fouled.

Worthy missed both free throws with two seconds left, but it didn't matter. Carolina had its championship. In one of the finer moments in all of sports, Thompson stepped onto the court and hugged a disconsolate Brown.

TOURNAMENT NOTES: Worthy was named tournament MVP. Perkins and Jordan were named to the All-Tournament team, along with Georgetown's Floyd and Ewing.

1982

Georgetown (62)	fg-fga	ft-fta	rb	pf	tp
E. Smith	6- 8	2- 2	3	5	14
M. Hancock	0- 2	0- 0	0	1	0
P. Ewing	10-15	3- 3	11	4	23
F. Brown	1- 2	2- 2	2	4	4
E. Floyd	9-17	0- 0	3	2	18
E. Spriggs	0- 2	1- 2	1	2	1
A. Jones	1- 3	0- 0	0	0	2
B. Martin	0- 2	0- 0	0	1	0
G. Smith	0- 0	0- 0	0	1	0
Team			2		
Totals	27-51	8- 9	22	20	62

North Carolina (63)	fg-fga	ft-fta	rb	pf	tp
M. Doherty	1- 3	2- 3	3	0	4
J. Worthy	13-17	2- 7	4	3	28
S. Perkins	3- 7	4- 6	7	2	10
J. Black	1- 4	2- 2	3	2	4
M. Jordan	7-13	2- 2	9	2	16
B. Peterson	0- 3	0- 0	1	0	0
J. Braddock	0- 0	0- 0	0	1	0
C. Brust	0- 0	1- 2	1	1	1
Team			2		
Totals	25-47	13-22	30	11	63

Half time: Georgetown 32, North Carolina 31. Officials: Dabrow, Dibbler, Nichols. Attendance: 61,612.

An Interview With Dean Smith

North Carolina Coach Dean Smith has taken teams to the Final Four seven times. His Tar Heels won the championship in 1982.

Packer—Looking back at the NCAA tournament of 1952 when you played at Kansas, I did not realize what a great tournament Clyde Lovellette had. He scored 31 against TCU, 44 against St. Louis, 33 against Santa Clara, and had 33 points and 17 rebounds against St. John's.

Smith—He was just a tremendous player and we obviously went to him. With Clyde inside, it was automatic.

Packer— That was really a great run of games for the Kansas club because, with the exception of TCU when you won by four points, you won by 19, 19, and 17. The night you played St. John's, their coach was Frank McGuire. What was your first impression of Coach McGuire?

Smith—Well, as you know from being a former player, players don't really pay much attention to the other coach. We knew we were playing St. John's. We played them in '51 and beat them by one point in the Garden. So our confidence was established. We had a seven-man rotation, of which I wasn't one, and I was sure we were going to win. But I never really met Frank until '57 when Frank was the coach at North Carolina. Bob Spear, Ben Carnevale and I, along with some other guys who worked for Bob, shared a two-bedroom suite with Frank in Kansas City. I was assistant coach at the Air Force Academy. I was in the same suite for a whole week with Frank. In fact, I was trying to get some information on North Carolina that I could run over and tell Dick Harp, the Kansas coach. Frank knew I was cheering for Kansas because I had helped coach the Kansas seniors, Maurice King and Gene Elstun, when I was a graduate assistant there and they were freshman.

That's when he asked me, after the championship game, if I wanted to be his assistant. At the time, I didn't know that Carnevale and Spear had been bragging on me. But I told him, "No, I don't think I'd enjoy it."

Packer—Kansas had a chance to be two-time champs. In '53, Kansas lost by one point, a game when Don Schlundt had a great performance.

Smith—It really was, but Bob Leonard really won the game when he made the two foul shots with 29 seconds remaining. We had Jerry Alberts open in the corner, but his shot rimmed out. That year, we were picked sixth in the conference, but the defense was even better than the year before. Al Kelley and Dean Kelley were just sensa-

tional, and Gil Reich came in from Army, and he was a real quick athlete, an All-American football player. We had another guy named Harold Patterson. He was 6-1, but he could actually touch his head to the rim, and he went on to be Player of the Year in Canada in football. We had B.H. Born, and all these guys were just good athletes. Schlundt was very good in that game, but Leonard was sensational. In that same, there were four excellent pivot men, Schlundt, Pettit, Born, and Houbregs, but Born was the MVP of the whole tournament. I remember, Dean Kelley and I went to see Dr. "Phog" Allen, our coach, and Dick Harp, his assistant, before the season and said, "Gee, could we play Nicholson at center, he's 6-7." We didn't think B.H. Born could help us at all. Born was real awkward, but he had a sensational year.

Packer—As a kid from Kansas, what is your first recollection of the Final Four?

Smith—I listened to the 1940 Indiana-Kansas game. I was 9-years-old, listening on the radio to the game in Kansas City. Of course, the term Final Four was unheard of.

Packer—In '67, you get your first chance at North Carolina to go the Final Four, the beginning of your great NCAA tournament record. But you ran into Houston, a great Houston team.

Smith—Billy, when I took over the team in '62, I didn't even dream of the Final Four. NC State and Carolina couldn't recruit and played a limited number of games, so I didn't think about it. In '67, when we won the regular season, I remember Smith Barrier, the Greensboro sports editor, picked Duke as the easy favorite for the tournament. Larry Miller tore that newspaper clipping out and stuck it in his locker and said, "I'll wait for that guy three days."

Packer—Yeah, I can relate to that, because a lot of people don't remember what a task it was, not just to get in the NCAA tournament, but just to get out of the conference, because only one team went, the conference tournament winner.

Smith—One team went, but it wasn't the best team necessarily. It was the team that could win a three-day tournament. It was even tougher on the regular season winner because, as you remember, all the other fans kind of ganged up and cheered against the season winner. I remember saying back in '67, '68 and '69, the NCAA is just like a bowl game, gravy. You know we just relaxed. We had accomplished our goal, to win the ACC tournament. That got us worn out. So just to get to the NCAA tourna-

North Carolina Head Coach Dean Smith.

ment was everything, After the ACC tournament, I told the guys just to stay in shape; go out and have some fun.

We had to beat a good Boston College team in the regional finals just to get to the Final Four. The funny thing in '67 was we'd beaten Virginia Tech, a good Virginia Tech team, by 30 or something in our last home game. Dayton and Virginia Tech played overtime in the finals of Mideast Regionals, but everybody was talking about how our sophomores would do against Lew Alcindor. As much as I kept saying to my players, "Hey, Dayton is dangerous," I couldn't convince those sophomore starters, and Dayton put on a great exhibition and beat us.

I fought to do away with the consolation game. I told our players, "No practice tomorrow, we'll just show up at game time." And we happened to play Houston, an angry Houston team. I think the consolation game was a horrible situation. I don't count the consolation game as part of my record, victories or defeats. Through the National Association of Basketball Coaches Tournament Committee, I wrote every coach who had been in a consolation game and asked, "Were your kids happy to be there?" Not one of them said "yes." So we got rid of it finally.

Packer—You come back in '68 and now you get a chance to play against UCLA.

Smith—I'd rather talk about St. Bonaventure with Bob Lanier. We played them in the regionals when they were undefeated. First of all, however, we had had to win the ACC tournament. We beat South Carolina in overtime and then killed State in the finals by 37 points. I mean this team was ready, and it's the only time that I can remember any of our teams that won the ACC Tournament played well the next game. We had St. Bonaventure and we had to play well.

Packer—Talking about '68, we have Wooden having his tremendous string of wins. What was it like going up against a person like that?

Smith—I never try to say we're playing this coach or that. I was concerned because we'd seen our guys lose to Dayton the year before. We were looking ahead in '67 to UCLA. You know, we preach don't look ahead. The next year in the Holiday Festival, we were supposed to play UCLA again. But we played St. John's in the semifinals and lost by one point. So we finally get our chance in the '68 NCAA finals. In '69, we thought we might have another chance, and what ruined that was when Grubar went down in the ACC tournament finals, and we were lucky to even get to the Final Four. Duquesne outplayed us in the regionals, but we won by a point. And then Purdue beat us on the way to playing UCLA.

In Alcindor's three years, we thought we'd have four chances to play against them, and then we only played once.

Packer—That team with Kareem, a lot of people talk about that maybe being one of the great teams in the history of collegiate sports. UCLA had Lucius Allen and Mike Warren in the back court.

Smith—I said after the game that was the best team in history. Even if Elvin Hayes had played for UCLA, they wouldn't have been as good. They had a perfect complement with Shackelford outside, the great quickness of Allen and Warren, and Heitz was a tremendous passer into Jabbar. Their chemistry was tremendous, and they were all so motivated.

Looking back at an old tape recently of that game, we did a great job defensively, except for the lob pass to Jabbar. You know we were fronting him and Heitz did a good job lobbing it over.

Packer—You played Florida State in the semifinals in '72, but you lost. Did you have high expectations going into that tournament?

Smith—That's the year I think UCLA was ranked number one, and we were ranked number two. Florida State was an extremely quick team, but we had a big rally after Robert McAdoo fouled out with 13 minutes to play. But Florida State had beaten Kentucky in the regionals, and they played very good basketball.

Packer—I thought the semifinal game in '77, the Vegas-Carolina game, was one of the great semifinal games of all time. Leading up to the Final Four, your team had struggled with injuries that hampered Walter Davis and Phil Ford.

Smith— Rich Yonakor was our starting center, and in January he had been our fourteenth man. We just barely beat Purdue, but I don't know how without Walter Davis. Then we were behind Notre Dame by 13 with about 10 minutes to play, but we came back and beat them, 79-77. That was when Phil Ford got hurt. Next we played Kentucky, and I was sure that would be almost impossible, and we win that one, 79-72. We felt just grateful to get to the Final Four. And then we hit what I felt was a great basketball game, the Vegas game.

Packer—What do you remember about Al McGuire when you played Marquette in the finals?

Smith—Al and I had been very close when he was at Belmont Abbey. We'd always scrimmage, I tried to recruit his son, Allie, and Al gave me my first stock tip. We'd hang around together at coaches' conventions in the 60s. So I was very happy for Al, because he had told me when they were losing in December,"I have a terrible team." In the Final Four, they played poorly against North Carolina-Charlotte in the semifinals and still won. Against us, they were really sharp with their stuff. And we were sharp, too. We played awfully well.

Packer—The four corners that you put in was something during that period of time.

Smith—Well, we put it in way-back-when, but it became famous then.

Packer—Where did you get the idea for the four corners?

Smith—The idea came from Bob Spear, the coach of the Air Force Academy. In 1956, the NCAA put in a rule that in some situations a defensive player had to be within three feet of the ball. So we came up with the four corners. If you ever got the lead, you had to come out and play. It was a crazy rule, but that was fun.

Packer—In that game with Marquette, you were playing with the "walking wounded." You made the decision to go to the four corners.

Smith—We played Vegas the last nine minutes in the four corners. You know we hadn't lost all year with it. We made a great comeback against Marquette at the beginning of the half. We cut a 12-point lead to two in four minutes. With 10 minutes to go, we finally got the lead. No, we didn't get the lead; it was tied. We went to the four corners, and Al wisely chose not to chase us, staying instead in a 2-3 zone.

Packer—It was a cat-and-mouse game there.

Smith—I had Mike O'Koren on the sidelines ready to come in. I had Bruce Buckley in the game giving me the tired sign. Al was shouting to his players, "Move back, move back!" I thought if I take a timeout now to get O'Koren in the game, it gives Al the chance to set up the defense. His players would come out when they had to to play man-to-man, but then would run back into their zone. And so it went on. Then, Buckley broke through for

a layup, and Bo Ellis wiped it off the glass. I thought it was goaltending. But I looked at the videotape later, and it wasn't. If we had gotten those two points, you know, the game would have been over. Of course, it ended up with Marquette leading by three.

Packer—Would you have been willing to hold the ball the rest of the way for the last shot?

Smith—Yes, but Phil Ford couldn't shoot outside against the zone with his injured elbow. Otherwise, it would have been a boring, national final, but we were going to take a layup. I'm surprised we didn't get the layup with what we were doing.

Packer— You've had a long association with Bobby Knight. What are some of the things that make him especially tough to play come major tournament time?

Smith—By tournament time, his players know exactly what their roles are. I mean, during the course of a season, Bob will yank a guy and start a different lineup. That first game of the tournament he is better than anybody else. They didn't have a close game in their drive to the 1981 championship. Our game in the finals was the closest game they had had for a month. Isiah Thomas had a great final game. If Landon Turner hadn't been paralyzed in the accident, who knows how good Indiana could've been again the next year.

Packer—In '82 comes the championship year. You had a team that had the ingredients from the get-go. From the first day of the season, people were pointing to North Carolina.

Smith—That's what's remarkable about that team. I don't think that will happen again: To be the team that's shot at and then go through the whole year and still be sharp in the end. They were mad they weren't champions in 1981, and I was too. And I think that helped us. When you get that second crack with the same team, you usually respond. Of course, we'd lost Al Wood, our best scorer, and Michael Jordan came in as a freshman and, as you know, Michael was up and down his freshman year, as any freshman would be. But his best game in his whole freshman year was the finals against Georgetown. If he hadn't made that shot, it would still have been the best game he played all year Defensively, he played well.

Packer— In the finals, you're going up against another guy you've had a close association with, John Thompson. He had worked with you on your staff in the Olympics. Going up against a guy with whom you had that type of personal relationship, was there anything you did to gear yourself up not to change your system?

Smith—Nobody should change what they have been doing all along. If you hadn't been successful, you wouldn't be there. That's why I still believe I was right in holding the ball in '68, though we hadn't had to do it in a long time. But we hadn't played a team like UCLA either. I think if we had played otherwise, they'd have beaten us too. You know they were just better. As for John, I was happy for him, just like I was for Al. But again, my job is with the young men, not the coaches. I want them to feel like they're champions. And so that part was easy.

A funny thing that happened at half time. You know Patrick Ewing took so long to shoot a foul shot. At half time, I told Hank Nichols, the official, "I'm serious, please don't call a technical foul on Patrick." And I was serious as I could be. I thought that would mar the game. I didn't want to win that way. But John thought I was trying to get Nichols to call the technical. John laughed, at least at the time he laughed. I said, "No. I mean it." I shouldn't have said anything because I really didn't want a technical foul called on Patrick. He takes 20 seconds to shoot each free throw.

Packer—In that game, you go inside right away to James Worthy, and Ewing blocks the shots. All four are ruled goaltending.

Smith—I knew that didn't bother James in the least. Some guys hate to see their shots blocked, but James was so sky high.

Packer—All right, James has the great ball game and now you go down to the wire in one of the great finals of all time. For the final shot, what did you have in mind?

Smith—Well, they came back and scored and they had a two-point lead. I don't see how they made it, but the shot bounced around and went in. We missed a foul shot, and we're one down with 32 seconds. Usually, I don't like to take a timeout there. We should know what to do. But I called a timeout. I expected Georgetown to come back to the zone and jam it in. I said, "Doherty, take a look for James or Sam, and, Jimmy, the cross-court pass will be there to Michael." As it turned out, Michael's whole side of the court is wide open because they're chasing James. If Michael had missed, Sam would've been the hero because he'd have had the rebound. Then John was wise not to take the timeout. Michael makes a heck of a play to cover Floyd, and James goes for a steal and doesn't get back in. To this day, I think that if Georgetown had been in their white uniforms that they had worn all during the tournament instead of wearing their dark uniforms, Brown would not have thrown the ball to James. James had gone for a steal on a fake moments earlier and was out of position. He shouldn't have been where he was on the court, and it fooled Brown, and James went for the steal. It would've been so much nicer if we had gotten the ball after they shot in the corner, and it had rimmed out. We would've gotten the rebound. You know, there's no guarantee they would have made it even if Brown hadn't thrown it away. I think John was very smart not to let us set up our defense after that.

Packer—You have known the feeling of winning the Final Four as a player. Was the feeling different as a coach?

Smith—In '82, I thought we had the best team and to win was special. Jimmy Black was a senior, and he wasn't going to get another chance and I didn't know if James Worthy would be back the next year. I don't think we should have won in '67, '68, or '69, nor '72 in Los Angeles with Walton. I was happy we got there. In '77, we were just lucky to get there with all the injuries. Actually, maybe '81, we and Indiana were the two best teams. So, yes, for 1982, I thought we had the best team, and to win was special.

Packer—I want to ask you about your particular system as a coach. Now that the Final Four and the NCAA tournament is so different from the time you took over the job at North Carolina, with multiple teams in conferences allowed in the tournament and moving teams around to balance the regionals, has that altered your system as a coach?

Smith—In the old days, our long-range goal was to win the ACC tournament championship. That's all we talked about from October 15th on. And then in '75, when they allowed two teams from a conference in the tournament, we started talking about winning the regular season to get in. Two of our best games this year were Notre Dame and Michigan. And I thought we'd make the Final Four, but in one game, anything can happen. You know, the regionals are so balanced. I think we have a great tournament the way it is. I thought they'd do away with the bye; I hated that bye. You get that bye in the tournament and you're down to 32 teams, and you're going against a very good basketball team in your first NCAA game.

Packer—Do you think it's more difficult now to win the NCAA tournament than it was when you were a player?

Smith—There are just so many good players now. The best athletes are just spread out and the teams are evening up. Try to name the teams in the Final Four next year. To make the final 16 anymore is great.

Packer—What are the best individual performances by non-Carolina players you can remember?

Smith—Bill Bradley comes to mind right away, and I'd say Wood, if you hadn't said not counting Carolina players. Abdul-Jabbar in '68—I've never seen him so fired up. I mean he was leading cheers on the bench. And Walton against Memphis State.

Packer—You said you were 9-years-old when you heard your first NCAA tournament game on the radio. Where do you think the Final Four will be 20 years from now?

Smith—Why did people get excited about the old ACC tournament? Because everybody had a chance to win it. Now so many are involved in the NCAA tournament, I just think it's unreal. I can't see how it could get much better unless we go to a double-elimination.

Valvano's Voodoo

North Carolina State was not exactly a Wolfpack in sneaking its way to the 1983 NCAA championship in Albequerque, New Mexico. Coach Jim Valvano's team was more coyotelike, stealing into the henhouse and snatching the trophy while the nation's top teams preened themselves.

That's not to take anything away from the Wolfpack's championship. In fact, their last-second victory over top-ranked Houston in the NCAA finals was one of the greatest, gutsiest performances in tournament history.

Somehow State cast a magic spell over the entire field, a bit of roundball voodoo that began in the Atlantic Coast Conference tournament. There, the Wolfpack upset North Carolina and Virginia to gain a berth in the NCAAs with a 20-10 record.

The conference championship was sweet for Valvano and seniors Dereck Whittenburg, Thurl Bailey and Sidney Lowe. But things got even sweeter, some might say stranger, in the NCAA West Regional. The Pack seemed gone in the first round until they worked a miraculous comeback and overtime victory, 69-67, against Pepperdine.

Then they dazzled sixth-ranked Nevada-Las Vegas with another handful of magic dust, when Bailey tapped in a missed jumper by Whittenburg just before the final buzzer to win, 71-70. Bailey, a lithe 6-foot-11 forward, had 25 points.

After blowing out Utah, State faced Virginia and Ralph Sampson in the regional finals. It was the same team they had defeated in the ACC finals, and again Valvano found some upset potion. The Cavaliers were up by five at the half and as many as seven later on, but they hesitated and State danced past.

Virginia held a 63-62 lead in the final minute, until State's sophomore forward, Lorenzo Charles, was fouled and made two free throws. Virginia got two shots at winning it, but missed both.

NC State's opponent at the Final Four was Hugh Durham's Georgia Bulldogs, who had nipped Virginia Commonwealth, then upset third-ranked St. John's and North Carolina in the East Regional.

The oddsmakers, however, paid little mind to all the underdog heroics. Their attention was focused on top-ranked Houston, which had entered the NCAAs with a 27-2 record. Phi Slamma Jamma did little to dispel their image in the Midwest Regional. They jammed their way past Maryland, Memphis State and Villanova in a whirlwind of dunks as Akeem Olajuwon, Larry Micheaux,

The Georgia defense collapses around Dereck Whittenburg in the 1983 semis.

Clyde Drexler and Michael Young all took turns starring.

Denny Crum made his face more familiar by bringing Louisville back to the Final Four. Milt Wagner, Rodney and Scooter McCray and Lancaster Gordon were his key players. This time, the second-ranked Cards picked their way through a patch of overtimes in the Mideast. They outdistanced Tennessee before struggling with Arkansas and Joe Kleine. The sweetest test came in the finals against cross-state rival, Kentucky. Jim Master pumped up a late bomb to send it to overtime at 62 all. Once there, the Cards lifted their wings and flew, 80-68.

In the first semifinal, NC State had surprisingly little trouble with Georgia, 67-60. In the other game, Louisville seemed in command until the midpoint of the second half, when Phi Slamma Jamma bounded to a new plane, wiping away the Cards' eight-point lead in the process.

The Cougars mounted an eight-point lead of their own, then cruised to victory, 94-81. Akeem turned in 21 points, 22 rebounds and eight blocked shots.

The whole Final Four crowd figured the final for a blowout. What they got instead was a tight squeeze, just tight enough for Valvano and the Pack to work one more trick.

"If we get the opening tip, we won't take a shot till Tuesday morning," Valvano joked in a press conference before the game.

Instead, the Pack played almost arrogantly in the first half, scoring frequently and controlling the game . They moved to an eight-point lead and coasted there. But in the back of their minds, in the back of everyone's mind, was the display Houston had put on in the second half against Louisville.

Sure enough, it didn't take long for the anticipated blast from Slamma Jamma to occur. The Cougars opened the second half with a 15-2 run and seemed poised to dash off to the championship. Then strangely, with about nine minutes left, Houston Coach Guy Lewis decided to slow the pace.

Valvano and his Pack were waiting to collect the turnovers and toss bombs over the Houston defense. NC State tied the score at 52 heading into the final two minutes, and Lewis opted for still more stalling. Whittenburg interrupted those plans with about a minute left

when he fouled Houston's Alvin Franklin. The Cougar guard missed his one-and-one opportunity, and Valvano had a shot at the national title with 44 seconds or so left.

Valvano opted to take the game's last shot. With the seconds draining from the clock, Whittenburg launched an off-balance air ball. But Charles rose up from near the basket, where Olajuwon had failed to box him out, and slammed home the winner at the buzzer, a la alley oop.

As Valvano and the State crowd erupted, disappointment fell over the Cougars. Phi Slamma Jamma had suffered a death by dunk, 54-52.

TOURNAMENT NOTES: Olajuwon, with 20 points, was named MVP. Thurl Bailey led State with 15, and Whittenburg scored 14.

Right—Thurl Bailey shoots over Akeem Olajuwon. Below—Sidney Lowe penetrates the Houston defense.

1983

North Carolina State (54)	fg-fga	ft-fta	rb	pf	tp
T. Bailey	7-16	1- 2	5	1	15
L. Charles	2- 7	0- 0	7	2	4
C. McQueen	1- 5	2- 2	12	4	4
D. Whittenburg ...	6-17	2- 2	5	3	14
S. Lowe	4- 9	0- 1	0	2	8
A. Battle	0- 1	2- 2	1	1	2
T. Gannon	3- 4	1- 2	1	3	7
E. Myers	0- 0	0- 0	1	0	0
Team			2		
Totals	23-59	8-11	34	16	54
Houston (52)	fg-fga	ft-fta	rb	pf	tp
C. Drexler	1- 5	2- 2	2	4	4
L. Micheaux	2- 6	0- 0	6	1	4
A. Olajuwon	7-15	6- 7	18	1	20
A. Franklin	2- 6	0- 1	0	0	4
M. Young	3-10	0- 4	8	0	6
B. Anders	4- 9	2- 5	2	2	10
R. Gettys	2- 2	0- 0	2	3	4
D. Rose	0- 1	0- 0	1	2	0
B. Williams	0- 1	0- 0	4	3	0
Team			1		
Totals	21-55	10-19	44	16	52

Half time: North Carolina State 33, Houston 25. Officials: Nichols, Housman, Forte. Attendance: 17,327.

Thompson's Troops

The 1983-84 season could best be described as the year of the big man. Kentucky had the twin towers of Melvin Turpin and Sam Bowie. Houston featured Akeem Abdul Olajuwon. And Georgetown put forth Patrick Ewing.

Although the NCAA tournament had expanded to 54 teams, the dominant centers still prevailed. Turpin, Bowie, Olajuwon and Ewing all gathered at the Final Four in Seattle to settle who was the most dominating big man in college basketball. When it was over, the answer was clear. It was Georgetown's other tower: 6-foot-10 coach John Thompson.

After being denied the title in 1982 against North Carolina, he returned with a vengeance in '84. When he was through, veteran sportswriters were talking dynasty. Certainly, his Hoyas were the stuff of dynasties. The 6-foot-11 Ewing at center. Freshman Reggie Williams at forward. Bill Martin as sixth man. David Wingate as the shooting guard. Michael Jackson at the point. Freshman Michael Graham was the resident bruiser. Guard Gene Smith was the defensive specialist. And Fred Brown, back in action after a year's absence with a knee injury, added a veteran's wisdom.

They bolted through the regular season and rolled into the Big East Tournament like a bowling ball, sending Providence, St. John's and Syracuse reeling.

With a 29-3 record, the Hoyas entered the West Regional and immediately found trouble in SMU's stall game. Only Ewing's incredible effort in the game's last minute saved them. He muscled past the Mustang's Larry Davis to rebound Gene Smith's missed free throw and score on the putback for a 36-34 Hoya lead. After a final exchange, the game ended, 37-36, Georgetown. From there they lanced Nevada-Las Vegas and Dayton to claim at seat for Seattle.

Kentucky, the number one seed in the Mideast, has a satisfying route to the big event. The Wildcats drummed Brigham Young, 84-68, then zapped their old Bluegrass rival, Louisville, 72-67, and eased past Illinois in the finals, 54-51.

Guy Lewis' Houston Cougars made the Midwest Regional business as usual by dropping Louisiana Tech, 77-69, Memphis State, 78-71, and Wake Forest, 68-63.

The only surprise was in the East with Virginia, the ACC's sixth place team with a 17-10 record. With Ralph Sampson having graduated, the Cavaliers and coach Terry Holland were forced to combine an ugly-duckling offense with a tight little zone. Somehow the formula carried them through a series of upsets in the regional

Patrick Ewing puts it to the glass and Michael Graham soars for the possible put back. Georgetown's Broadnax (32) and Houston's Michael Young (43) watch.

over Iona, Syracuse, Arkansas and Indiana. In Seattle, it almost took them a step further.

Taking it slow and easy, they pushed Houston to overtime and had a shot to win it in regulation. But in the extra period, the Cougars escaped, 49-47.

The other semifinal was one of the more memorable in tournament history, not for its close score but for its astounding turnaround. Ewing was called for three fouls in the first 11 minutes as Kentucky raced to a 27-15 lead. With their center on the bench, the Hoyas jump started their dreaded full-court press and narrowed the gap to 29-22 by halftime. With three minutes left in the half, Turpin had scored on a jumper.

Kentucky wouldn't score again for another 13 minutes, as Georgetown encased the Wildcats in defense and suffocated them. There were more than 300 coaches in the audience at Seattle's Kingdome. The second half left them stunned. "No one had ever seen anything like it," said

Patrick Ewing swats away yet another shot as Georgetown stifles Kentucky in the 1984 semifinals. Georgetown held Kentucky scoreless through the middle part of the game in one of the most awesome defensive displays in Final Four history.

Georgetown defenders swarm around a frustrated Akeem Olajuwon in the 1984 finals against Houston.

Miami coach Bill Foster. "Incredible."

The most stunned of all was Kentucky Coach Joe Hall. "I can't explain it," he said afterward. "What happened is beyond me."

The numbers explain it simply. Kentucky failed to score on its first 14 possessions of the second half. For the half, the Wildcats made 3 of 33 attempts or 9 percent, an NCAA record. The five starters missed all 21 shots they attempted in the second half.

The Hoyas had moved to a 34-29 lead before Winston Bennett scored for Kentucky. Then Georgetown ran off another 11 points for a 45-31 lead. After a few more depressing minutes, it ended, 53-40.

"They took everything away from me," Melvin Turpin lamented afterward. "Every time I turned around they were in my face."

The championship match with Houston wasn't as dramatic, but it was convincing. The Cougars jumped out to a 10-2 lead, then watched Georgetown close the gap and take over. Akeem was called for his third foul just before the half. Then just 23 seconds into the last half, with the Hoyas leading 40-30, he was whistled for a fourth.

Houston closed to 51-47, then to 57-54, but could get no closer. The two powers raced toward a 84-75 close. Thompson had dreamed the sweet dream.

TOURNAMENT NOTES: The teams in the Final Four were awarded $614,000 each as their share of tournament revenues. Patrick Ewing was named tournament MVP.

1984

Houston (75)	fg-fga	ft-fta	rb	pf	tp
R. Winslow	0- 1	2- 2	6	4	2
M. Young	8-21	2- 3	5	3	18
A. Olajuwon	6- 9	3- 7	9	4	15
A. Franklin	8-15	5- 6	2	3	21
R. Gettys	3- 3	0- 0	1	2	6
B. Anders	2- 2	0- 2	0	0	4
B. Clark	0- 0	0- 0	0	0	0
G. Anderson	1- 1	0- 0	2	0	2
E. Dickens	2- 3	1- 2	0	5	5
R. Thomas	0- 0	0- 0	0	0	0
D. Giles	0- 0	0- 0	0	0	0
J. Weaver	0- 0	0- 0	0	0	0
G. Orsak	1- 1	0- 0	0	0	2
M. Alexander	0- 0	0- 0	1	0	0
S. Belcher	0- 0	0- 0	0	0	0
Team			3		
Totals	31-56	13-22	29	21	75
Georgetown (84)	fg-fga	ft-fta	rb	pf	tp
D. Wingate	5-10	6- 9	1	4	16
R. Dalton	0- 0	0- 0	2	1	0
P. Ewing	4- 8	2- 2	9	4	10
F. Brown	1- 2	2- 2	4	4	4
M. Jackson	3- 4	5- 5	0	4	11
M. Graham	7- 9	0- 2	5	4	14
R. Williams	9-18	1- 2	7	2	19
H. Broadnax	2- 3	0- 0	0	2	4
B. Martin	3- 6	0- 0	2	0	6
V. Morris	0- 0	0- 0	0	0	0
Team			7		
Totals	34-60	16-22	37	25	84

Half time: Georgetown, 40, Houston 30.
Officials: Ron Spitler, Mike Tanco, Booker Turner. Attendance: 38,471.

An Interview With John Thompson

John Thompson has built Georgetown into a NCAA tournament regular since becoming coach there in 1972.

Packer—John, when you were a player at Providence from 1960-64, what was the bigger deal, the NIT or the NCAA?

Thompson—When I was at Providence, I didn't have much awareness of the NIT or the NCAA. A lot of that was related to segregation. I knew a lot about the CIAA and the CIAA tournament because most of the guys who played ball with me talked about the CIAA tournament. Once I got to college, I started to hear about the NIT and the NCAA tournaments, but at Providence the NIT had more significance that the NCAA. In fact, several times when I was in college, we chose to go to the NIT rather than go to the NCAA tournament. In my senior year, our players voted to go to the NCAA, and we talked to the athletic director and coach about it. We had a player on our team from California named Jimmy Hadnot who used to talk about the NCAA tournament. He was the only one who really talked about the NCAA. We thought he was kind of crazy because we thought in terms of the NIT. The year that Loyola-Chicago won the NCAA, we had passed up the NCAA to go to the NIT. The big question in our minds was whether we could've beaten Loyola. As you know, we won the NIT that year. All our players were saying that they would have loved to have played Loyola.

Packer—In 1964, you get to play in the NCAA tournament, but you lost an opening round game to Villanova 77-66.

Thompson—The thing that I remember about the game is that George Leftwich, who played in high school with me, was on that Villanova team. We played in the Palestra, Villanova's home court. Even then, there was a lot of politics; every time I hear about someone having to play on someone else's home court or in their home town, I reflect on that game.

Packer—That year also has significance because it was the first time that John Wooden won a national championship at UCLA. Did the name John Wooden mean anything special to you?

Thompson—When I was a player, it didn't mean anything to me, except that 1964 was also an Olympic year, and I had an opportunity to try out for the Olympic team that was coached by John Wooden. After I met the man, I was quite impressed. I really liked him because he was more of a players' coach than a coaches' coach. What

I mean by that is that during the whole Olympic trials, he associated with the players more than he did with the coaches. John Wooden was always mingling with the players, and he ate with the players a lot of times.

Packer—In 1975, you have the opportunity to take your first team to the NCAA. What was your feeling knowing that you had finally made it to the tournament?

Thompson—It was a trememdous feeling. To get to the NCAA, we had to beat West Virginia University at West Virginia. The game was decided in the final seconds. West Virginia was leading by one point, but they missed a free throw with five seconds to play. We came down with the rebound and scored on the break. I just remember everybody yelling and jumping up and down, realizing that we finally had made it to the NCAA tournament.

We went down to Alabama to play Central Michigan in the NCAAs. That game ended in controversy when we lost the game at the buzzer on a shot where one of our players was called for an offensive charge. The time had run out and they went down to the other end of the court and shot free throws with the time expired.

Packer—A name from that '75 game with Central Michigan jumps out at me. That is Dan Roundfield, who was a great player. What did your scouting reports tell you about Roundfield?

Thompson—We had scouted him and we knew he was an exceptional player. At that time, they had another fine player, James McElroy. We knew that Roundfield could block shots really well and that he also had great jumping ability. Around the basket, he was tough.

Packer—You reached the Final Four in 1982, and you play the championship game against Dean Smith. What was your feeling about having an opportunity to go against a guy you had worked with in the Olympics?

Thompson—Two things. I think that to reach the Final Four itself was a tremendous feeling and a tremendous accomplishment. We called it the "Georgetown Bigtop." You know it's like the center ring of the circus. We had worked real hard to get the program to this point, and I felt we had a bunch of kids who deserved it. Beyond that, I had mixed emotions about playing against Dean because I have a great deal of respect and affection for him. Dean was instrumental in helping me understand what the college game is about and helping me to structure my thoughts about what I had to do and how I could carry out the things I wanted to accomplish. And here, at the biggest moment of my career, I was playing against the guy who had as much to do with my thinking as anybody.

Left—Patrick Ewing at the center and Michael Jackson at the point were a big part of Thompson's dream team. Above right—A touching moment as Big East Commissioner Dave Gavitt (R) congratulates John Thompson following the 1984 championship. Gavitt was an assistant coach at Providence when Thompson played there. Former CBS broadcaster Gary Bender (Behind Gavitt) and I look on. Bottom right (L-R)—Georgetown's Patrick Ewing, John Thompson and Ralph Dalton embrace after the championship.

So I had to generate a little bit of competitiveness and stubbornness in order not to think of him as my friend. Because it was Dean, it caused me to be even more fired up.

Packer—When the game started, Patrick Ewing was blocking everything in sight. Was that something that was the result of his natural abilities or was that part of a special psyche that you had nurtured?

Thompson—I think it was a combination of both. Patrick was an excellent shot-blocker. We wanted to establish ourselves inside as much as we possibly could. I still question some of the goaltending calls.

Packer—The game flowed back and forth, with some sensational plays, but it came down to a last-second shot by North Carolina. You knew Dean, you had worked with him, and you knew his personnel like the back of your hand. You knew he would go for the last shot, but who did you think would take it?

Thompson—We thought that Worthy hurt us more

that anybody. You hear a lot about Michael Jordan's shot. That certainly broke our backs, but we were having a lot of difficulty with Worthy. He was quick enough to create problems for our big people and strong enough to create problems for our little people. Worthy was really hurting us, and at that point I thought they would get the ball in to James. What we did was to go into a match-up so we could have people on the ball. Carolina sent Michael to the side opposite the ball, and we wanted to collapse back if James got the ball and not give him any room. James is what I call an "inch player." You know he'll get an inch closer to the basket than you want him to all of the time. Doherty threw it to Jordan on the opposite side, and he hit the jump shot. It wasn't really a tough shot because we had shifted to put as much emphasis as possible on James.

Packer—Then, of course, there was "The Pass," when Freddie Brown threw the ball to Worthy. Everybody who ever saw that game has his own theory. What do you think happened?

Thompson—I think it was more of a reflex action because Worthy had run out of the defense.

Packer—He was out of position, really.

Thompson—Right, and we were playing five against four. Worthy was coming from the direction an offensive player normally would come from, and I think Freddie reacted reflexively. It was like the old playground thing where the defensive player stands out where the offensive player should be and calls for the ball. But Worthy didn't call for it, he was just coming from the other side and by reflex Freddie threw him the ball. A lot of people talk about that costing us the game. What a lot of people forget is that we still had to get it to an open person and score. Eric "Sleepy" Floyd was open in the corner and I thought he was in pretty good position, but we had to make the shot. We had made other mistakes during the game and I think Freddie's mistake is overrated as the reason we lost. Freddie recovered from that extremely well, and I was pleased that the team used it as a learning experience.

Packer—When that game ended after a season of hard work, did you wonder if you would ever get another chance to win the championship?

Thompson—I don't think you really focus on that as much as the fact that you're disappointed. Winning is a big satisfaction, and losing is a big disappointment. The higher you climb, the more you feel the disappointment when you don't get it. But you know you've accomplished an awful lot to be one of the last two teams. The guy who loses on that last night feels just as bad as the guy who loses the first night. And he might even feel worse.

Packer—Because he knows he was so close?

Thompson—Right. Because he was so close. I can never forget the expression on Ewing's face. It's a deep pain, but everybody who tries to accomplish something takes the chance of a big disappointment.

Packer-In '84 you come back and put on an awesome display in moving through the tournament field. The Kentucky game has to go down in history as an awesome display of talent. What was the catalyst for that incredible effort?

Thompson—We had lost to Carolina, and we just said, "Hell, you know, we've got to win this thing." Everybody had talked about Kentucky as one of the best teams ever assembled because of their size and talent. Our kids were just stubborn, and that might have been the most satisfying victory I've ever had in terms of execution and determination. Those kids were stubborn, and they worked and made a commitment and did the things that you wanted them to do. The championship game was extremely important because that's the crown on your head.

Packer—After that Kentucky game, I think that there was a feeling in the gymnasium that the championship game with Houston was kind of anticlimatic.

Thompson—And that scared me, Billy. I knew what those kids had accomplished in winning the Kentucky game 53-40. They played tremendous defense, they worked like hell, and really did the job. And then we lost Gene Smith for the game with Houston. I said to myself, this is going to be tough. But to be very honest, I'm not certain that, in a weird way, losing Gene might not have helped us more than it hurt us because it returned extra fear and caution. Had we not lost Gene, complacency might have been there a little bit more.

Packer—The game with Houston did not go down to the buzzer like your Carolina game. I want to ask you about three people in particular. First, Gene Smith. You seemed to have a special rapport with him.

Thompson—It's because Gene had scholarships to Morgan State and to Georgetown. I had to go in and talk to him and tell him that he would never be a starter at Georgetown, that I wanted him for a special purpose. Then the kid worked his behind off, and he was the person who spearheaded our defense. He was just hard-nosed and tough. He was like the storybook kid who pulled himself up by his bootstraps among all the All-Americans. Here's a kid who by rights didn't belong in the Final Four, but who fought his way up, and I always respected him for that.

Packer—What about Freddie Brown?

Thompson—Real special feeling, because I always thought that his pass in the '82 final was taken out of perspective. I always felt bad that he would have to carry that with him. So it was like a tremendous relief when we won it. I grabbed him, and he and I just felt, you know, that it's over, that we had come back and won.

Packer—And up in the stands there was a guy who by his mere presence was special, Bill Russell.

Thompson—Yeah. I can remember now seeing Russ. You know I have always had a great deal of respect for Russ because I thought he was one of the most intelligent human beings I had ever been around in sports. He combined his ability with intelligence, and I thought that seeing him right at the end was just the thing that topped it all off. Here's a guy who's coming over to congratulate me, and this was sort of like my little day. It was a tremendous compliment for me to see him make the effort to be there, because you know Russ runs away from crowds and fanfares. I knew that he had to be very happy for me if he would come out of the stands and get involved in all of that.

Packer—Now comes '85, and if a team was ever favored to win, it was yours. You think back to your first years at Georgetown and then, in 1985, everybody says you're the guy to beat. The Big East puts three teams in the tournament, which in itself is historical for the NCAA. You face Louisville in the semis and then you go up against a team in Villanova that will have to play the perfect game even to stay competitive. Did you think they could do it?

Thompson—No, I didn't. I thought we would win it. You know, I definitely thought we'd win it. But the thing that irritated me most about it, and you know I don't say it in a negative sense, but in an affectionate sense, is it's the damn Big East teams again. You know you're playing Louie, you're playing Rollie, and you're saying, "Hey, I'd rather play anybody else." You're happy that the league is doing well, but you don't want to get in the situation where you've played people two and three times and they keep coming back. I still feel that we had played them well; we played them three times and beat them twice. That was a great effort on their part. They shot the ball extremely well against a great defensive team and a confident team. But Villanova believed that it was good.

Packer—John, you won one national championship very easily. You could've had three under your belt; three in four years. Is there such a thing as a winning formula for fellows like you, Bobby Knight, Dean Smith, and Denny Crum?

Thompson—You have to have a system or a way of doing things that you believe is sound. You also have to have kids with ability, but ability alone is not enough. You have to have kids who have the cohesiveness and the willingness to believe in the system, who believe in the tradition that you've tried to establish, and who want to work toward your goals. You're not going to do it with kids who are just All-Americans; kids who have status but don't have togetherness. You need unity and a belief in what you're doing, and you've got to be a little stubborn. And you have to do the job under all circumstances. Under adverse circumstances or real happy circumstances, you have to sustain a certain level of concentration. You can go your lowest in certain situations, and you go your highest in other situations, but you have to maintain a certain level of concentration to win consistently. At Georgetown, we emphasize defense because I think that you can sustain a certain amount of consistency with defense that you might not be able to get with offense. It's easier to get five guys, year after year, to play consistent defense than it is to get guys who can shoot outside or run fast and make layups and those kinds of things.

Packer—On the one hand, we talk about kids and sports and having fun, and then we talk about 166-million-dollar contracts. You've been criticized for some of your methods during the NCAA tournament. But things have changed so much since your team voted in 1964 to go to the NCAA. How do you feel about this?

Thompson—I bet you that there hasn't been any group of kids who've gone to any NCAA tournament who've had any more fun than Georgetown. It's just that we had our fun together. Because we didn't walk up and down Bourbon Street or mingle with the alumni didn't mean that we didn't enjoy the Final Four. We maintained our own little controlled group, so that we could focus on basketball. The greatest fun of all is to have won it. There's fun in disciplining yourself and controlling yourself and knowing that, in the end, you accomplished something together. We carried on the foolishness and joking that comes along with every team. But we ran a controlled environment, and I believe in that, particularly when you are trying to carry out a specific function, a specific mission. Had we mingled with the alumni, we couldn't have told them it's time for you to go, we've got to get to work. Times are changing. There's more money involved in the tournament, there's more pressure, there's more media, there's more scheduling involved in it, and there's a need for more controls. We certainly had as much fun in those Final Four presentations as anybody did.

Packer—You've become a part of the history of the tournament. Where will it be 20 years from now?

Thompson—It's very hard to tell, but I don't think society will accept de-emphasizing. That's like going back to the horse and buggy when we're in the jet age. We need to put in the controls and do the proper monitoring of things. The money, the bigness, television; that's the real world that these kids live in outside the athletic environment. Everything has moved simultaneously. It's not like athletics is moving and everything else is standing still. Athletics is moving along with the rest of our society and I think that it's utterly ridiculous in educational institutions for people to think that one aspect of our society should move and the other aspect of it should stay back. I think we have to emphasize athletics in conjunction with the educational system. We're not going to go back to having fewer teams in the NCAA or less money. That's ridiculous. Everybody's getting paid more money for everything in society. And I think athletics has always served to prepare our kids for the real world. So I don't think it's bad, really.

The Year of the Cat

The 1985 Final Four became a Big East Conference convention when Georgetown, St. John's and Villanova all won their regionals. Never before had any conference sent three teams to the grand event in one year.

It was a nice angle for the media, but there was little doubt concerning the outcome of the tournament. Everyone knew that the Georgetown Hoyas would win a second consecutive title, becoming the first team since UCLA to repeat as champions. The team least expected to win was Villanova which had entered the tournament with a mediocre 19-10 record.

So much for expectations.

Memphis State was the only team not from the Big East when the Final Four convened at Rupp Arena in Lexington, Kentucky. Coach Dana Kirk's Tigers had eked a ticket out of the Midwest Regionals with a pair of squeakers, 59-57 over Boston College, and 63-61 over Oklahoma.

Keith Lee and William Bedford gave State height along the front line, and Andre Turner ran things from the point. But Villanova punched the Tigers' ticket with little trouble, 52-45. The victory was enough to get Massimino's Wildcats a tip of the hat from the press but nothing more.

St. John's, on the other hand, had players aplenty in shootist Chris Mullin and frontliners Bill Wennington and Walter Berry. For role power, rebounding and defense, Coach Lou Carnesecca added Willie Glass at forward. For confidence, they had a 66-65 win over Georgetown during the regular season that had propelled them into the top ranking for a while.

But at the Final Four, it did them little good. Georgetown's David Wingate played grand defense on Mullin and allowed him a puny 8 points. Reggie Williams and Ewing rammed in 20 and 16 points respectively as the Hoyas walked, 77-59.

When it was over, Carnesecca compared Georgetown to the great San Francisco dynasty with Bill Russell. "We tried everything," Looie said. "But when a club like Georgetown is executing and performing at that level of proficiency, there's very little you can do."

The prospect of Villanova playing Georgetown for the title produced mostly guffaws. One Lexington columnist suggested that the NCAA not even bother to hold the final.

Asked what his team would have to do to win, Massimino replied, "We're going to have to play a perfect game... And that may not be enough. We can't turn the ball over too much against their various pressure de-

The Villanova Wildcats prepare to battle Memphis State in the 1985 semis.

fenses. And we have to shoot in the 50 percent range."

Considering that the Hoyas had held most of their opponents to near 40 percent shooting, Coach Mass seemed to be wishing for a lot. Yet if his team had shot a mere 50 percent, Villanova would have lost the championship by 14 points. The Wildcats had to shoot nearly 80 percent to win by a hair. In the second half, Villanova shot 90 percent from the floor. Guard Harold Jensen was 5 for 5 from downtown range.

To go with the shooting, Gary McLain gave Massimino errorless ballhandling. And the Wildcats' match-up zone smartly squeezed Georgetown's offense outside. The inside, meanwhile, was a standoff with Ed Pinckney, Harold Pressley and Dwayne McClain battling Ewing and company.

There were other factors that figured in the outcome. The Hoyas had to get the lead early and keep it to prevent Villanova from slowing the tempo. Reggie Williams pushed in a string of jumpers to stretch a 20-14 lead, but

Patrick Ewing defends against Villanova's Harold Pressley inside.

The Cat's victory led to wild celebration in Philadelphia

a nagging ankle injury cut into his playing time. With him on the bench Villanova worked its way back to take a 29-28 lead at the half.

The Hoyas' uneasiness stretched into the second half, as Villanova extended its advantage to 36-30 and maintained it to 53-48. Georgetown kept pressing, though, and finally it worked, forcing a run of turnovers. Suddenly, the Hoyas took the lead, 54-53, and the ball with four minutes remaining. The Georgetown crowd roared as Horace Broadnax brought the ball up the floor. But the Hoyas opted not to play against the Villanova zone, and the Cats eased out of it momentarily. Then came the turnover. Bill Martin's pass glanced off Broadnax's foot, and Villanova scooped up the loose ball. The momentum shifted again, and the Hoyas could never recover it.

The crowd of 23,000 had seen Villanova whip Georgetown, 66-64, producing one of the most unexpected outcomes in tournament history. The Wildcats had hit a tournament record 78.6 percent from the floor. In the second half alone, Villanova shot 90 percent of their field goals, many of them long jumpers over the Hoyas' scrambling defense.

TOURNAMENT NOTES: Villanova's Ed Pinckney was named tournament MVP with 16 points, six rebounds and five assists in the title game.

1985

Villanova (66)	fg-fga	ft-fta	rb	pf	tp
H. Pressley	4- 6	3- 4	4	1	11
D. McClain	5- 7	7- 8	1	3	17
E. Pinckney	5- 7	6- 7	6	3	16
D. Wilbur	0- 0	0- 0	0	0	0
G. McLain	3- 3	2- 2	2	2	8
H. Jensen	5- 5	4- 5	1	2	14
M. Plansky	0- 0	0- 1	0	1	0
C. Everson	0- 0	0- 0	0	0	0
Team			3		
Totals	22-28	22-27	17	12	66
Georgetown (64)	fg-fga	ft-fta	rb	pf	tp
B. Martin	4- 6	2- 2	5	2	10
R. Williams	5- 9	0- 2	4	3	10
P. Ewing	7-13	0- 0	5	4	14
M. Jackson	4- 7	0- 0	0	4	8
D. Wingate	8-14	0- 0	2	4	16
P. McDonald	0- 1	0- 0	0	0	0
H. Broadnax	1- 2	2- 2	1	4	4
R. Dalton	0- 1	2- 2	0	1	2
Team			0		
Totals	29-53	6- 8	17	22	64

Half time: Villanova 29, Georgetown 28.
Officials: John Clougherty, Bob Dibler, Don Rutledge. Attendance: 23,124.

Destination Dallas

Tournament time 1986 brought the new, expanded, 64-team format. Some observers predicted problems. But the reviews were glowing. When it was over, the basketball community had witnessed yet another in the Final Four's run of classics. The season came down to a clash of senior dominated teams: Duke vs. Louisville. Yet the glory would belong to a freshman. Louisville center Pervis "Never Nervous" Ellison scored 25 points and sought out 11 rebounds to earn the MVP award, the first time a freshman had claimed the honor since Utah's Arnie Ferrin captured it in 1944. Ellison not only had the big numbers, he also made key plays late in the game that reversed the outcome.

Up until the closing minutes of the championship game, the year seemed destined for Duke with four prominent seniors: All-American guard Johnny Dawkins, center Jay Bilas and forwards Mark Alarie and David Henderson. The other keys were junior point guard Tommy Amaker and freshman Danny Ferry in the frontcourt. With a 32-2 record, Coach Mike Krzyzewski's Blue Devils won the ACC regular season and tournament, claiming with them the top-ranking in the polls and the number-one seed in the NCAA East Regional.

In the early rounds of the tournament, Duke ran into quick trouble, falling behind Mississippi Valley State. But Dawkins scored 20 of his 27 points in the second half, and the Blue Devils avoided the upset, 85-78. The next round brought an 89-61 blowout of Old Dominion, and again Dawkins led with 25 points. Dawkins continued that pace in the regional finals at the Meadowlands in New Jersey. He scored 25 with 10 rebounds in a 74-67 win over DePaul. Against Navy that Sunday, he rang up 28 points as Duke dropped David Robinson and the Middies, 71-50.

Seniors Milt Wagner, Jeff Hall and Billy Thompson drove the Louisville Cardinals through the West Regional, cruising past Drexel, 93-73, Bradley, 82-68, North Carolina, 94-79, before stalling briefly against Auburn and Chuck Person in the finals. The Cards' balanced scoring, led by Herbert Crook's 20 points, propelled them to the Final Four in Dallas, 84-76.

The surprise team of '86 was LSU, which gasped through a two-overtime upset of Purdue, 94-87, in the opening round of the Southeast Regional. Dale Brown's Bengals then crept past Memphis State, 83-81, Georgia Tech, 70-64, and Kentucky, 59-57, in the finals to reach

Dallas. Brown's team had run on emotion the whole way. When they reached the Final Four at Reunion Arena, they still had fuel. It just didn't burn hot enough to outlast Louisville's superior athletes. Senior Don Redden scored 22 in the semis, and the Bengals held the lead at the half, 44-36. But from there, the Cards took wing, as Thompson and Wagner both scored 22. Thompson made 10 of 11 field goal attempts. In the closing minutes, Louisville extended the margin to 11 points, 88-77.

Duke's last obstacle before the finals was Kansas, coached by Larry Brown and powered by sophomore Danny Manning and seniors Greg Dreiling, Ron Kellogg and Calvin Thompson. In the Midwest, the Jayhawks had zipped North Carolina A&T and Temple before struggling past Michigan State, 96-86, in overtime. The Michigan State game was marred by a clock malfunction that allowed Kansas extra time to stage a comeback, a development that still has State Coach Jud Heathcote fuming. In the regional finals, the Jayhawks pushed aside NC State, 75-67, to give the Final Four a Neapolitan flavor— one team each from the ACC, Big Eight, Metro and Southeastern.

The Jayhawks almost worked a trick on Duke in the national semifinals, but Danny Ferry came up with a rebound and a stickback late to propel Krzyzewski's team to the finals, 71-67. Once more, Dawkins was Duke's main man with 24 points.

Dawkins, the Naismith Player of the Year, sustained that pace into the championship right up until the final three minutes. With a jumpshot four seconds before the half, Dawkins gave the Blue Devils a 37-34 lead. Duke ran the lead as high as six at the 12:20 mark of the second half. But with 4:08 left, Ellison powered inside and scored to pull Louisville to 63-62. From there, the teams traded one-point margins, until the Cards began their stall at 2:48, holding a 66-65 lead. At 0:40, Hall launched an air ball from the perimeter, Ellison seized it and scored from three feet out, pushing the lead to 68-65. From there, it was a matter of whistles and free throws until Denny Crum claimed his second NCAA title, 72-69.

"It's unbelievable a freshman can handle that kind of pressure and play as well as he did," Crum said of Ellison.

TOURNAMENT NOTES: Ellison was joined on the All-Tournament team by teammate Thompson. Dawkins, who scored 24 in the final, and his teammates, Amaker and Alarie, also made the team.

Louisville's Billy Thompson goes for the block from behind on Duke's David Henderson. Left—Louisville's Pervis Ellison pulls down a rebound in the 1986 final.

1986

Louisville (72)	fg-fga	ft-fta	rb	pf	tp
H. Crook	5- 9	0- 3	12	2	10
B. Thompson	6- 8	1- 3	4	4	13
P. Ellison	10-14	5- 6	11	4	25
M. Wagner	2- 6	5- 5	3	4	9
J. Hall	2- 4	0- 0	2	2	4
M. McSwain	2- 4	1- 2	3	1	5
K. Walls	0- 1	0- 0	1	2	0
T. Kimbro	2- 4	2- 2	2	1	6
Team			1		
Totals	29-50	14-21	39	20	72

Duke (69)	fg-fga	ft-fta	rb	pf	tp
D. Henderson	5-15	4- 4	4	5	14
M. Alarie	4-11	4- 4	6	5	12
J. Bilas	2- 3	0- 0	3	4	4
T. Amaker	3-10	5- 6	2	3	11
J. Dawkins	10-19	4- 4	4	1	24
D. Ferry	1- 2	2- 2	4	2	4
W. Williams	0- 1	0- 0	0	0	0
B. King	0- 1	0- 1	0	2	0
Team			4		
Totals	25-62	19-21	27	22	69

Half time: Duke 37, Louisville 34. Officials: Hank Nichols, Don Rutledge, Peter Pavia. Attendance: 16,493.

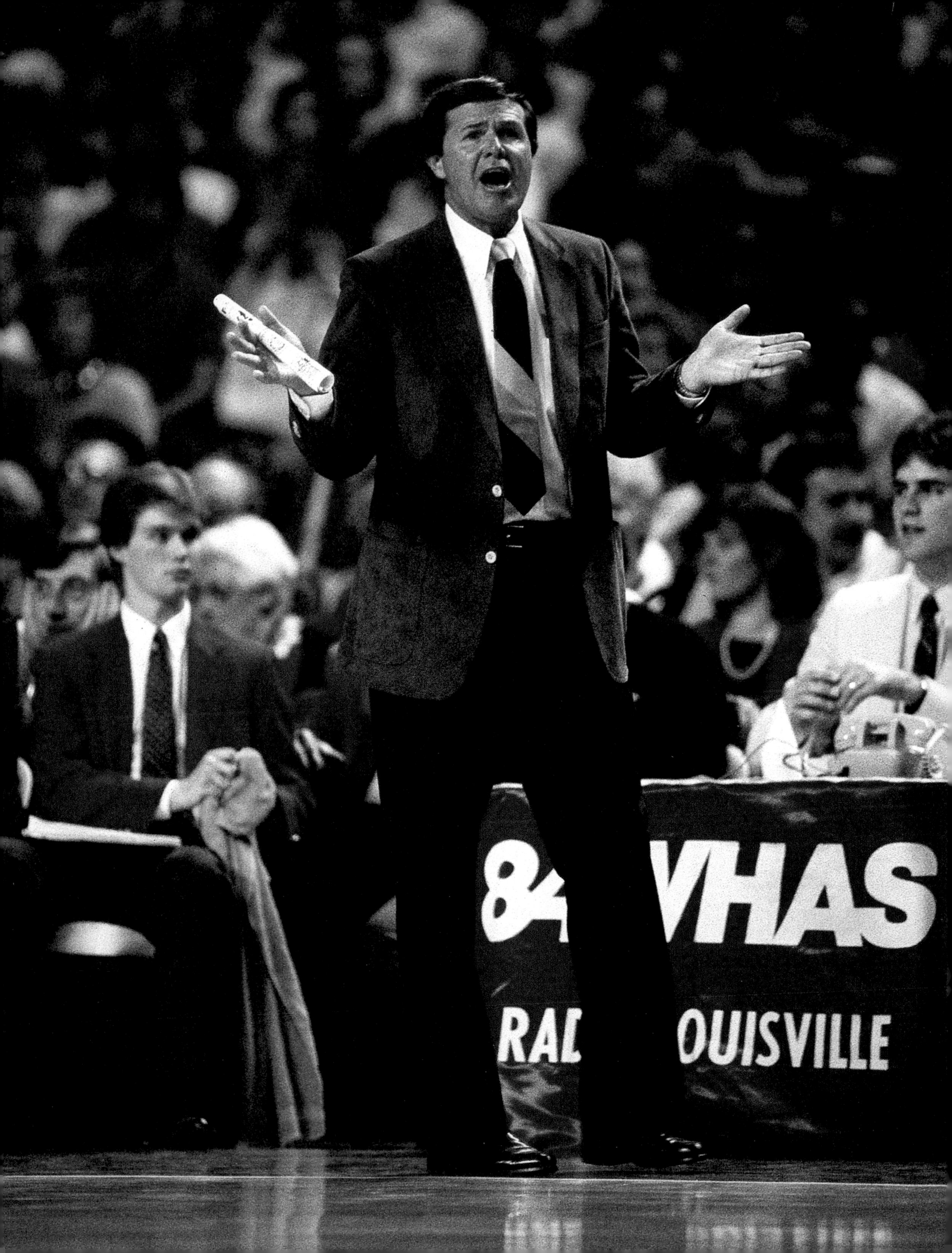
84
HAS
RAD
OUISVILLE

An Interview With Denny Crum

Denny Crum, a former UCLA player, served as an assistant to John Wooden from 1969-72, when he became head coach at Louisville. His teams have won two NCAA championships.

Packer—There are only a few guys in the history of the sport who have had the opportunity to experience success in the Final Four both as an assistant coach and as a head coach. I realize the emotions have to be a great deal different. Since you're one of the few, explain to me the difference.

Crum—When I was an assistant coach at UCLA, I didn't feel any pressure because we honestly felt we were the best team, and I knew we had the best head coach. It was just like any other game to me. I guess I didn't understand the importance of the Final Four and how hard it was to get there. I was kind of spoiled initially because it was an every year occurrence with UCLA. Even before I became Coach Wooden's assistant, I was at a local junior college, and UCLA was in the Final Four every year. The pressure was on Coach Wooden because he's the head coach. As an assistant, you're just kind of in limbo.

When we won our first championship at Louisville in 1980, I had a feeling of total relief. I wasn't really happy, or joyous, or excited. I was totally relieved that we had finally won one. We'd been in two other Final Fours and had lost both of them to UCLA. When we won the championship in 1986, I was relaxed and I really had a good time and enjoyed the coaching. In '80, it was just too much pressure.

Packer—You won your first championship against UCLA, kind of ironic for a person with your UCLA background. The semifinal game against UCLA in 1975, Coach Wooden's last year, was one of the great games in NCAA history. That had to be a game you thought you could win.

Crum—Yeah, we really played well in that one. We had played well that whole year, and I really thought we were going to win that game. We had the right opportunity to win it. We had a two-point lead. Coach Wooden instructed his freshman guard to foul Terry Howard right at the end of the game. We had a one-and-one, but we missed the free throw. Richard Washington hit a turnaround jump shot with two seconds to go to put the game into overtime, and we lost by one. I'm not saying we lost because we missed a free throw, because we had thrown the ball away a couple of times down the stretch. Good teams like UCLA have a way of winning. They never

thought they were going to lose, and I think our kids weren't sure because we had not been there before. That was a great game, and if we had to lose, I'm glad it was to Coach Wooden and UCLA.

Packer—The events that followed that game were bizarre. I had run into J. D. Morgan, and he said he had just talked to John and that John had an announcement to make. You had been with Coach Wooden a long time, not only as an assistant but also as a friend and a player. Was there anything that tipped you off that he was going to retire?

Crum—I had no inkling whatsoever until the press conference. Then, all the reporters were coming up to me and wanting to know if I was going to take the UCLA job. I had only been with Louisville a few years and we had not won a championship, and that was one of the things that I really felt strongly about doing there, and I told them I was not a candidate for the job. Not that it wasn't a great job, but I hadn't accomplished what I had wanted at Louisville. UCLA went on to beat Kentucky in the finals, which was a double-downer for us because we had wanted to play Kentucky for a long time during the regular season, and they refused to play us.

Packer—Going back to your high school days, how did you end up playing for UCLA?

conference championship, the first ever at the school. The president of the junior college knew Coach Wooden and he knew how badly I wanted to go to UCLA. So he invited Coach Wooden to come watch us play. We were playing a big rival, Compton I believe, and I played really well in the game. Coach Wooden then invited me to come and watch UCLA play, and he sent me two tickets in the mail. I never talked to him; he invited me through the president of the college. So I went to the game with my girl friend. I didn't talk to anybody, and nobody saw me, but when I got back home, I got a phone call and he asked me if I would like to come and watch them practice. And I said I'd love to. I went and watched the whole practice, and I really enjoyed it. When it was over, Coach Wooden said, "Come on, we're going to go eat at the training table." So we walked out of the gym and went to the little room where the team came to eat. He and I sat together, and I met a few of the other players. He never mentioned a scholarship and of course I didn't know anything about that stuff. When we got ready to walk out of the cafeteria, he asked, "Well, are you coming or not?" I said, "Yeah, I guess I am." That's what I always wanted to do anyhow, play basketball at UCLA. But there was no recruitment or high pressure. It was a different ball game in those days.

Packer—UCLA always had great players and, of course, that was true while you were an assistant there. What did UCLA do to get Bill Walton to come play at UCLA?

Crum—Well, we were very fortunate in a way because Bill Walton's older brother Bruce was on football scholarship to UCLA. I first found out about Bill through his brother and a guy named Frank Cushing, who was a UCLA graduate and a retired colonel in the Air Force who happened to live in San Diego. I started corresponding with Bill, and when I finally went down and watched him play, I came back and told Coach Wooden he was the best high school player I'd ever seen. I think he was a junior at the time. We were sitting in his office, and he got up and closed his door and he said, "Denny, don't you ever make that stupid statement again. It makes you look like an idiot to say that some red headed, freckled-faced kid from San Diego is the best high school player you've ever seen. First of all, there's never ever been, since I've been here, a major college prospect from San Diego, let alone the best player you've ever seen." And I said, "Coach, there's a lot of them I haven't seen play in high school, but he's still the best I've seen." Coach Wooden didn't like to recruit, didn't like to travel. He liked to be home with his wife. He enjoyed the coaching and teaching, but he didn't enjoy recruiting.

To get to take a look at Bill, I asked him what he was doing a certain Tuesday night. He said nothing, so I told him to tell Marion that he wouldn't be home for dinner. I told him I needed him to go somewhere with me. He

Crum—Tell you how my recruitment went. Coach Wooden told my high school coach that I wasn't good enough to play for UCLA. I knew that I was. At least in my mind I thought I was, and I wanted to go there so badly that I decided to go to junior college. I was a B-plus student, so I didn't have any grade problems or anything. I was going to prove to Coach Wooden that I could play there. They had recruited junior college kids before. My freshman year at LA Pierce Junior College, I led the state in scoring with a 27.1 points-a-game average. We won the

Coach Denny Crum of Louisville gives a little long-distance encouragement.

didn't know where we were going, and he didn't ask. We went to Bill's high school, and Coach Wooden wanted to sit way up in the corner of the gym to be obscure. Of course, everybody recognized him anyway. When the game was over and we were in the car, I asked him, "Well, what did you think about him." He said, " He is pretty good, isn't he?" And that was a real compliment because he didn't say real positive things about high school kids. He was usually real low key about that kind of thing.

So, I kept in contact with Bill. There is an interesting story about Bill's recruitment. Usually you get summer jobs for the kids when you're out to recruit them. Bill's brother and a couple of friends had rented a beach house down on the ocean front, and I asked Bill if he wanted a summer job. He said, no, he wasn't going to work that summer. He was going to read, which he did a lot of, and lie on the beach. I told him to call me if he needed something or had a problem or decided he wanted a job. Well, about halfway through the summer, he called me and said, "Coach, I've run out of money and I need a job." I said I'd see what I could do. So there I was in LA trying to find a job in San Diego, and I didn't know anybody. So I went to the Alumni people and they gave me a few names. I called this guy at a construction place and he said, sure, I'll hire him. He said he'd get $3.50 an hour to clean up. I called Bill and told him where to go and who to report to and he worked Monday, Tuesday, Wednesday and Thursday. Then I got a phone call from the guy and

he was worried. He said, "Bill didn't show up and I don't know what happened. Is there some problem or something I should know about?" I said I didn't know, but that I'd find out and get back to him. That evening, I called and asked him why he didn't show up for work. And he said, "Coach, all I needed was enough money to last me the rest of summer." And that's a true story, and it tipped me off that material things never meant anything to Bill Walton. He always ran around campus with cut-off Levis and T-shirts and thongs, or whatever you call them on his feet. He rode a motor scooter and was a champion of all the minority classes on campus. He had a different philosophy and he and Coach Wooden clashed a number of times, not about basketball, but other things.

Ironically, that year we had a great recruiting class, with Greg Lee, Jamaal Wilkes, who at that time was Keith Wilkes, and a couple others, including Gary Franklin. That was the year I left UCLA and went to Louisville. Then I had to turn right around my first year at Louisville, go back to LA, and play Bill Walton and that crew in the Final Four. Everybody said, "Well, they're just sophomores." And I said, "Listen, let me tell you something about sophomores who come from California. They play in organized leagues all year round. When I was in high school, we played in summer leagues five nights a week, with officials and uniforms, and in the spring, when the season was over, we played four nights a week. Not pick-up games, but organized basketball. By the time the kid is

a college sophomore, he's played more games than most other college seniors." So I said, don't underestimate sophomores. Of course, they beat us like a drum. We played as well as we could play and still got beat by 18 points or something.

Packer—Denny, you had an opportunity to compare UCLA teams. Which two teams do you would think were the toughest to beat?

Crum—Kareem's team in 1968, when they had Lucius Allen and Mike Warren as the guards, had such great quickness and was awesome. They could dominate teams with their quickness and their great playing ability. Another team I liked was Coach Wooden's first championship team with Hazzard and Goodrich. Talk about two great guards.

That team didn't have the size, but they were relentless with the zone press, which was relatively new to college teams. As the game wore on, they started anticipating passes and moves and they might be down 15 points, and, all of a sudden, boom, they'd be right back in the game and just beat you with their quickness. A third team, one of Walton's, the one with Greg Lee and Jamaal Wilkes, would have been competitive with any team I've ever seen in college basketball.

Packer—Your two clubs that won at the Final Four followed clubs that, the year before, weren't your best. You get a lot of credit for bringing teams along and having them gel in March at tournament time. Is that something you do consciously?

Crum—I think it's something inherent in the system that I learned from Coach Wooden. His teaching process is a building process based on repetition. By year's end, they're doing everything they can do to the best of their ability. We play one of the toughest schedules in the country year in and year out. Confidence is a crucial thing at tournament time, because it's a do-or-die situation, and the pressures are such that if you don't think you can win

it, you probably can't. I don't care how good you think you are. Our kids, because we played everybody in the country by tournament time, knew we were competitive and that we had gotten better each week. That's one of the things we used, get a little bit better each week. Learn something this week that you didn't know before. By year's end, with the level of competition we played, our kids knew they were competitive and that they could win. In '80, when we won, it's ironic because we won with freshmen centers. Rodney McCray, a freshman, took Scooter McCray's place when Scooter got hurt in the third game of the tournament. And I didn't even have much chance to play Rodney during the season except as a backup center or something. In the championship game against UCLA in Indianapolis, he had 11 rebounds and played super. Then in '86, Pervis Ellison played great in the championship game. But the teams were a lot different. The '80 team had three sophomores, a freshman, and Darrell Griffith. So it was an exceptionally young team but they had Darrell, a superstar who could carry you through all the tough spots. The '86 team had Milt Wagner, but he had been injured the year before, and it took him half the season to get into the swing of things. As he started playing better, our team got better and better, and by year's end, I think we had won 14 or 15 in a row. Coming into the tournament, we were really playing well. But that was a senior-dominated team, although we had a freshman center, Billy Thompson.

Packer—Today the NCAA tournament is much different in terms of the number of games you have to play; multiple teams from a given conference, the seedings process, the geographical changes. If today's tournament format had existed, say, back when UCLA had its run of championships, do you think they would have had as much success?

Crum—I don't think it would have changed the results because UCLA was the best team year in and year out anyway. They had the best players, the best coach, the best program, and they were just dominant over everyone else. Today, nobody is clearly dominant. There are more good teams today than there were then. The level of play is higher, the coaching is better, the format is different, and it is probably more difficult today. That's not to take anything away from UCLA, because if they had those teams playing today they would win the majority of the games.

Packer—Your teams have been involved in some great games. Although that wasn't a championship game, I feel the Louisville-Houston game was probably one of the great all-time performances in the Final Four. In your opionion, what would be the great games you have seen in the Final Four?

Crum—I go back to the '75 Louisville-UCLA game, when we lost 75-74 in overtime, as a game that was as well

UCLA Coach John Wooden sends reserve Bill Seibert into a 1970 game.

played by both teams as you can play. The teams just executed everything as well as it could be done.

Packer—What was the best individual performance that you've seen?

Crum—I think I'd have to go with Greg Lee's and Bill Walton's performances against Memphis State in the finals. I think Greg Lee had 14 or 15 assists, and Bill Walton hit 21 out of 22 field goals.

Packer—You've won two national championships, and you were associated with Coach Wooden, who won 10. Is there a formula for success that you see?

Crum—I don't think there is any one system that is better than any other. You have to do what you do best. You can't teach what you don't know. The little things make the difference when something is working or not working, and they can only be learned over the years by trial and error. Something I think is very important is to play the toughest competition that you can play. Because you have to win six in a row in the tournament, you can't have an off night. And the only way you can learn to play your best every night is to play your best throughout the year.

The Three-point Showdown

Happy days again returned to Hoosierland in 1987 as Indiana Coach Bobby Knight found the championship formula—a pair of junior-college transfers to align with All-American Steve Alford. Knight's team brought his third and Indiana's fifth national title home with a sizzling late-game victory over Syracuse in the national finals.

Knight had departed from his previous policy of not recruiting junior-college players when he brought in Dean Garrett and Keith Smart to bolster his core team of Alford, Rick Calloway, and Daryl Thomas. The move

needed no better confirmation than Smart swishing the winning shot in the closing seconds of the national finals.

Although the Hoosiers claimed the championship, the consolation prizes weren't bad for everyone else. Syracuse Coach Jim Boeheim found some peace of mind and relief from his critics by assembling a solid team and coaching it into the national finals. The Big East Conference again basked in the warm glow of the spotlight by having two teams—Syracuse and surprising Providence—in the Final Four at New Orleans. After the season, Providence Coach Rick Pitino parlayed his success

Indian's Steve Alford looks for an opening against Derrick Coleman of Syracuse

into a job as head coach of the New York Knicks.

The only disappointment came for Nevada-Las Vegas Coach Jerry Tarkanian, who put together a sleek unit—the nation's top-ranked club much of the year—and nervously chewed his towel as the Runnin' Rebels pitched and pulled their way to the Final Four only to meet Indiana in a classic shootout. The Hoosiers, of course, emerged from the smoke and Tarkanian's Rebs went home.

History will remember the 1986-87 season as the year of the three-pointer, a controversial new rule that had some coaches fuming and some smiling the entire season. The abruptness of the change left some coaches—Louisville's Denny Crum, for example—without time to recruit players who could drill jumpshots from downtown, or at least past the 19-foot, 6-inch perimeter.

The teams that did emerge had long-range shooters in residence: Steve Alford at Indiana and Gerald Paddio and Freddie Banks at UNLV. And ultimately, the three-pointer would play a major role in determining the national championship, as Alford hit seven of 10 attempts in the finals.

UNLV earned a reputation early for the three-pointer and gunned their way to the top seed in the West Regional. Their real strength, however, was in the frontcourt with senior Armon Gilliam. The regionals proved that as much as anything. The Rebels mowed down Idaho State, 95-70, Kansas State, 80-61, and Wyoming, 92-78, before fighting it out with a nifty Iowa team in the regional finals. There Gilliam did most of the slinging with 27 points and 10 rebounds as UNLV won a tight one, 84-81.

The Hoosiers also came out smoking in the Midwest, drilling Fairfield, 92-58, in the first round, then sending Auburn home, 107-90 (Smart had 20 points, nine rebounds and 15 assists). From there, however, the regionals were a sweat. Duke had lost Dawkins and company from the season before but was still pesky in the semifinals before losing 88-82. And Dale Brown was waiting with another Louisiana State Cinderella team in the regional finals, hoping to sneak into the Final Four back in the home state. But Alford led four teammates in double figures with 20 points, and Indiana snipped Brown's hopes, 77-76.

For Providence and Pitino, the magical mystery tournament was keyed by senior guard Billy Donovan and Delray Brooks, a transfer from Indiana. Donovan got the Friars' tour rolling with 35 points and 12 assists in an opening round win over Alabama-Birmingham. Then Providence threw cold milk on another Cinderella, Austin Peay, 90-87, in overtime and dumped second-seeded Alabama 103-82. But the real delight for the Friars was whipping Big East rival Georgetown, 88-73, in the Southeast finals. For all the Providence joy, a pallor was cast over the regionals by death of Pitino's six-month-old son, Daniel Paul.

Alford brings the ball up against Syracuse's pressure.

Boeheim's bunch came alive on the emergence of guard Sherman Douglas, the maturation of center Rony Seikaly, and the fact that the Orangemen played the first two rounds of the East Regional on their home floor. Syracuse won two straight tournament games for first time in 10 appearances, downing Georgia Southern, 79-73, (as Sherman Douglas scored 27 points), and a good Western Kentucky team, 104-86, (Greg Monroe scored 20 for the Orange).

Then they punched Florida's ticket, 87-81, in the regional semifinals and traveled on to the Final Four with a 79-75 win over NC State in the regional finals.

The semifinal in New Orleans was a Big East matchup, Orange versus Friars, but Syracuse pretty much solved the riddle early and coasted, 77-63, with all five starters in double figures. Howard Triche had 12 points and 11 rebounds; Derrick Coleman had 12 and 12.

The atmosphere in the other semifinal was anything but sleepy. Banks scored 38, including an incredible three-point performance and Gilliam slipped in 32 for Vegas. Alford matched that with 33 for Indiana, but he had more help from his teammates, as Calloway, Garrett and Smart all rang up double figures. Tarkanian chewed his towel and watched as Indiana pushed away, 97-93.

The final was an odd, tight game that twisted the fans in knots. Bob Knight played nine Hoosiers, but only four scored: Daryl Thomas had 20 with seven rebounds; Steve Alford knocked in 23 points with five assists, two steals and three turnovers, (including seven of 10 from three-point range); Keith Smart scored 21 with six assists, two turnovers, and two steals.

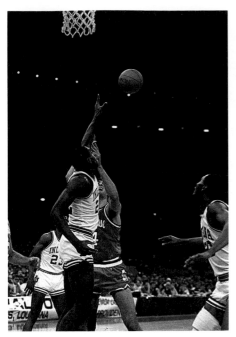

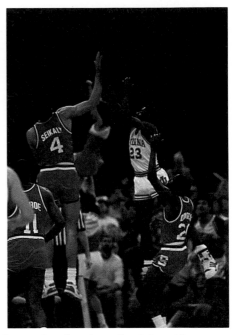

Left—Dean Garrett knocks away Rony Seikaly's shot. Center—Garrett and Seikaly duel inside. Right—Keith Smart launches a jump shot. Below—The Syracuse defense seemed like a canopy at times, but Alford still managed to get his shot off.

It almost wasn't enough against Syracuse's balance. Douglas led with 20 points and seven assists, and Seikaly was aggressive inside with 18 points and 10 rebounds. The Hoosiers had a 34-33 lead at the half, and that pace persisted. Going into the closing seconds, Syracuse held a 73-72 lead, until Smart launched his swisher sweet from the left baseline to give Indiana a 74-73 lead. The Orange first fumbled the notion of a timeout, then flubbed the inbound pass and the final lifeblood drained from the clock.

TOURNAMENT NOTES: Indiana had made seven of 11 three point attempts in the final, for 63.6 percent accuracy, much better than their 23 of 51 from two-point range for 45.0 percent.

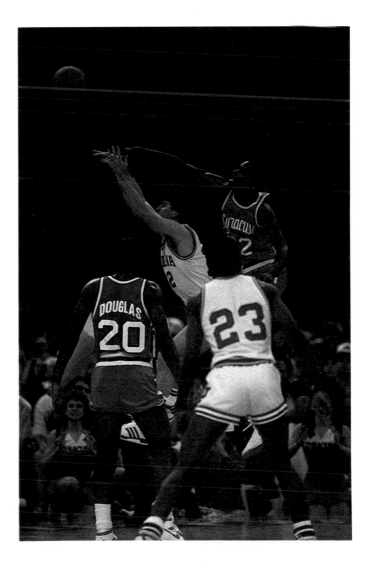

1987

Syracuse	(t)fg-fga(3)	ft-fta	rb	pf	tp
H. Triche ...	3- 9 0- 0	2- 4	1	4	8
D. Brower ...	3- 3 0- 0	1- 3	1	3	7
R. Seikaly ...	7-13 0- 0	4- 6	10	3	18
G. Monroe ..	5-11 2- 8	0- 1	2	1	12
S. Douglas ..	8-15 2- 2	2- 2	2	3	20
S. Thompson.	0- 2 0- 0	0- 0	3	0	0
D. Coleman..	3- 7 0- 0	2- 4	19	2	8
Team			0		
Totals ...	29-60 4-10	11-20	38	16	73
Indiana	(t)fg-fga(3)	ft-fta	rb	pf	tp
R. Calloway..	0- 3 0- 0	0- 0	2	3	0
D. Thomas...	8-18 0- 0	4- 7	7	1	20
D. Garrett ...	5-10 0- 0	0- 0	10	4	10
S. Alford	8-15 7-10	0- 0	3	2	23
K. Smart	9-15 0- 1	3- 4	5	2	21
T. Meier	0- 0 0- 0	0- 1	1	0	0
S. Eyl	0- 0 0- 0	0- 0	1	2	0
K. Smith	0- 0 0- 0	0- 0	0	1	0
J. Hillman ...	0- 1 0- 0	0- 0	2	2	0
Team			4		
Totals ...	30-62 7-11	7-12	35	17	74

Half time: Syracuse 33, Indiana 34. Officials: J. Forte, N. Fine, J. Silvester. Attendance: 64,959.

An Interview With Bobby Knight

Bobby Knight first experienced the Final Four as an Ohio State player in 1960. He has won three championships as coach at Indiana.

Packer—Bob, when did you first hear of Pete Newell?

Knight—When you and I started playing in college, the top team was California and Pete Newell was the coach. Cal won the NCAA championship in '59, and played in the championship game again in '60, although they were beaten by our Ohio State team. When his '60 team won the Pacific Coast championship, it was his fourth straight title.

Fred Taylor, my coach at Ohio State, had spent a lot of time with Pete Newell. The summer before the 1959 season, Coach Taylor spent a week with him at the Moore-head, Minnesota clinic. Pete was speaking for four or five days, and Coach Taylor went up there and spent the whole time talking with Pete about defense. What he learned paid off, because as the '60 basketball season wore on, we became a better and better defensive team. When we played Pete's Cal team in the NCAA championship game that year, we defensed them very well, and it was ironic that Coach Taylor had learned so much about defense from Pete.

I can tell you exactly where I met Pete the first time. It was in 1969 in a little bookstore in the St. Francis Hotel in San Francisco. We were playing California in the Cable Car Classic and Stu Inman, who was the general manager of the Portland Trailblazers, was there to see the games. Pete was there, too, as the general manager of the San Diego Rockets. I told Stu I'd really like to meet Pete. So, he arranged a meeting. When I walked into the bookstore, I saw Pete at the newsstand. I introduced myself, and we sat down from noon until five o'clock talking basketball.

One of the ironies of Pete's coaching career was that he only coached in college for 14 years. He was at USF for four years, at Michigan State for four years, and at California for six.

Packer—You were 19 years old and were playing on a team that, in effect, had kicked highly regarded California's tail. What was your impression of Coach Newell after that game?

Knight—Although Cal was 27 or 28 and 1 when we played them and had lost only to USC early in the season, I really didn't think it was a very talented team. I felt that anybody who could go to the final game with that kind of talent had to be an extraordinary coach.

Packer—On your ball club, you had Jerry Lucas, Mel

Nowell, and John Havlicek returning for two more years. How disappointing was it not to repeat as NCAA champions?

Knight—We had a really good forward named Joe Roberts, who was 6'6," about 220 pounds, a tremendous jumper, a good shooter, and a good defensive player. At that time, he was a pretty good-sized forward. We lost him and we had nobody else nearly as good. And then the next year we lost Siegfried. Siegfried, in my thinking, was the best guard in the Big Ten. He was 6'4," weighed 195 pounds, and he was ruthless player, great on defense. He could shoot the ball really well. He was a helluva player. When we lost those guys, we could never replace them.

Packer—You were a sub on those teams. Did that influence you in your philosophy about substitution patterns?

Knight—Coach Taylor settled on five guys to start and stayed with that five. I bet in the three years that I played there, there weren't 10 changes in the starting lineup. I have always started a bunch of guys. Hell, everybody on my team starts at some time. I think its great for a guy who plays well to come back and start. When we played you in Winston-Salem in '61, you got us down by about five points. I came into the game with about 10 minutes left in the half. I scored four or five points and got a few re-bounds. We were up six points at the half, so in the locker room I was really anticipating what I was going to do in the second half. But I didn't get to start the second half, and I was really disappointed. That was maybe the most disappointed I've ever been. Coach Taylor went back to the starting lineup. I've never done that. I want the guy who has gone into the game and done well to have a chance to continue to play, plus I want the guy who started, but hasn't played real well, to say, "Well, I've got to work like hell to get that chance back again."

Packer—Jumping to an entirely different era, I can think of one game in particular when Isiah Thomas played against LSU in Philadelphia in 1981. Ethan Martin??? was right in his face and Isiah had a bad first half, and I don't think Isiah even played much in the second half. How does that fit in with your coaching philosophy?

Knight—We took Thomas out at the end of the first half and sent in Jimmy Thomas. At the start of the second half, Isiah got his third foul, so we just kept on playing

Bobby Knight in a moment of frustration on the sidelines.

Jimmy. As long as we're doing well, I'll let the guys in there keep playing. I like to have them think that everybody has a chance to play.

Packer—When was the first time you ever heard of the Final Four?

Knight—I was first aware of the Final Four when San Francisco beat Tom Gola and LaSalle in 1955. Gola was my favorite player. I thought he was a great player. I can remember watching him play against Dick Ricketts and Si Green, both of Duquesne, in the finals of the Holiday Festival in Madison Square Garden that year. I was a sophomore in high school. K.C. Jones guarded Gola, and Gola scored 16 points. But USF won. Then in '56 I listened to the Iowa-USF game on the radio, and Iowa had USF, Bill Russell's team, down 17 to 4 to start the championship game. Those were probably the first two I paid any attention to or listened to.

Packer—When did it cross your mind that you'd like to coach in a Final Four?

Knight—In 1963, I went to the finals with a buddy of mine from Union Town, Pennsylvania. I was an assistant coach in high school, and the finals were in Louisville. We were screwing around up in Akron until about midnight. We didn't have a room, so we were in no hurry to leave. We were going to drive down to Louisville. We made it to Cincinnati and we were taking a back road through Indiana when we ran out of gas somewhere near Aurora, Indiana. Aurora is just a little town on the Ohio River, and it's dark and it's five in the morning, and I don't know how the hell my buddy had this, but he had a gasoline can and a length of rubber hose in the back of his car in the trunk. And I thought, "How in the hell is he going to get gas?" He said, "Come on." So we take this gas can and hose and we sneak into some farmer's garage and take the gas cap off his tractor, and we suck the vacuum in the hose, and I get sick off the fumes, and we stick the hose down into the can and drain the gas out of the guy's tractor. We put it in our tank and drive to Louisville, and that was the first NCAA championship I went to as a fan.

So we get down to Louisville and go to the Brown Hotel, where my boss, Harold Andrews, was rooming with Tony LaTuesa, the Akron University coach. We knock on the door and they're just showering, so we just walked into the room and crawled into their beds. I mean as they got out of them, we got into them.

Packer—After all this, did you have tickets to the game?

Knight—Yes we had tickets, but I forget where the hell we got them. The four teams that year were Duke, Loyola, Cincinnati and Oregon State. I remember saying to myself, "If you're going to coach, it would be really great to have a team here some day."

Packer—So, a few years later, you're the rookie coach at Indiana. George McGinnis has turned pro and left school. What was your reaction toward the loss of McGinnis?

Knight—McGinnis left about a week before I got there. But ever since then, George has been just great for us. He's a helluva recruiter and he has stayed really close to our basketball team. Every game, he comes down to the locker room at the half. I tell him that leaving school early cost him a million dollars: "If you had stayed for two more years, you would have been a high-priced guy to go into the NBA. We'd have won the NCAA with you playing."

Knight—I can remember telling Dave Bliss that sometime in five years, by 1975, that we'd play in the NCAA finals. That would have been our fifth year, and the first players we had recruited would be seniors. Our objective was to play in San Diego. When San Diego came around, we happened to have the best team in the country. But that's when Scott May got hurt and couldn't play.

Packer—But you ended up going to the Final Four before 1975.

Knight—We ended up going in '73. We won six straight games in the Big Ten that year. Since we were only playing 14 conference games that year, a 6-0 start made us hard to catch. We went to the NCAA regionals and beat Marquette and Kentucky. Then you only had to win two games to get to the finals. Now, of course, you've got to win four games, and I think that is really hard.

Packer—So you faced Johnny Wooden in your first tournament final. By the time you faced him in '73, you're talking about a legend. What was it like going up against him?

Knight—I think the hardest thing was to get our kids to believe they could win. UCLA won their first championship in 1964, when my players were still in fifth, sixth, and seventh grade. So now we're in 1973, nine years later, and all they've ever heard is UCLA. I mean they don't know anybody but UCLA. And, all of a sudden, we've got to play them. And we have to play them in a semifinal game.

But I really thought we could do a good job on them. I thought Steve Downing could play Walton. I didn't think we could shut Walton out, but I thought he could score against Walton. Downing ended up scoring 26 and holding Walton to 14. Quinn Buckner and Jimmy Crews were our guards and they were freshmen. Steve Green was just a sophomore at one forward. Most of the team were sophomores and freshmen. At the half we're down 20 or 21, and we go 22 down, but then we score 18 straight. Then we get the worst official's call I've ever seen. Downing is guarding Walton. Walton pivots and makes a crossover to his right. Now where the official is, I can see why he would call blocking on Downing, but what he doesn't

Bobby Knight scores on a layup for Ohio State in 1961.

see is Walton giving Downing the forearm just like a defensive end. He just knocks Downing right on his ass and that should be Walton's fifth foul. We're only down two points at the time. Instead of Walton picking up his fifth foul, it's Downing's fourth. Then we get to within two points with about seven minutes to play, and Steve fouls out, and we end up losing by 11. Wooden said after the game that he felt sure they would have won even if Walton had fouled out. But I don't think there was any way because we had just scored 18 in a row, and with Downing playing the way he was. . . .

Packer—You said you set a goal at Indiana to be at the Final Four in San Diego in 1975.

Knight—I think you can get caught up with getting there. That's not the objective for me. The objective was getting there and winning. Getting there only transpires on the day of the regional finals. We play to get into the finals and win the championship.

Packer—You didn't get there in '75. Scott May was injured, but even without Scott you came close. Any thoughts on the season?

Knight—That year, I think I made the biggest mistake I've ever made in coaching. When May broke his arm in the Purdue game, I had to decide whether to replace him with Tom Abernethy or John Laskowski. Abernathy is the normal replacement for May because he's a helluva defensive player and rebounder, but Laskowski is a great scorer. So I play Laskowski at the point against Illinois. At the workout on Sunday, I tell John to shoot the first three times he gets the ball, and I tell him that I'll let him know if I want him to shoot anymore. He hits his first two shots and scores 28 points against Illinois. We win 113 to 89, and I remember thinking 113 points is great, but we shouldn't be giving up 89 points. We had two regular season games left, and I'm struggling trying to decide whether to play Abernethy or Laskowski. If I play Laskowski, I've got to break up our guard combination of Wilkerson and Buckner because Wilkerson has to guard the opposition's high scoring forward. With Abernethy I don't have that problem because he can guard whoever is at forward. Abernethy's our best defensive forward; he's even a better defensive forward than May. We're playing Texas-El Paso in our first round game at 12:30, and I'm sitting there at quarter til twelve undecided about who is going to start. I think I should start Abernathy, but Laskowski is just too good a scorer. So we go with Laskowski, and that broke up our guard combination and really hurt us. When we played Kentucky, we start May, who was on the verge of being ready to play, but he can't handle the ball or throw it at all with his left hand. So he was in the game only for a minute and we take him out. We struggle, struggle, struggle, and they keep scoring against us and end up beating us 92-90. Nobody should score 92 points against us, and I think if we had played Abernethy, he

could have played Kevin Grevey, but the way we played it, I had to put Wilkerson on Grevey while and Laskowski and Buckner guard Flynn and Connor out on top. Our normal guard combination, Wilkerson and Buckner, would have eaten up Flynn and Connor. Abernethy would have done a good job on Grevey. We might have held the score down in the 70s. I'm not positive we would have won, but we would have been a much better team. Not going back to the best defensive team we ever had was the biggest mistake I made in coaching. And that '75 team might have been good enough to have won it all.

My biggest regret in coaching is that our '75 team didn't win because that team included Steve Green, Laskowski, Steve Ahlfield, and Kamstra, guys who really started with me. They were the guys I had recruited before I ever coached a game.

Packer—The '76 team has to go down in history as one of the best teams. Do you agree?

Knight—The '75 team was better.

Packer—In '76, you not only get to the Final Four, you win the championship. About the only bad thing that happened that night was the injury to your great defensive guard, Bobby Wilkerson.

Knight—Bobby had gotten 19 rebounds in the semifinals against UCLA. You think of our front line of Benson, Abernathy, and May, all three NBA players for at least five years. And UCLA's front line was Marques Johnson, Richard Washington, and David Greenwood, all three 10-year pros. But in that choice company, Bobby was the leading rebounder in the game by far.

In that game, we didn't play very well the first half. In the second half, we came on and played really well. We got a lot of good plays from everybody. With 10 minutes to go, the score was even, but five minutes later, we were ahead by seven or eight. We ended up winning the game by 14.

Packer—What was the emotion like winning the first one.?

Knight—The first time we won it should have been in '75. That team was a great one, one of the best I've been around, including the teams I was on and the teams I've seen play. There just hasn't been a better one. So it was a tremendous disappointment not to win the title that year. One of the major emotional feelings in '76 was relief at winning the championship. I was just so pleased that that team won because it was one of the truly great college basketball teams. You know your team will always identify with that accomplishment. I still go home to athletic events in Ohio State, and I'm a member of the only Ohio State team that ever won the NCAA championship. That stays with you and you like to see kids have a part of it. I tell our players that some day they will be watching the tournament with their kids or grandchildren and they'll say, "Hey, I played in that." And it's a helluva lot better,

goddamn it, to say you won it. I talk to our players about how it was with all of us who played on the 1960 championship team. When we have a team with a chance to go to the finals, I put up a mathematical equation that shows a player's chances of winning the national title. The odds are a little over 4000 to 1. You take 280 some teams and multiply that by 12 scholarships and you're up to 4200 players in the division. Only 30 will play for the championship, and just 15 are going to win it. I've seen how winning the title has affected our kids. It gives them something. That's a hell of a thing for a 21- or 22-year-old kid to be a part of. And I honestly think it gives them a confidence to continue to do things in their lives. Our players have done very well as pros or as business people or professionals.

Packer—In the game against Syracuse this past season, you put Keith Smart back into the ball game. What were you thinking about?

Knight—Calloway hadn't been playing very well. We were struggling even before the Monday night game. We went in to work out on Sunday and I was real tired, the players were tired, and I thought I was making a mistake to go in and work out at all. But I was afraid not to. But we didn't stay very long. When the game unfolded on Monday night, I thought we were too tired to win it. Calloway played very poorly. We had had such a tough game with Vegas on Saturday, and Calloway didn't score a point in the game Monday night. I put Hillman in for Smart, but Smart was our most active kid, so we had to get him back in the ball game. I wanted Smart playing in Calloway's position as a scorer because Calloway wasn't giving us anything, with Hillman handling the ball.

Packer—How about the last shot. Who did you want to see get it?

Knight—I see all that bullshit about how we called timeout and talked about setting up a play. First of all, we didn't have a play. We wanted to run our offense and try to screen off the goal. I didn't want a shot taken until 10 seconds were left. We went inside to Thomas, and Thomas made a great play getting the ball back out to Smart. I didn't know if his shot was going to go in or not, but hell, he got an open 16-foot shot from the base line and he drilled it. I keep saying I didn't think this was a great team, but there was a great quality to this team with its ability to play in crucial situations and its ability to make points. They went through tight games with Duke, LSU, and Vegas and made almost every play that had to be made.

Packer—On the day of the tournament final in 1981, President Reagan was shot. Was there talk of canceling the game?

Knight—I was asleep that afternoon. I didn't know the President had been shot until five or six o'clock. I couldn't imagine canceling the game because that's just not the way we do things in this country. Historically we rise to the occasion and put things in perspective and go on. It just never dawned on me that we would not play the game. The first time it dawned on me that it was even an issue was as we were walking down the ramp into the arena. Here come about 50 writers, who look like they came out of the wall. I'm walking down the ramp behind Benson, who is squeezing a rubber ball I'd given him as a freshman when I told him, "Goddamn it, get some strong hands." And here we are three years later, and he's still squeezing that rubber ball going to the championship game. The writers are asking if I think the game should be played. Dean Smith and I had talked about it, and we both thought we should play. The two people who settled the issue were Chancellor Friday of UNC and Indiana's President Ryan. They got together and said we were going to play the game and they told the NCAA tournament that. They already had the semifinal game in progress, so it didn't make sense not to play our game.

Packer—Short answers. The finest Final Four game you ever saw that your team didn't play in?

Knight—The North Carolina - Georgetown game in '82 was a really good game. Also Georgetown against Kentucky. The biggest upset was the '77 game when Marquette beat North Carolina.

Packer—Best individual performance you can recall.

Knight—I saw Goodrich's game against Michigan on television. That same night, Bill Bradley scored 56 against Wichita. Walton, hitting 21 of 22, was excellent.

Packer—What do you think will be the future of the Final Four?

Knight—It has to be one of the best two or three sporting events in the country, and that's not going to change. It's at least the equivalent of the World Series, better than the Super Bowl. I don't think the excitement is there at the Super Bowl. In the NCAAs, you've got to win six times and you've got to win twice within three days to win the championship.

Packer—What are your goals now. Do you take it year by year, or do you say you want to win three more?

Knight—I never really think of winning. We've had more good teams than the three teams that won the championship. This year, after we played Iowa really tough at Iowa, I thought we had a team capable of beating anybody. Of course you never know if they can win six in a row and win it all.

Author's Acknowledgements

The authors wish to express their appreciation to their copy editors and production assistants—Richard Lovegrove, David Meador, Karen Lazenby, Toby Hunt, Deborah Geering, Barbara Packer, Virginia Lazenby, Tim Orwig, and Rick Remensnyder. Special thanks to The Naismith Memorial Basketball Hall of Fame, CBS Sports, NBC Sports, the National Collegiate Athletic Association, and to the numerous people who granted us interviews for this book.

Photo Credits

P.2 Villanova University Sports Information; P.3 UCLA Sports Information; P.5 UCLA; P.6-7 Indiana University Sports Information; P. 8 Princeton University Sports Information; P. 10 CBS Sports; P.13 Archives, University of Oregon; P. 15, CBS Sports; P.16 NBC Sports; P. 17 NC State Sports Information; P 18, Marquette University Sports Information; P.20-21 University of Oregon; P.22-23, Indiana University; Naismith Memorial Basketball Hall of Fame; P. 24-25, University of Wisconsin Sports Information; P. 26, Standford University; P. 27, Basketball Hall of Fame; P. 30, DePaul University Sports Information; P. 31, Archives, University of Wyoming; P. 33-34, University of Utah Sports Information; P. 37, Oklahoma State Sports Information, Hall of Fame; P. 38 Hall of Fame; P. 39 Oklahoma State, P. 41, Hall of Fame; P. 43 University of North Carolina Sports Information; P. 46-47, Holy Cross Archives; P. 48-51, University of Kentucky Sports Information; University Archives; P. 52-53 City College of New York; P. 54-55 University of Kentucky; P. 56-57, University of Kansas Sports Information; P. 58-59, Indiana University, Kansas; P. 60-61, Hall of Fame, LaSalle University Sports Information; P.64-67, University of San Francisco Sports Information; P. 69-73, universities of Kansas, North Carolina; P.74-75, Kentucky; P. 76-79, University of California Sports Information; P. 80-83, Photo Archives, Ohio State University; P. 84-87, University of Cincinnati Sports Information; P. 88-89, Loyola University Sports Information; P. 90-91, UCLA; P. 92, Duke University Sports Information; P. 95, University of Utah Sports Information, Kentucky; P. 96-11, UCLA; P110-113, NC State; P. 114-126, UCLA; P. 128-129, Indiana University; P. 130-131, Marquette; P. 132-37; University of Kentucky, Duke University; P. 138-139, Photo by Steve Lingenfelter; P. 139-143, Michigan State University Sports Information, Indiana State Sports Information; P. 144-145, University of Louisville Sports Information; P. 146-147, Indiana University; P. 148-151, University of North Carolina, Georgetown University Sports Information; P. 154-55, NC State, P. 156-57, Georgetown University; P. 158-161, Georgetown University; P. 162-63, Villanova Sports Information; P. 164-171, Duke University, University of Louisville; P. 172-177, Indiana University. P. 179, Ohio State Archives; P. 181, Indiana University.

MANHOOD,

· A NEW DEFINITION ·

STEPHEN A. SHAPIRO

G. P. PUTNAM'S SONS · NEW YORK

The author gratefully acknowledges permission from the following sources to reprint material in their control.

Coward-McCann, Inc., for material from *What Do Women Want* by Luise Eichenbaum and Susie Orbach, copyright © 1983 by Luise Eichenbaum and Susie Orbach.

Doubleday & Company, Inc., for material from *Homer, the Odyssey*, translated by Robert Fitzgerald, copyright © 1961 by Robert Fitzgerald.

Gerald Duckworth & Co., Ltd., for material from *Against the Self-Images of the Age* by Alasdair MacIntyre, copyright © 1971 by Alasdair MacIntyre.

E. P. Dutton, Inc., for material from *Martin Buber's Life and Work: The Middle Years* by Maurice Friedman, copyright © 1983 by Maurice Friedman.

Farrar, Straus & Giroux, Inc., for material from *The Essential Earthman* by Henry Mitchell, copyright © 1983 by Henry Mitchell.

Harcourt Brace Jovanovich, Inc., for material from *Prophecy From the Past* by Benjamin Constant, edited and translated by Helen Byrne Lippmann, copyright 1941 by Helen Byrne Lippmann; and *The Seven Storey Mountain* by Thomas Merton, copyright 1948 by Harcourt Brace Jovanovich, Inc., renewed 1968 by The Trustees of the Merton Legacy Trust.

Harvard University Press for material from *Moralia* by Plutarch, copyright © 1927 by Harvard University Press.

Holy Cow! Press for lines from "Safely" in *Brother Songs* by David Ignatow, edited by James Perlman, copyright © 1979 by Holy Cow! Press.

Meridian Books, Princeton University Press, for material from *The Hero with a Thousand Faces* by Joseph Campbell, copyright © 1956 by Joseph Campbell.

William Morrow & Company, Inc., for material from *Male and Female* by Margaret Mead, copyright © 1949 by Margaret Mead.

The New York Times Company for material from "New Stirrings of Patriotism" by R. W. Apple, Jr., copyright © 1983 The New York Times Company; "Russia: A People Without Heroes" by David K. Shipler, copyright © 1983 by The New York Times Company; and "Unhappy Families," copyright © 1983 by The New York Times Company.

Sage Publications, Inc., for material from *Criminal Violence* by Marvin E. Wolfgang and Neil A. Weiner, copyright © 1982 by Marvin Wolfgang.

Schocken Books, Inc., for material from *Dearest Father* by Franz Kafka, edited by Max Brod, copyright © 1953, by Schocken Books, Inc.

Viking Penguin, Inc., for material from *Black Lamb and Grey Falcon* by Rebecca West, copyright 1940, 1941 by Rebecca West, copyright © renewed 1968, 1969 by Rebecca West.

The text of this book is set in Granjon.

LIBRARY OF CONGRESS CATALOGING IN PUBLICATION DATA

Shapiro, Stephen A.
Manhood: a new definition.

Bibliography: p.
Includes index.
1. Men—Psychology.   2. Conduct of life.   3. Trust
(Psychology)   4. Social values.   5. Interpersonal
relations.   I. Title.
HQ1090.S47   1984   305.3'1   84-11565
ISBN 0-399-12992-8